The Packraft Handbook

The Packraft Handbook

AN INSTRUCTIONAL
GUIDE FOR THE CURIOUS

LUC MEHL

ILLUSTRATED BY SARAH K. GLASER

MOUNTAINEERS
BOOKS

MOUNTAINEERS BOOKS is dedicated to the exploration, preservation, and enjoyment of outdoor and wilderness areas.

1001 SW Klickitat Way, Suite 201, Seattle, WA 98134
800-553-4453, www.mountaineersbooks.org

Mountaineers Books and its colophon are registered trademarks of The Mountaineers organization.

Printed in Korea
Distributed in the United Kingdom by Cordee, www.cordee.co.uk

25 24 23 22   1 2 3 4 5

Design and layout: Molly Golden
Illustrations: Sarah K. Glaser
All photographs and illustrations by the author unless credited otherwise
Cover and frontispiece photographs: Chickaloon River, Alaska

Library of Congress Cataloging-in-Publication data is on file for this title

Mountaineers Books titles may be purchased for corporate, educational, or other promotional sales, and our authors are available for a wide range of events. For information on special discounts or booking an author, contact our customer service at 800-553-4453 or mbooks@mountaineersbooks.org.

Printed on FSC®-certified materials

ISBN (paperback): 978-1-68051-602-9
ISBN (ebook): 978-1-68051-603-6

An independent nonprofit publisher since 1960

FSC
www.fsc.org
MIX
Paper from
responsible sources
FSC® C140526

CONTENTS

DEDICATION

For Rob Kehrer

ACKNOWLEDGMENTS

It was humbling to discover how badly I needed peer reviewers to make *The Packraft Handbook* what it has become. I am especially grateful to Sarah K. Glaser for her insights and patience during illustration revisions. Brad Meiklejohn, Trip Kinney, and Francis Mitchell dove deep and provided help with the big picture. John and Paul Schauer provided a new-to-me and greatly-appreciated perspective on the principles of river-running, and Tony Perelli helped translate it into something packrafters can relate to. Bretwood "Hig" Higman was a huge help regarding open-water crossings, where I lack experience. Eric Riley provided a critical review of the concepts in the rescue chapters. Jeremy Wood gave a doctor's assessment of the Medical Emergencies chapter. Thanks to Joseph Bell, Hugh Canard, Amy Christeson, Gregg Christopher, David Coil, Roman Dial, Chris Erickson, Clinton Hodges, Shasta Hood, Timmy Johnson, Galen Johnston, Becky King, Will Koeppen, Zorba Laloo, JoAnne Mehl, Mark Oates, Sven Schellin, Zak Sears, John Shook, Ben Sullender, Dmitry Surnin, Thor Tingey, and Tom Wetherell for their contributions. Molly Golden designed the layout; Lisa Delaney copy edited the text; and Lizzy Scully provided a marketing plan. Joe Stock and Kelsey Gray helped me navigate self-publishing. Finally, thank you to my wife, Sarah Histand, for encouraging me to give up the stability of a full-time desk job for the instability of promoting a packrafting Culture of Safety.

PREFACE

I bought my first packraft to extend hiking trips, never expecting that the adorable blue boat would change my life.

I grew up on the banks of a cold, brown, and swift Alaska river, known as the Kuskokwim. I was always intimidated by it. The river was dangerous. Kids were warned about the river, and none of us learned to swim until we grew up and left town. One of my early memories is shivering while wrapped in a blue tarp after I got wet riding a raft of firewood logs.

In rural Alaska, there are no actual highways; you have to fly to the villages or navigate the rivers by boat. This river was our highway. At the same time, it was a barrier that blocked overland travel. I carried this impression into adulthood: the blue lines on the map defined the boundaries of exploration.

Many years and rivers later, my eyes are now drawn to those same blue lines, but for different reasons. The rivers are highways again, but now I see them as liberating instead of limiting. These days, my packraft sneaks its way into my luggage on every family vacation. I routinely plead with my wife Sarah Histand to pull over so that I can study the flow of a roadside river.

I started packrafting rivers the way I hiked trails—pointing the boat downriver and plowing through any obstacles. After a season of "boating like a backpacker," Roman Dial recruited me into his team of whitewater packrafters. Roman was on a mission to prove that packrafts were viable whitewater boats. Under the mentorship of Roman's team and the river kayakers who looked out for us, I learned to love boating like a boater.

My learning curve included many mistakes and even more swims, but I enjoyed the process and felt invincible. That all changed in 2014 when, just days after traveling together, Rob Kehrer capsized, was separated from his packraft, and drowned. Rob's death was shocking to me because we cut the same corners—incomplete safety equipment and no swiftwater training—it could've just as easily been me. His death forced me to reassess my relationship with recreation, especially my risk assessment and tolerance. I took a course from the Swiftwater Safety Institute, then shadowed as an instructor and eventually earned a teaching position.

I wrote *The Packraft Handbook* to prevent packraft incidents like the one that took Rob's life.

ILLUSTRATOR'S PREFACE

I was born and raised on the banks of Victor Creek, a steep, rocky tributary into Kenai Lake, Alaska. But I didn't discover whitewater until I was a homesick college student. I was bewildered by the lack of accessible wilderness and mountain peaks from the tightly fenced-off trails and miniature parks of mid-coast Maine.

The college outing club offered a semester of whitewater kayaking. I had never seen anything like those clear, thundering rivers (green instead of a glacial gray), and they engulfed me. The rivers could swallow me up and spit me out in a single afternoon, and they often did. In the confusion of college and classes, I so badly needed that. I was smitten.

I dove in with enthusiasm. I learned to roll, then taught pool sessions twice a week. I bloodied my lip, scraped my chin, got ear infections, surfed tidal waves, and ran glorious dam-release rivers over and over.

And then, too soon, I graduated.

I'm back home in Alaska, where there are fewer roads and more rivers (thank goodness), and my paddling has converged with my love of backpacking and hunting. With a packraft, I still get that same joy of running rivers. I've walked hundreds of miles with my saucy little whitewater packraft on my back.

I hope *The Packraft Handbook* helps you share in the joy of discovering rivers. Ideally, my illustrations will help you imagine scenarios and visualize techniques. I'm grateful to benefit from Luc's knowledge and want to make this material more accessible to people like myself, who prefer pictures over words.

-Sarah K. Glaser

DISCLAIMER

The Packraft Handbook should supplement, but not replace, in-person training. You should seek relevant courses in swiftwater rescue, packraft instruction, and wilderness medical training. Careful study, diligent practice, and capable partners can provide an appropriate learning environment if you don't have access to formal courses.

The opinions in *The Packraft Handbook* are mine and should be understood as the perspective of just one person. There is no definitive standard on matters of style, technique, equipment, and safety. While I have been strongly influenced by a wide array of instructors, mentors, and peer editors, I am solely responsible for this book's contents.

Ultimately, you are responsible for your safety. There are very few actual accidents in packrafting; the things that go wrong are often predictable. It is up to you to anticipate risks and be properly equipped and trained to mitigate them.

CULTURE OF SAFETY

The best action to prevent packrafting incidents is to create a "Culture of Safety." We want it to feel normal to wear proper safety equipment, train before getting on the water, and be willing to change plans. You can further develop the Culture of Safety by helping others and sharing your learning journey.

PRANZ Packraft Meetup. Acheron River, New Zealand. © Mark Oates

Shasta Hood, joyous freedom. Skwenta River, Alaska.

INTRODUCTION

There is joyous freedom in having a little boat that you can take anywhere, and that can take you everywhere. Packrafts make possible the simplest family outings and the most ambitious adventures. Wherever you are starting from, there is a place for you in a packraft.

Whether you are entirely new to packrafting or are a seasoned paddler, your experience will be most enjoyable if you are prepared to handle the surprises that come your way. Your safety will be determined by your preparation and your ability to react appropriately. If you aren't good at this now, you can look forward to a fun and rewarding learning curve.

The Packraft Handbook is dense with information in order to meet the needs of novices and experts alike. Start by browsing the Table of Contents, glossary, and illustrations to identify gaps in your current skills and knowledge base. You will likely want to revisit the advanced sections to dive a little deeper as you gain first-hand experience.

The Packraft Handbook is organized into sections that promote a natural progression as you work your way through the book:

Part I: Foundations. This section presents the foundational skills new packrafters should develop before heading far from shore or through rapids. *Part I* captures what we would do together on a lake during the first day of an in-person course: review our equipment, practice paddle strokes, wet re-entries, and discuss risk.

Part II: Rivers and Open Water. After understanding the limitations of your equipment and how to control your boat, you will likely want to move to rivers or open-water crossings (lakes and the ocean). *Part II* presents how rivers work and how to navigate river features. Open-water crossings are host to a unique set of opportunities and hazards; specific preparation and navigation techniques are presented.

Part III: When Things Go Wrong. Even with the best training, things will go wrong in the water. Honestly, that's usually part of the fun. *Part III* covers rescue and recovery techniques from the boat and from shore, repairing equipment, and preparing for medical emergencies.

Part IV: Putting the 'Pack' in Packrafting. For packrafters who want to choose their destinations and plan their own trips, *Part IV* presents trip-planning principles, such as how to load backpacks, bikes, and skis on your packraft, and considerations when choosing backpacking and camping equipment.

HOW TO USE THE PACKRAFT HANDBOOK

How you use *The Packraft Handbook* depends on your experience and objectives. Whether you are just getting started or planning the trip of a lifetime, there is something in this book for you.

Many topics in this book won't seem relevant until you experience missteps. It is more important to know what is in the book than to understand it all. Revisit the text as you gain curiosity or identify gaps in your knowledge.

The first use of a term in the glossary is indicated with a bold font.

BEING SMALL AND POWERFUL

Packrafting is humbling and empowering.

Water is powerful; our small boats feel even smaller when the ocean gets choppy, the river gains another tributary, or the creek constricts through a canyon. Since we can't control the water, we have to embrace its power, and in so doing, the water forces us to recognize how small we are.

> **Be bold enough to be small enough to let the world be awesome, and it will.**
>
> James Snyder, *The Squirt Book*

Being small is not the same as being powerless. Since water doesn't care about our safe passage, we have to. And through caring, we develop preparedness, which allows us to thrive in the water environment. Developing packrafting skills can be deeply rewarding; don't be surprised if the confidence you gain on the water extends into other aspects of your life.

Preparedness requires an understanding of what can go wrong and how to respond when it does. Your best companion on this adventure is curiosity. Curiosity can motivate you to learn how rivers and open water work, how to provide a metaphorical **safety net** for your partners, and what your body is capable of.

INHERENT RISK

Moving water, open waterways, and remote environments all have inherent risks. While some packrafters will seek risk (and its companions: adrenaline and dopamine), others will fail to recognize that packrafting is a risky activity.

The hardest part of recognizing risk is identifying what we don't know. The failure to recognize danger will likely stem from a failure to identify vulnerability and the consequences of what can be lost—family and friends. Rob Kehrer's drowning was a wake-up call that diminished my self-confidence and forced me to reevaluate what I thought I knew.

Ultimately, safety is caring. Caring will motivate you to learn to anticipate what can go wrong and respond appropriately when it does. There will be surprises; an intentional learning strategy is your best preparation to manage them. Nothing about water is guaranteed safe, but packrafting can be fun and meaningful if you approach it with intention, curiosity, and practice.

LEARNING AND PROGRESSION

Regardless of your initial expectations, you are likely to feel the allure—or the necessity—of reading moving water and navigating rapids. Being familiar with rough water prepares you for unexpected conditions around the bend, or when the wind picks up during an otherwise easy open-water crossing.

Cultivating continuous learning and curiosity is critical when interacting with a substrate you can't control. The river doesn't care what you think you know. Rivers are constantly changing, and we must keep our attitudes flexible.

As packrafters, our progression is hindered by an unexpected foe—the relative stability of our boats! Packrafts are unlikely to capsize while sitting flat on the water, but very likely to capsize when you lean too far to one side. The stability of packrafts on flat water promotes overconfidence that quickly disappears when things get rowdy. In contrast, river kayaks are less stable on flat water, motivating kayakers to seek formal instruction and progress more slowly.

Train for the worst: When things go wrong, your training will determine where you fall in the spectrum between ineffectiveness and composure, and whether you can keep yourself and your party secure. The best training strategy is to seek in-person instruction and to frequently practice rescues and gear recovery. The decisions and skills developed *before* getting on the water are as important as the act of paddling.

Celebrate your accomplishments: There will be mistakes and frustrations, so make sure to recognize your advancing skills and accomplishments.

A Note for Beginners

If you are anything like me, you are eager to get in the water (or maybe you already have). Be careful. Half of the known packraft fatalities have involved beginners, and their deaths might have been avoided with simple precautions like wearing safety equipment and outfitting their boats to minimize hazards. Embrace intentional progression if you want to have a long and deeply fulfilling packrafting career. Play the long game; it's worth it.

Formal instruction is the fastest way to learn. In-person courses create an appropriate learning environment, and your instructor will likely introduce you to concepts that would otherwise take a long time to discover. Courses also connect you to other paddlers and potential partners.

If you don't have access to instruction, practice the essential safety skills with partners. Going alone might be your only option, but it should be your last option. If you don't have a packrafting community in your region, start one! (See inset, following page.)

Swimming pools, ponds, and small lakes are ideal locations to adjust your outfitting, practice paddle strokes, and get odd looks from people. Rapids and whitewater are not the right places for your first few packraft outings.

If you don't own packrafting equipment, borrow or rent to help you decide what to purchase. Check the internet for a packrafting group or forum in your region. Packrafters are generous with their equipment and love to recruit new adventure partners.

BUILDING A COMMUNITY

Zorba Laloo discovered a love for packrafting at home in Meghalaya, India. His dedication to community-building, conservation, and river safety outreach was recognized with the American Packrafting Association Golden Paddle award in 2013. Zorba shares his community-building experience here.

The steps needed for collecting humans together for sustained and similar-interests are not unlike starting an extremist group or a neighborhood gardening club. By no design of our own, here are some points of what transpired in Meghalaya. Except for the first, they are in no particular order.

Pioneers: *You need one or two of these to bring the experience home.*

Paddle with friends: *It is critical to attempt trips that build skill and excitement early. Ensure that the least experienced team member is enjoying themselves.*

Research and document: *Collect information about rivers, chat with folks, explore maps and satellite imagery. Always research routes before committing to them. Maintaining trip reports and notes supported by media and GPS data is a time-tested way to increase collective knowledge while generating more interest.*

Train: *As often as possible, do safety drills to build skills individually and as a team. If one cannot get proper training from more experienced folk, connect virtually with mentors, and train slowly and carefully.*

Build and connect: *Packrafting communities are tightly knit, supportive both on and off the water. It may be useful to create formal bodies like clubs or associations. Reach out to global paddling communities—it won't be long before you find friends, plan trips, seek advice, and find gear to swap or buy. Experienced paddlers might be excited to travel and explore rivers with you in your area.*

Utilize: *From tying laundry lines to conservation programs in remote areas, river skills have become a part of my life. The only limitation is your imagination.*

An outreach event organized by Zorba Laloo. Meghalaya, India. © Zorba Laloo

"Paddle up a Level"

A common theme in my learning, and now instruction, is "paddle up a level." Paddling up a level allows you to choose when to be challenged. When you decide to make the river more difficult (by paddling harder lines), you get to practice techniques without the consequences of actually being on more difficult water.

The "paddle up a level" strategy allows you to master challenging moves before you need them. For example, paddle Class II water while using the techniques required for Class III difficulty. Then, when you step up to Class III, your body will already have muscle memory for Class III maneuvers. This approach helps instill an understanding that controlled technique is more important than "getting through" rapids. Controlled technique is also more fun and rewarding, and we learn well when we're having fun.

The "paddle up a level" approach works well for groups with varying skill levels. Experienced paddlers will want to catch every **eddy** and surf every **wave**, while the less experienced paddlers can stick to less ambitious goals.

Repetition

Familiarity with a run allows you to become comfortable with that environment, which gives you the confidence to try new lines and techniques. It takes intentional practice to improve—logging hours isn't enough. If you get serious about progressing, have a friend video record your run. Review the video in slow-motion to identify ways to improve.

Ways to utilize repetition include:

- Try to catch smaller eddies as your boat control improves.
- Count the number of strokes (or times you take a blade out of the water) and try to reduce that number.
- Intentionally veer off the familiar line in small increments to learn corrective strokes.
- Choose a more difficult line.
- Return to the same section at different water levels to get a feel for various degrees of pushiness.

HOW PAUL GOT TO BE SO GOOD

I was extremely fortunate to learn the way I did. I learned from my dad, and I grew up on and around the river. Learning from my dad made it so that I didn't have any say in what I got to do. My dad made it so that I never progressed above my skill limit. When I wanted to paddle the hardest stretch on the Nenana, my home river, he said I couldn't do it until I could paddle the hardest rapid on the easier stretch, backward, trying to surf every wave. So, the next time I ran that stretch, I ran it backward, trying to surf every single wave, and I got my butt kicked. By the time I could do that, my dad let me paddle the canyon stretch, and it was easy, not scary at all. I was really lucky to learn that way. I learned by making hard moves in easy whitewater, and I think that is the key to learning successfully.

-Paul Schauer

Paul Schauer, Bird Creek, Alaska. © Joe Stock

Find a Mother Duck

A Mother Duck is someone who is excited to teach you and who can provide a safety net. The right Mother Duck can help you determine when to try new things. The wrong Mother Duck might cheer you on but not know how to help if something goes wrong.

Indications that your Mother Duck is dependable include patience, communication, and a willingness to set up a throw rope or safety boat. Signs that your Mother Duck may be unsafe include poor communication, distraction, impatience, pressure, and no clear plan to help if something goes wrong.

As a duckling, try to follow the Mother Duck on their exact route down the river. Pay attention to how the Mother Duck orients their boat, when and where they change speed, and how they use different strokes. Match the Mother Duck's paddle placement stroke-for-stroke. If anything isn't clear about their line or technique, ask for an explanation.

Sarah Histand "Mother Ducking" her parents. Kennicott, Alaska.

TIMMY JOHNSON'S 1,000TH RAPID

I joined Timmy Johnson, Jule Harle, and Tony Perelli for a packraft descent of the remote Class IV Kuskulana Canyon in 2009. We loaded up in Timmy's Student Driver business vehicle for a 5-hour drive to the Wrangell Mountains.

Timmy is a very skilled kayaker and, to my knowledge, was the first to install thigh straps and roll a packraft. Tony and I felt confident after our first autumn paddling all the Class IV water we could find. Jule was still not convinced about packrafts, but she sure didn't want to carry her kayak on our 13-mile (21-km) approach.

We scouted an early rapid, and Timmy, our Mother Duck, walked us through the best line, then announced he would portage it. I was shocked. Timmy was the expert, and the rapid didn't look that hard. Tony decided to run it. Timmy told Tony what could go wrong and where he would end up. Sure enough, it went wrong, and Timmy was waiting in precisely the right position to fish Tony out of the water.

On the next rapid, Timmy described the best line and announced, again, that he would portage. Tony agreed, but this time I decided to give it a shot. Like the first rapid, Timmy set up in a position where he easily plucked me out of the water.

It was a lesson that stuck with both Tony and me. The consequence of those swims didn't turn out to be serious, but that was in large part because Timmy read the hazards so accurately. When I asked Timmy why he was so comfortable portaging, he said, "There are a thousand other rapids. Walking one doesn't make a difference."

Timmy Johnson and friends scouting Kuskulana Canyon, Alaska. © *Jule Harle*

Spend Time in a Kayak

If you discover that paddling whitewater is your passion, spend time in a whitewater kayak. I felt like I learned more about boat control after four hours in a kayak than after four weeks in a packraft. Kayaks provide instant feedback and force you to lead with your head, learn edge control, and recover by rolling. Rolling is easier in a kayak, and having a reliable roll allows you to quickly recover from mistakes, which might make you more willing to try new things. Everything you learn in the kayak will make you a better packrafter, including an appreciation for how much easier packrafts are to carry!

WHAT GOES WRONG

Even with perfect planning and an ideal group of partners, things will go wrong on the water. Some of the following terms and concepts might not be familiar yet, but will be soon. You can also refer to the glossary.

What goes wrong:

- **Risk assessment**: The most critical piece of safety equipment is your brain. We have to train our brains to assess risk and respond appropriately when things go wrong. Underestimating risk and overestimating preparedness leads to close calls, or worse.

- **Cold water**: It is easy to underestimate how quickly cold water can debilitate a swimmer. Cold water has been a major factor in nearly all known packraft fatalities.

- **Paddling alone**: Half of the known packraft fatalities to date have involved solo paddlers. Paddling alone rips a massive hole in your safety net.

- **Too little or too much gear**: Not wearing a life vest can result in an otherwise preventable drowning. Overloading your boat with equipment can make your boat hard to maneuver.

- **Wind and waves on open-water crossings**: Open-water settings (lakes, oceans, and large rivers) are prone to rapidly changing conditions that can lead to capsizing and separation from gear and the group.

- **High water**: Rising water makes river currents faster and more forceful, and potentially carries in debris. Many boating incidents could have been avoided simply by waiting for water levels to drop.

- **River features:** Packrafts commonly broach and capsize on river features like confluent channels, water pile-ups, and cutbanks. Hazardous river features include rocks, dams, holes, and sieves.

- **Strainers:** Strainers are obstacles that allow water to pass through but can trap a body. Strainers are transient: a rapid that was clear last week might not be clear today.

- **Alcohol:** Drinking alcohol is a preventable cause of drowning.

PRO TIP!

Water conducts heat away from our body 25 times faster than air, and the larger the temperature gradient, the faster the transfer. *All but one* known packraft fatality occurred in cold water (Alaska, British Columbia, Russia, Greenland, Iceland, Argentina). The best way to protect yourself from cold water is to wear appropriate layers ("dress for the swim") and a drysuit (see *Chapter 1: Packrafting Equipment*). Refer to *Chapter 11: Medical Emergencies* for a discussion of how the body reacts to cold water.

WHAT GOES RIGHT

Safety is caring. It takes discipline to care, to really honor the dangers involved, especially after we get away with several low-consequence incidents. Caring is hard work. Things go right when you *intentionally* learn and practice good technique.

What goes right:

- **Learning:** Take every opportunity to learn, reflect, and debrief.

- **Planning:** Create a trip plan that recognizes hazards and includes risk mitigation. We make our own success.

- **Communication:** Create an environment that applauds communicated objectives, concerns, and mitigation plans.

- **Equipment:** Wear appropriate safety equipment. Outfit your boat to limit entrapment hazards. Note the role that leashes play on open water, and that they are not appropriate on rivers.

- **Partner-up:** Paddle with competent partners who provide safety and the opportunity to help others.

- **Swim smart:** Use both defensive and offensive swimming techniques to work your way through hazards. *Keep your feet up to avoid foot entrapment.*
- **Wet re-entry:** Frequently practice wet re-entries, our go-to self-rescue technique.
- **Paddle under control:** Recognize your limitations and choose appropriate destinations.
- **Respect the river:** Use the river's current and features, such as eddies, to control your progress down the river.
- **Set up safety:** Know how and where to set up safety systems.
- **Avoid unusual conditions:** High water, high winds, and cold temperatures can turn a low-consequence mistake into a high-consequence incident.
- **Leave No Trace:** Do your part to keep rivers pristine for future visitors.
- **Fitness:** You don't need to be fit to packraft, but it sure helps. Core-strength and flexibility make packrafting easier and more enjoyable.

PUSH-UP CHAMPIONS

In the summer of 2018, Luc and I were in the habit of doing a set of push-ups each day. Then we left for a 10-day packrafting trip that started with 60 miles (97 km) on the Yukon River. We'd estimated that the Yukon moves at about six miles per hour (10 km/h), and expected to be on it for two days. What we hadn't anticipated was a strong headwind. We worked really hard to make those miles, even strapping our single packrafts in a line with driftwood to be more aerodynamic.

After our time on the Yukon, we hiked into the hills and floated down Hot Springs Creek to the Melozi Hot Springs waterfall. The trip finished in a little town called Ruby, after 50 more miles (80 km) of flatwater without much current. When we got home after the trip, Luc started a set of push-ups and then exclaimed that I needed to join him. Our hard work to paddle into the headwind made us significantly stronger—we couldn't believe the difference. Ever since, we've started doing extra push-ups before our trips, and factoring in extra time in case there is a strong headwind.

-Sarah Histand

Sarah Histand. Melozi Hot Springs, Alaska.

PART I

FOUNDATIONS

The best way to begin packrafting is to understand the safety features and limitations of your equipment, followed by paddling on a lake or other controlled setting. Day-one priorities include: using appropriate safety equipment, outfitting your boat for a proper paddling position and to minimize entrapment hazards, and practicing different paddle strokes and wet re-entries. Note that not all packrafts can be re-entered by all paddlers. Expect to capsize and be sure to know your options when you do.

Developing familiarity with equipment and boat control will prepare you for fun and healthy experiences in *Part II: Rivers and Open Water.* Frequently revisit these concepts; improvement requires intentional practice.

Part I ends with a chapter on risk assessment, which is the framework to govern your decisions about equipment, objectives, and destinations as you progress into more difficult or exposed settings.

Brooks Range, Alaska.

Alan Rogers and Lee Helzer. Talkeetna Mountains, Alaska.

CHAPTER 1

PACKRAFTING EQUIPMENT

To the extent possible, *The Packraft Handbook* is informed by the known pack-rafting fatalities and many close calls. The only thing that all of these incidents had in common is that they involved packrafting equipment. In retrospect, it is easy to identify equipment decisions that might have saved lives.

Packrafting equipment includes the packraft, paddle, personal protective equipment (life vest, helmet, etc.), and additional river equipment. See *Chapter 12: Backpacking, Camping, and Cargo* for non-packrafting equipment considerations and how to load cargo onto your boat.

WHAT YOU NEED TO KNOW

Packrafts are small and light inflatable boats that can be carried in a backpack. The right packraft for you is probably the one you already own, can afford, or can borrow. What matters most is that the outfitting doesn't pose an entrapment risk and that you choose appropriate destinations.

Packraft models are designed for different uses (fishing, fast-and-light, whitewater, etc.). It is easier and safer to choose water that matches your boat's abilities than to force the boat through unintended conditions.

Other paddling equipment considerations include:

- If you will experience unstable conditions—intentionally or not—knowing how to adjust the seat and backband to provide a proper paddling position will be important.
- Use a paddle suitable for your size and objectives.
- Choose appropriate safety and protective equipment for your purposes: helmet, life vest, clothing, drysuit, throw rope, footwear, and accessories.

COMMON USES OF MODERN PACKRAFTS

Packrafts are commonly used as utility boats, to gain access to hard-to-reach areas, to travel down rivers, or a combination of all of these.

Utility boats: Deckless utility boats are popular with hunters, anglers, ultralight hikers, dog owners, and parents. Utility boats are great for carrying cargo, including other people, skis, meat, or bikes. The variety of applications are endless: bikerafting enables bikers to cross water or use rivers to extend their trips, hunters and anglers can cross rivers and lakes, and so on. The National Park Service, wildland firefighters, search and rescue professionals, and environmental scientists use packrafts to access remote waters.

Utility paddlers might give little attention to questions of packrafting skills and safety if they view the boats simply as accessories to their main activity (hunting, fishing, etc.). This mindset can lead to unexpected consequences. It would be a mistake to assume that using a packraft to haul cargo across flat water does not expose you to danger.

Loading cargo is discussed in *Chapter 12: Backpacking, Camping, and Cargo.*

Access: From the packraft pioneers in Tasmania and Alaska to today's explorers across the globe, packrafts have been paddled or carried to hard-to-reach pockets of the world. With a boat that fits in a backpack, carry-on compartment, and trunk of your car, the options are endless. Lightweight and compact, they are the right tool for the job. Packrafts have been strapped to backs, bikes, mules, and other boats while crossing continents, ice fields, and deserts. Packrafts are used as sleds on snow and as shelters in the rain.

River-running: Whether for hard-to-access rivers or road-side paddling, packrafts are an excellent tool for running rivers. Whitewater-specific packrafts are built to maneuver through rivers and stay upright in turbulent water.

Paddlers who aren't seeking whitewater will still benefit from experiencing it. Whitewater forces you to learn proper paddling techniques and how to accommodate the river's force. These skills come in handy when your lake crossing gets choppy, or you are surprised by a log jam around the corner.

A BRIEF HISTORY OF PACKRAFTING

Lightweight and portable boats have been used by cultures worldwide for millennia (see: coracle). The first inflatable boats closely followed the development of the process to vulcanize rubber in 1838.

In the 1840s, Lt. Peter Halkett designed an inflatable boat that, when deflated, could be worn as a cloak. A walking stick doubled as a paddle shaft, and an umbrella served as a sail. The boat featured four air chambers for redundancy and weighed 7.5 lbs (3.4 kg).

Lt. Halkett tested the boat on the River Thames and the open sea. A second model fit two passengers and could be carried in a backpack. Despite being useful in several expeditions in the Canadian Arctic, Halkett never gained naval or commercial support to make the boats available for general use.

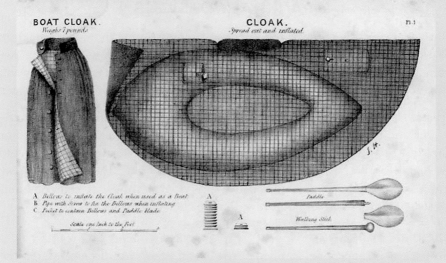

One of the first recreational hike-and-float trips with an inflatable boat was Dick Griffith's 1952 journey to Barranca del Cobre in Mexico. Dick carried a military surplus raft.

Recreational use of packrafts was advanced in the 1970s and 1980s by small groups of explorers on opposite sides of the globe. These packraft pioneers extolled the blending of mountain travel and river-running. In Tasmania, flat-water inflatables, including air mattresses, were modified to access and protect Tasmanian rivers threatened by hydroelectric dams. On the other side of the world, recreational packrafting co-evolved in Alaska to access and traverse the vast wilderness. The packraft manufacturers in these decades included American Safety, Sherpa, and Curtis Designs.

Packraft design underwent its most significant revolution in the early 2000s when Sheri Tingey started building boats in her garage in Anchorage, Alaska. Sheri's "Alpacka Raft" packrafts were the first designed specifically for backpackers and wildland access; they were light, compact, and intended for down-river travel.

Since the 2000s, packrafts have benefited from design and manufacturing improvements across the globe. There are over 30 brands at the time of publication, providing a full range of options to meet specific needs. Modern packrafts include niche designs for specific applications but share the primary characteristics of being lightweight and packable.

PACKRAFT DESIGNS

There are many different packraft designs. This means you can find just the right boat for your needs, but you'll have to sort through the options. Packrafts vary from 2-lb (1-kg) ultralight boats that are appropriate for short floats on flat water (and nothing more) to high-performance boats capable of difficult whitewater.

Several factors govern the cost of packrafts: quality and weight of raw materials, the complexity of the design, and the quality and process of manufacture. The cheapest option is to build your packraft, and there are excellent kits and instructions online (for example, www.diypackraft.com). The most expensive options are precision engineered boats with specialty fabrics and eco-conscious construction. Identify your objectives before choosing a packraft.

Packraft Hull Shape

The packraft's shape is determined by the hull, the part that displaces water. The most affordable boats have the simplest hulls: a uniform-diameter tube attached to the floor, creating a "bathtub boat." More expensive packrafts generally have more complicated hulls, distributing the tube volume to place the paddler's center of gravity in a more centered position. For example, a high-volume stern creates buoyancy to counter the paddler's weight, pushing the boat's center of gravity forward.

Stability: The stability of a boat is its ability to resist capsizing. Wider boats are more stable, but stable boats are slower and less maneuverable.

Boat stability is described in two parts:

- **Primary stability:** The boat's stability when sitting flat in water. Due to the wide and flat floor, packrafts have substantial primary stability. Normal body movement in a packraft does not result in tipping.

- **Secondary stability:** The boat's ability to stay stable when on edge. The packraft's perfectly round side tubes result in poor secondary stability. This means that when a packraft is on edge, due to turbulent water or wind, the boat is unstable.

The packraft's excellent primary stability convinces many novice paddlers that they are ready to run rapids. But as turbulent water and river currents push the packraft up on one side, the poor secondary stability can quickly result in capsizing. Proper paddling position and outfitting allow us to make the best of poor secondary stability.

Basic and utility packrafts: Typical applications for this type of packraft include family days on the lake, hunting, fishing, dog packing, bikepacking, ultralight packrafting, and Class I/II rivers.

- Most affordable.
- Ultralight models (as light as 2 lbs, 1 kg) are only appropriate for water crossings, not river-running. Heavy models built with PVC fabrics are the most durable.
- An open cockpit allows for easy entry/exit and extra cargo.
- Anticipate getting cold in splashy water. You will need to stop frequently to dump the water from an undecked boat.

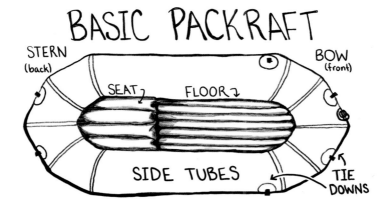

Whitewater packrafts: Whitewater packrafts are high-performance boats featuring advanced designs and more expensive materials and production.

- More expensive due to advanced hull design and construction. Specifically, asymmetrical bow and stern shapes are used to reduce drag, improve boat handling, and optimally position the paddler's center of gravity.
- A whitewater deck and spray skirt trap heat in and keep water out of the cockpit.

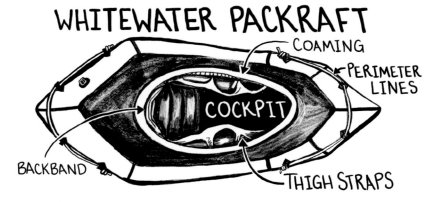

Two-person packrafts: Several brands offer two-person packrafts that weigh around 10 lbs (4.5 kg). Two-person packrafts vary in design from sit-on-top canoes to expedition whitewater boats. Two-person rafts are generally paddled with oars, like tandem canoes. It always takes me some time to adjust to the steering (stern) and power (bow) paddling roles.

The main advantages of a two-person boat are weight savings and the social aspect. Sarah Histand and I appreciate being in a two-person boat for leisurely conversation, sharing snacks, and taking breaks from paddling. Depending on the design, some two-person packrafts will be faster than single packrafts or more stable in whitewater.

Disadvantages of two-person packrafts depend on the design. Speed is a common pitfall: being larger than one-person boats, two-person packrafts experience more drag and wind resistance. Exposure is another downside: most two-person packrafts don't have decks, making for a colder paddling experience when exposed to wind, rain, or splashing cold water.

Sarah Histand steering a two-person packraft. Wulik River, Alaska.

MY FIRST PACKRAFT

In 2007, after a season of borrowing friends' packrafts, I did the math and committed to purchasing my own. The math involved how many one-way flights equaled the cost of the boat. I justified that if I could use the packraft four times instead of paying to fly in or out of a remote trip in Alaska, the packraft would pay for itself.

I met Sheri Tingey, creator of Alpacka Raft, at her house in east Anchorage. At that time, Sheri met the market demand by hand-building boats in her garage.

Financially strapped, I asked Sheri if she had any defective boats at a discounted price. Sheri set me up with a decked blue packraft with seams that had accidentally been welded twice, which sounded like a great defect to me.

DIG DEEPER

Most river-capable packrafts are made of nylon fabric coated on one or both sides with thermoplastic polyurethane (TPU). Nylon provides the material strength while the TPU coating makes the nylon airtight and allows the material to be heat-welded.

Fabric weights are described by denier, a measure of thread weight. In general, higher denier fabrics are stronger and heavier than lower denier fabrics, but the denier-strength relationship is not linear. Popular material weights are 200-denier for the tubes and 800-denier for the floor. Some ultralight packrafts are made with 75-denier fabric. For reference, a human hair is approximately 20-denier.

Other hull materials include PVC and Vectran. PVC packrafts are durable and less expensive but are heavier and bulkier. PVC can withstand higher pressures, making for a more rigid boat that will feel more familiar to kayakers. Vectran is a space-age fabric (used in airbags for Mars landings) that is stronger and lighter than nylon of the same denier. There's always a catch, though: Vectran is more expensive and susceptible to pinholes and tearing over sharp rocks.

Optional Packraft Features

Self-bailing floor: Packrafts from all three hull categories can have self-bailing floors, meaning that water drains through the floor. A thick inflatable mat elevates the paddler off of the wet boat bottom. The mat might fully or partially fill the floor (note that a partial mat can result in colder feet, since they will be in the water).

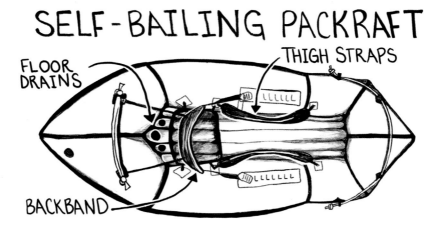

Self-bailing boats are easier to enter and exit at the shore and during wet re-entries. Self-bailing floors also provide the luxury of not having to stop to dump water from the cockpit. Most self-bailing packrafts don't have a deck, which means you might get cold from splashed water. Self-bailing boats can also feel more sluggish due to the extra mass of water in the cockpit and increased drag on the perforated floor.

Decks and spray skirts: Packrafts come with many deck options, varying from no-deck ("bathtub boat") to spray decks (permanent or removable) and spray skirts. Decks help keep water out of the cockpit, and skirts shed even more water. The drawback with decks and skirts is that they can make getting in and out of the boat more difficult.

Skirts are worn under a life vest and generally attach to the boat deck with Velcro or an elastic band that stretches over the coaming. The coaming is typically a hoop made of tubing (PEX, PVC) mounted at the opening of the cockpit that keeps water out.

Spray skirts are made of lightweight material to save weight when backpacking. Unfortunately, this means they are easily punctured and torn.

Cargo zipper: Some packrafts feature waterproof zippers or roll-top enclosures that allow you to store equipment inside the boat. There are several advantages to carrying cargo inside the boat, most notably that the cargo stays dry and that the cargo helps stabilize the boat by lowering the center of gravity. Cargo zippers are discussed in more detail in *Chapter 12: Backpacking, Camping, and Cargo.*

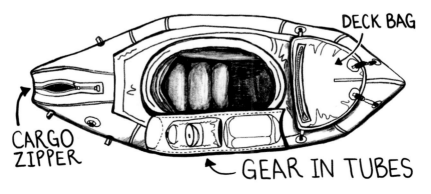

EXPEDITION MODE: CARGO ZIPPER

DECK BAG

CARGO ZIPPER

GEAR IN TUBES

Packraft Fit

Some packrafts are available in different sizes to accommodate different weight and height paddlers; check the brand's website for the sizing chart. The fit of the boat largely depends on your intended usage: casual or performance. For casual usage, such as paddling on calm lakes, the fit should be looser, with more room to shift and adjust your legs during a long day on the water (think "living space").

A performance fit is snug, ensuring that the boat moves in response to your body while navigating rivers. The soles of your feet should press against the bow with your knees slightly bent. Some packrafters place a foot brace, padding, or a block at their feet, to give them something to push against. An appropriate analogy is wearing tight rock climbing shoes instead of climbing in sneakers—tight climbing shoes allow you to make precise moves. As with climbing shoes, a long day spent in a boat with a performance fit can be uncomfortable.

Heavy paddlers and people planning to carry heavy cargo will want a more buoyant hull. The tube diameter and hull design determine buoyancy. For reference, at the time of writing, common tube diameters range from 10 to 12 inches (25-30 cm). A bigger paddler is better off in a boat with a large tube diameter.

PRO TIP!

Many paddlers will find themselves between sizes. Size down for performance (whitewater) and to save boat weight; size up for comfort (long days on the water).

INFLATING THE PACKRAFT

The inflation bag consists of a lightweight bag sewn onto a valve that threads onto the hull. It's hard to mess up inflation, but there are a few tricks to getting the bag as full as possible for each pump.

Using the inflation bag:

1. If there is any breeze, face the opening into the wind to fill the bag.
2. Without wind, hold the bag's edges and snap both hands vertically down and back up. This wrist snap helps fill the lower volume of the bag.
3. Seal the top of the bag and compress it with a bear hug as it inflates the tube.

Pressure: You will need to top off the boat manually after using the inflation bag. You want the highest pressure that your lungs can provide. Higher pressure results in a more rigid hull, which is more efficient to paddle and easier to control. Note that tube pressure will drop when the boat is placed in cold water. Add air to the boat after letting it sit in cold water and anticipate needing to repeat this process after a few minutes of paddling.

PRO TIP!

- I store the inflation bag in the pant leg of my drysuit unless someone in the group has a deck bag.
- Packrafts are more likely to puncture when at maximum pressure. At lower pressures, the tube material can deform around sharp objects. I'm most nervous about punctures during a portage—the pressure in the boat increases in the warmer air. Let some air out of the tubes before portaging on a hot day.
- During late-autumn boating in Alaska, the air can be colder than the water. When I notice my packraft getting more rigid after moving it into the water, I begrudgingly admit that the packrafting season is nearly over.

Electric pumps: You won't lose any friends if you show up to a put-in with an electric raft pump. And if you are an eligible bachelor or bachelorette, nothing says bona fide like a portable electric leaf blower. Place the blower on the valve and let 'er rip. The back-woods version of this technique is to attach the valve to your car's exhaust pipe, but you didn't hear it from me.

GALEN'S LUNG CAPACITY

The employees at Alaska Mountaineering and Hiking participate in a traditional "Challenge of the Month." One month, the challenge was to inflate a packraft by mouth. On his first attempt, Galen Johnston inflated an Alpacka Llama in 1 minute and 43 seconds! Galen is not normal. As a year-round ski coach, and having stood on the summit of Denali as an eleven-year-old, Galen's got lungs.

Supposedly, Alpacka Raft offered a free boat to anyone who could do it in under 1:30. Galen got his time down to 1:34 but has not yet earned a free packraft.

Next time you realize that you forgot your inflation bag at home, embrace your inner Galen and use your lungs.

PACKRAFT CARE

Packrafts should be rinsed with fresh water and hung to dry after any day of use. Given the option, drying gear in the shade is preferable since it limits UV damage. If the cockpit has sand or pebbles, use a vacuum to clean the tight spaces between the hull, floor, and deck. Store your boat clean, dry, and loosely rolled or folded.

If your boat features a cargo zipper, open the zipper after each use to allow the zipper chain to dry. Close the zipper for storage.

CLEANING YOUR PACKRAFT

Cleaning your packrafting equipment is especially important when traveling. Do your due diligence by following local guidelines to help prevent the spread of aquatic invasive species. Before entering any new body of water, the rules are: check, clean, and dry.

Check: Remove plants from the cockpit and bottom of the boat.

Clean: Use a household disinfectant such as biodegradable laundry or dishwashing detergent (5% solution) or bleach (2% solution) to clean all equipment that got wet.

Dry: Completely dry the packraft, inside and out. If you weren't able to use a disinfectant for cleaning, leave the raft inflated to dry for an additional 48 hours.

Eben Sargent due for a rinse. Susitna Flats, Alaska.

PROPER PADDLING POSITION

Depending on your objective, boat control might not be a high priority. However, you will appreciate—and possibly need—boat control as soon as the lake gets choppy or you find a surprise around the riverbend. *Floating* doesn't require proper positioning, but *boating* is a full-body endeavor. Not all packrafts allow this adjustment; experiment with your options in a lake or other controlled setting.

Installing and adjusting a seat and backband will improve comfort and place you in a proper paddling position. Proper positioning enables increased torso rotation, the use of strong core muscles, and engaging your legs for power and stability.

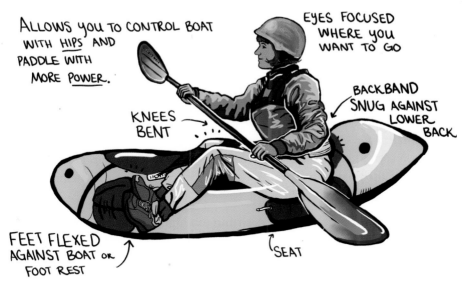

PROPER PADDLING POSITION

ALLOWS you TO CONTROL BOAT WITH HIPS AND PADDLE WITH MORE POWER.

EYES FOCUSED WHERE you WANT TO GO

KNEES BENT

BACKBAND SNUG AGAINST LOWER BACK

FEET FLEXED AGAINST BOAT or FOOT REST

SEAT

Seat

Your packraft seat should provide comfort as well as place you in the proper paddling position.

Fore-aft position: The packraft should lie flat in the water while you are seated. If possible, adjust your seat position until the bow and stern sit at equal levels in the water when you are seated.

Basic and ultralight packrafts might not have additional buoyancy in the stern. Since the paddler's center of gravity will be near the stern, the stern will drag deeper in the water. This stern-heavy geometry limits your boat-handling ability, but there isn't much you can do about it.

Height: A common problem with packraft seats is that they don't lift the boater high enough. Sitting low in the boat might feel more stable, but it has several disadvantages. Shorter and smaller paddlers will especially benefit from raising the seat height.

Problems with a low seat:
- You can't see over the bow.
- You can't engage your core muscles while paddling.
- You can't get full leverage from paddle strokes.
- It is less comfortable to sit with your butt at the same height as your feet.
- A reduced ability to get the boat on edge, which is an important aspect of boat control.

Fully inflate your seat, and if that isn't enough, raise the seat with closed-cell foam or a second seat. You might be able to run a single strap under the seat to lift it off the boat's floor, which has the added benefit of reducing drag on shallow rivers.

Conversely, there is such a thing as sitting too high—sitting higher raises your center of gravity, making the boat less stable. Find the seat height that allows you to use your core when paddling, but does not feel unstable.

Seat length: Some packrafts can accommodate different length seats. Short seats are lighter and less bulky, better for backpacking. Long seats make the boat more rigid and serve as an additional chamber if the boat were to deflate suddenly. Long seats are better for whitewater and open-water crossings.

Backband

A backband helps connect you to the packraft, increasing your comfort and ability to control the boat. A well-placed backband snugs you into the boat and promotes a proper paddling position and a long spine. Proper positioning enables increased torso rotation and the use of strong core muscles. Slouching limits the torso's ability to rotate and forces you to rely on smaller (and weaker) arm muscles for power.

Backband options include:

- No backband (lean against the bare tube or a backpack)
- Inflatable backband
- Adjustable foam or rigid backband

Inflatable options are light and compact, but might not be adjustable or durable. Rigid backbands can be adjusted to match your paddling needs. Pushing the backband toward the bow helps move the center of gravity forward and puts the paddler in a more aggressive paddling position. Moving the bankband toward the stern provides more legroom and comfort for long days on the water.

Foot Brace

A foot brace or foot block provides a connection point between your feet and the packraft. Whitewater and short packrafters will benefit from installing a foot brace.

Foot braces include inflatable blocks sold by packraft brands or stuffing something like a beachball into the boat. As with all of your outfitting decisions, be sure you're not inadvertently installing an entrapment hazard. Do not use a throw bag as a foot brace since the rope could come loose from the bag (an entrapment hazard) or get lost in the river (an entanglement hazard).

Thigh Straps

A well-positioned seat and backband are generally sufficient for boat control up to Class III water, but you will want the additional control provided by thigh straps beyond that. I use thigh straps for all of my packrafting, even flat water.

Thigh straps connect your legs to the packraft, which allows more of your body to control the boat and thus provides better coupling between you and your packraft. With thigh straps, when you move your body, the boat moves with you.

Thigh straps can be entrapment hazards. Packraft brands resisted installing thigh straps for many years because of this concern. If you use thigh straps, recognize that you are introducing an entrapment hazard to your boat. That said, there are no recorded packraft fatalities due to getting stuck in thigh straps.

If your packraft didn't come with thigh straps, you can install your own, as outlined in the *Permanent Glue Repairs and Modifications* section of *Chapter 10: Equipment Repair and Modification.*

Basic thigh straps have attachment points at the ankle and hip (two-point), while higher-performing straps include additional attachment points near the knees (four-point). Four-point straps provide more control and make the thigh straps less dangerous because the shorter span between strap segments is less likely to trap a foot or leg. Note that entrapment is a more significant concern in a soft or partially deflated packraft because it is easier to trap a foot on a loose strap.

PRO TIP!

- Thigh straps should be tight! I pull my straps tight against the hull *before* inserting my knee.
- Use accessory straps (flat webbing with a buckle) as ultralight thigh straps when weight is at a premium. Minimalist straps are inadequate to roll, but do help with boat control. Tie one end of the strap to the hip or ankle attachment point and use the buckle to tighten the other end. *Do not install anything with a loop or excessive tail*; these would be entrapment hazards.

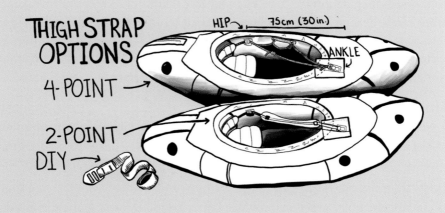

OUTFITTING YOUR PACKRAFT (RIGGING)

Entrapment and entanglement hazards are always relevant, even for a casual day of fishing on a lake. This is a big deal. It is critical that your packraft is outfitted as cleanly as possible. Sloppy outfitting can and has resulted in entrapment and death. Outfit your boat properly and let other paddlers know if you spot hazards on their boats.

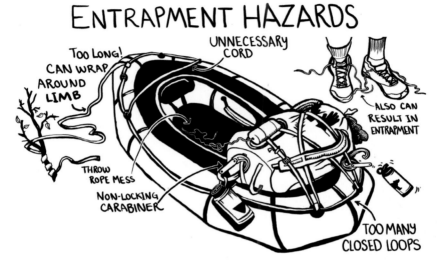

Anything that might keep you in the boat is an entrapment hazard. Possible entrapment hazards include:

- Getting wrapped by a long tail or perimeter line during a turbulent swim.
- A non-locking or unlocked carabiner accidentally clipping into webbing on your life vest or drysuit during entry, exit, or swim.
- Catching a foot or leg on a long strap or loop of material in the cockpit or on the bow. A partially deflated boat increases this risk.

To limit entrapment hazards, follow these best-practices:

- No long, loose, or looped straps, cord, or rope.
- Only use locking carabiners.
- Perimeter lines should be snug against the boat.
- Tails should be short enough to prevent wrapping around a body limb, if they are to be used at all.

- Cargo and cargo attachment systems should be clean and snug.
- Throw bags should not be attached to the boat in a way that allows them to move or feed rope.

Perimeter Lines

Most packrafts come with tie-downs along the perimeter of the hull. Tying a cord through these tie-downs creates a perimeter line—a line of cord along the boat's perimeter. If you don't run a perimeter line, it is important to have grab loops at both the bow and stern. Perimeter lines or grab loops should be on every packraft; you can install your own tie-downs if your packraft didn't come with them (see *Chapter 10: Equipment Repair and Modification*).

Perimeter lines serve many functions:

- A way for a swimmer, or safety boat, to grab a loose packraft
- A system for attaching a pack to the bow
- An attachment point for a leash to line the boat upriver
- Handholds so that you can flip a capsized boat upright

PRO TIP!

Perimeter lines on the sides of a boat are likely to snag on your life vest during a wet-entry attempt. For this reason, I only have perimeter lines on the bow and stern, leaving the snag zone free of cord.

SNAG ZONE (NO LINES)

SHORT TAIL

PERIMETER LINE

PERIMETER LINE

Attachment: There are two options for attaching perimeter lines. Each has advantages and disadvantages in regards to entrapment hazards; there isn't a correct option.

Perimeter line options:

1. Knot the perimeter line only at the first and last tie-downs, allowing it to run freely through the intermediate tie-downs. If something gets caught in any segment, cutting the line in any location will release the entire cord. The disadvantage of this system is that if your boat were to suddenly deflate (by dragging over a sharp rock, for example), you could end up with a long **bight** of loose cord, which becomes an entanglement hazard to a swimmer.
2. Tie the perimeter line to each tie-down. This way, no long loop would form during sudden deflation. The disadvantage of this system is that if something gets caught in a segment, that specific segment would need to be cut.

Cord diameter and material: Five-millimeter polypropylene accessory cord makes a nice perimeter line. Narrow-diameter cords are lighter and less bulky, but also more challenging to find during a swim, and can be hard to hold. Wide-diameter cords are easier to hold but add weight and bulk. Polypropylene is a better cord material than nylon because polypropylene floats.

Tail Lines

A tail line is a strap or cord attached to the stern of the packraft. The entanglement concern with a tail is that it can wrap around a paddle or body limb. If you choose to use a tail, it should be short enough not to allow a full wrap around a body limb.

Uses for tail lines:

- Holding the boat during a swim or boat recovery.
- Tying the boat to shore when scouting.
- Dragging the boat through shallow water ("walking the dog").

Best-practices for tail lines:

- Use polypropylene or other buoyant cord or webbing.
- Field testing suggests that flat webbing is less likely to wrap around a person's limb than tubular.
- Keep the end of the tail clean; don't tie a knot or bobber at the end of your tail. Knots can snag between rocks.

SHASTA'S TAIL: A CAUTIONARY TALE

Years after cutting his whitewater teeth on the Rio Savegre, Costa Rica, as a rafting guide, Shasta returned to packraft an upper canyon that was hard to access, even with a packraft.

Shasta capsized in the Class IV rapids and performed a wet re-entry. He pulled his chest over the tube and slid back into the cockpit, but somewhere in the swim, the packraft tail had entirely wrapped his arm and now held it pinned behind him. He couldn't free his arm or control his boat, and the turbulent water caused a second swim. Shasta then moved to the back of the boat, released his arm from the tail, and re-entered his packraft.

Shasta's tail was four feet of tubular webbing. He cut it off immediately, as did the rest of our friends, after hearing his story.

If you are concerned about entrapment (you are), and practice other ways to keep hold of your boat during a swim (perimeter line, thigh straps), consider removing the tail. I carry an accessory strap in my life vest that can be attached to the boat for tying, towing, or dragging but is then removed from the packraft when I'm in it.

Paddle

The most common paddles used for packrafting are four-piece fiberglass kayak paddles. River kayak paddles (197 to 205 cm) are preferred for moving water; sea kayak paddles (205 to 220 cm) can be better in open water. Paddles that are too long make maneuvering in whitewater more difficult; paddles that are too short make open-water paddling inefficient.

The key considerations when choosing a paddle are:

- **Breakdown size:** Four-piece paddles are the most convenient to carry
- **Length**: 197 to 205 cm is the most popular range
- **Blade shape**: Whitewater or flatwater paddling

- **Material**: Expense, weight, and durability tradeoffs of different materials
- **Leash**: Recommended in open water, not okay in turbulent water

Paddle Design

Four-piece paddles are preferred for packrafting because they break down into the most portable package. Two-piece paddles are more affordable, but they don't fit in a pack and can catch branches if they extend above the pack. One-piece paddles are more rigid, but they are inconvenient to carry.

Kayak paddles are designed for two environments: sea and whitewater.

- **Sea**: Sea kayak paddles are intended for long days on flat water. The blades are narrow, which keeps the weight down and allows for more efficient passage through both water and air. Sea kayak paddles are long (205-220 cm) and designed for low-angle strokes, keeping the paddle mostly parallel with the water, which reduces fatigue.
- **Whitewater:** Whitewater paddles are designed for power and quick maneuvering. The blades are wider, providing more surface area to transfer force to the water. Whitewater paddles are short (194-205 cm) and designed for high-angle strokes that quickly allow the next move.
- **Hybrid:** Sea kayak paddles are not designed for whitewater, so it is always risky to use them to run rivers. But we aren't the only boaters that want a paddle that can do it all, and several brands offer long and light paddles with whitewater blades (wide).

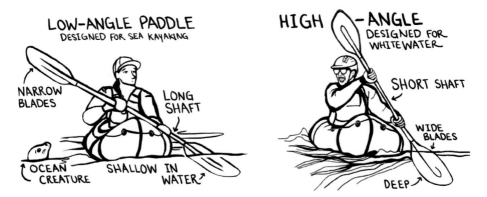

LOW-ANGLE PADDLE
DESIGNED FOR SEA KAYAKING
NARROW BLADES
LONG SHAFT
OCEAN CREATURE
SHALLOW IN WATER

HIGH-ANGLE
DESIGNED FOR WHITEWATER
SHORT SHAFT
WIDE BLADES
DEEP

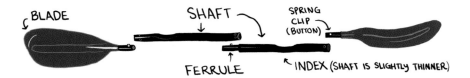

I recommend a paddle with whitewater (wide) blades in the 197 to 205 cm range for all adults and all-around use. If you anticipate primarily packrafting on flat water, you will probably want a paddle 205 cm or longer. If you know you will paddle rivers, stick with a high-angle paddle on the shorter end of the length spectrum. Anything less than 197 cm is generally too short for our (rather wide) packrafts. Note that high-end paddles are available with smaller shaft diameters to accommodate smaller hands.

Feather angle: The feather angle describes the angle of rotation between the two blades, with a default of 30 degrees. The feather angle allows the upper paddle to slice through the air, reducing air resistance, which makes a big difference on long days, especially when there is a headwind. Paddles come with either a fixed or an adjustable feather angle. If I'm using a paddle with an adjustable feather, I set it to 30 degrees for whitewater and increase it in windy conditions.

DIG DEEPER

Paddles are available in different materials. Light materials reduce paddling fatigue, but are more expensive. Generally, beginners start with plastic paddles, intermediate paddlers upgrade to fiberglass, and advanced paddlers may justify the expense of carbon fiber.

Paddle blade material:

- **Plastic (polymer, polypropylene, nylon):** Plastic blades are inexpensive, heavy, and flexible. A flexible blade makes for inefficient energy transfer to the water. Plastic blades can be durable, but they don't age well (UV damage) and are susceptible to cracking when pushing off or hitting rocks.
- **Composite (fiberglass, carbon fiber):** Composite blades are rigid and durable. Fiberglass provides a nice balance between cost and performance. Carbon fiber is the choice of high-performance paddlers.
- **Wood:** Wood paddles are lightweight, durable, rigid, and aesthetically pleasing. Wood paddles are rare in the packraft community because they are usually one piece.

Paddle Maintenance

Paddles should be cleaned, dried, and disassembled for storage. The connection between pieces typically gets looser with time, with some slop or play developing at the spring clip. It's time to upgrade when the connections get too loose.

PRO TIP!

The segment junctions on some paddles can swell and become difficult to separate, especially if stored wet. To loosen stuck segments, brace the blade vertically between your thighs and use both hands on the shaft to depress the spring clip, then twist. For really sticky shafts, have a friend brace the blade and push the spring clip while you twist on the shaft. Refer to *Chapter 10: Equipment Repair and Modification* for how to make the connections less sticky.

Paddle Leash

Paddle leashes are used to keep the boat nearby in case of capsizing. However, paddle leashes are a significant entanglement hazard, and thus are not recommended on rivers, because turbulent water can wrap the leash around a body limb. Leashes are recommended for open water because the consequences of you getting separated from your boat are more significant.

Some leashes are releasable, which might save you from entrapment . . . or result in you being separated from your boat. Leashes are a complicated safety concern; be intentional and make the right decision for your objective.

CASE STUDY: LEASHES

Paddle leashes are not recommended on rivers because the entanglement hazard is too high. Paddle leashes *are* recommended for open-water crossings. The leash is still an entanglement hazard, but the possibility of entanglement seems worth the risk of separation and drowning during an open-water crossing.

There were three packraft fatalities related to leashes in 2020:

- **Argentina:** The paddler was separated from his packraft during a 1.2-mile (2 km) open-water crossing. He might have been able to hold on to his boat if he had a leash.
- **Russia:** The paddler was entangled by his leash and drowned after capsizing in a river.
- **Japan:** The paddler was presumably entangled by his paddle leash and unable to recover from capsizing in a river.

LIFE VEST

Life vests (a type of personal flotation device, or PFD) should be standard equipment for all outings. Good vests can be as light as one pound (0.45 kg)—a small penalty to pay for increased safety. Life vests provide multiple functions, including buoyancy, warmth, and impact resistance. Replace your life vest when it starts to wear out, as indicated by fading colors and ripped straps or seams.

The key life vest considerations are:
- A snug and comfortable fit.
- Appropriate buoyancy for your weight.
- Impact resistance (for whitewater).

Standard Vests

Standard river life vests are Coast Guard-approved Type III life vests. A Coast Guard-approved life vest is required for permitted rivers, and some regulators will inspect your vest before allowing you to start your journey. The minimum buoyancy of a Type III vest is 15.5 lbs (7 kg), but a buoyancy range is available. 15.5 lbs lifts the average user's nose above the waterline so that they can breathe. Wear the right size vest; dense paddlers need more buoyant vests.

Wear your life vest on top of all other layers (e.g., rain jacket or drysuit). A jacket over a vest can fill with water during a swim and invert over your head.

When sizing a vest, start by tightening the waist straps and work your way up to the shoulders. If you can't get a snug-but-comfortable fit at the shoulders, choose a different vest. Vests also come in women-specific designs, though these aren't available with the same variety of models and sizing as unisex vests.

Make it a standard procedure to check your paddling partners before you get in the water. Look for unzipped zippers, unclipped buckles, a poor fit, etc.

Features of a properly fitting life vest:
- The base of the life vest is at the belly button level.
- The shoulder straps don't rise above your ears when a partner pulls the straps upward.
- There is enough space between your chin and the life vest's top to tuck chin to chest.
- The vest is snug but allows for full range of motion.

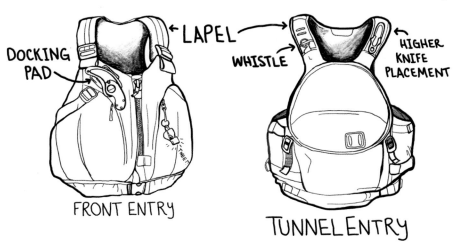

TYPE 3 PFD (STANDARD LIFE JACKET)

DOCKING PAD — ←LAPEL→ WHISTLE ↑ HIGHER KNIFE PLACEMENT

FRONT ENTRY

TUNNEL ENTRY

Life vests were not designed with packrafters in mind, and several common features are inconvenient for us.

Evaluate these details when selecting a life vest:

- **Knife attachment plate:** The knife attachment plate is often in a position that makes the knife hard to access or likely to snag when trying a wet re-entry. You might be able to use cord or zip ties to hold the sheath's tip closer to the life vest, reducing the likelihood of snagging.

- **Storage pockets:** Bulky front panels make it difficult to re-enter your packraft. I like the convenience of storing things in the life vest's zipper pockets—some vests include a throw rope—but everything you store will hinder your re-entry. Also, keep in mind that carrying dense items (hardware) reduces the vest's buoyancy.

- **Multiple-use:** Front-entry life vests can be unzipped and used to sit or sleep on. Sitting and sleeping on vests compresses and degrades the foam, but some packrafters justify this multi-use trade-off.

PRO TIP!

Many life vest zipper-pulls are designed to lock when the zipper-pull is in the down position but to release when the zipper-pull is in any other position. Some vests feature a subtle elastic "keeper" to hold the zipper-pull in place in the sealed position. Use this feature and check your partners to see that they use it too.

Do not attach a whistle to a zipper-pull; a bouncing whistle (in waves or rapids) keeps putting the zipper-pull in the release position and can unzip your vest. *I've seen this happen many times!*

DIY and Inflatable Vests

Do-it-yourself vests: Some expedition packrafters have gotten away with wearing do-it-yourself flotation, either by stuffing rain jackets with sleeping pads or wearing a thin vest with zipper pockets filled with empty water bottles. These options technically increase your buoyancy, but they won't stay on in rough water or protect from impact. My opinion is that safety gear is not the right place to get creative.

Inflatable vests: To my knowledge, there are no Coast Guard-approved inflatable life vests for use in whitewater. The concerns are durability, protection from impact, and buoyancy.

Graham Kraft in a homemade life vest. Russell Fjord, Alaska.

LET'S PLAY IN THE SURF

After hiking and packrafting on the Olympic Peninsula, David Coil and his companions made an impromptu decision to play in the surf.

The sun was setting as we headed into the ocean, and we were unable to hear each other over the roar of the waves. I made it over the first few waves, and then I saw a big one and thought, 'there's no way that I'm not flipping.' I was right.

We had been testing the use of Thermarest sleeping pads as flotation devices—wrap one around your body and then hold it in place with a rain jacket. As I submerged, the Thermarest tried to stay afloat, and the pressure became too much for my jacket, which tore open.

In addition to losing his makeshift life vest, David was shocked by the cold; he was soaked through, had swallowed a significant amount of saltwater, and lost his packraft when the leash broke at a plastic clip. His partners speculate that the only reason he didn't drown was because he held onto the loose Thermarest.

My first thought was, 'Oh shit, there goes an expensive raft. I'm not going to lose this 250 dollar paddle as well.' But as I headed to shore, I quickly realized that the paddle was the least of my worries; I might not make it at all. I ditched the paddle and tried to swim. This is where my memory gets hazy, but I started to realize I could die.

Fortunately, David's partners noticed him heading toward the bigger waves and anticipated him needing help. Andrew Mattox reached David and pulled him into his packraft. The boat could only fit one person, and because Andrew was wearing an actual life vest, he jumped in the water to swim to shore. Andrew started swimming and was met by another friend who towed him to shore. David was effectively unable to help himself, but by laying low in the packraft, he stayed upright and was pushed to shore by the waves.

I've never been so relieved as when I washed up on the beach.

Rescue Vest

Rescue vests are a class of Coast Guard-approved Type V vests popular in difficult whitewater. Rescue vests are designed to withstand significant impact and hydraulic pressure, and include technical features to assist with rescues. However, without training, rescue vests pose new entanglement hazards.

Rescue vest features can include a belay strap, pockets for hardware, and a releasable belt. The releasable belt can be used to belay a rescue swimmer or tow a boat. In both cases, the rescuer must be able to release themselves from the belt—to escape the rescue system and protect themselves. If the release mechanism fails, the rescuer might become another rescuee.

Do not modify a standard life vest by adding a belt or strap. Every strap is an entanglement hazard and should be releasable on both ends. If you are interested in upgrading to a rescue vest, be sure to get trained on its proper use. Also, if you purchase a tow strap ("cow-tail"), strongly consider replacing the stock, non-locking carabiner with one that locks.

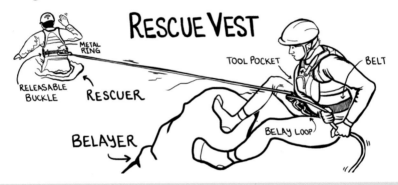

PRO TIP!

The rescue belt passes through a friction plate and buckle that typically features a tethered ball for quick release. If there is too much friction on the belt, or the release mechanism breaks, the belt becomes an entanglement hazard. If your anticipated use of the releasable belt is to tow a packraft, you should only thread through one side of the friction plate or bypass it entirely. Trim the excess belt length to two inches (5 cm) beyond the buckle to ensure intentional release.

HELMET

Early packrafting photos and videos feature people wearing bike or hockey helmets, if anything. The problem with these helmets is that they are designed for a single impact on dry land, not use in water.

Packrafters should wear water-specific helmets. Water-specific helmets feature materials and construction to ensure that the helmet stays intact during multiple impacts underwater. The key helmet considerations are fit, coverage, and special features, such as a short bill that creates an air pocket over your mouth.

BIKE HELMETS: IN ROMAN'S DEFENSE

Roman Dial is widely recognized for his role in popularizing packrafts as white-water boats. In playing that role, Roman spent a decade receiving criticism—from both the kayaking and packrafting communities.

When chided for sharing videos with packrafters wearing bike helmets instead of river helmets, Roman countered, "But this is an improvement! Packrafters weren't wearing any helmets before we started wearing bike helmets!"

Roman's initial motivation was wanting his son to wear a helmet. Seeing Cody Roman paddle whitewater in a helmet made Roman realize that he should wear one too.

When Roman progressed to Class IV rapids and pulled me along, one of our mentors, Timmy Johnson, told me:

> *I know it sucks to buy another helmet. But think of it this way, if you could only have one 'right' helmet, choose the one where your head is bouncing on rocks underwater.*

It was a compelling argument.

Considerations for water-specific helmets:

- **Durability:** River helmets are designed to withstand multiple impacts and are built with materials that will not (easily) break down while wet.

- **Coverage:** River helmets generally extend farther down the back of the skull than bike helmets, and some models include ear and jaw coverage. Full face protection is only necessary for paddlers on shallow, difficult rivers.

- **Fit:** Your helmet should be snug but comfortable.

- **Drain holes:** Drain holes can help water flow through the helmet, reducing suction during a deep plunge. Drain holes are not a critical feature.
- **Visor:** The stubby visor on some water helmets is designed to propel water away from the face, creating an air pocket. Sit with your back to the current and you will quickly appreciate this feature.

A SMASHED BIKE HELMET

Gregg Christopher upgraded his bike helmet to a whitewater helmet after watching a friend's helmet disintegrate during a swim.

I wish I had been able to get better pictures of the damage to this bike helmet after my friend's swim on McCallum Creek. The visor had been ripped off, and the front of the helmet was deformed. The foam had cracked/shattered and wasn't going to take another hit. The bike helmet was visibly disintegrating from the short swim, especially where the foam didn't have any hard plastic cover.

CLOTHING AND FOOTWEAR

Appropriate clothing for watersports follows the same principles as for land-based recreation. The layering of non-cotton fabrics allows for versatility and thermal regulation in mixed and varying conditions.

The general layering strategy for backpacking and packrafting is to wear a thin moisture-wicking base layer; thicker, warmer layers as insulation; and finally, rain gear, or a dry top, or a drysuit as an outer shell. I prefer wool base layers for their odor management, but synthetic base layers are cheaper and dry faster. Fleece or thin, insulated jackets and pants make for good middle layers.

Dress for the swim: From a safety perspective, our concern is capsizing and going for a swim. Therefore, you should wear layers that will keep you warm during a swim. It's easier to cool off than it is to warm up, so err on the side of too many layers, especially on open-water crossings where you might not get the chance to swap layers. Cold water has been a significant factor in most packrafting fatalities and many incidents.

Insulate your legs: Your legs hold a lot of blood, and it is common to under-estimate the effectiveness of insulating them. I wear lightweight, insulated puffy pants and thick, warm socks in oversized shoes when paddling cold water.

MARK OATES: STANDING COLD

After a 7.5-mile (12-km) flatwater paddle at the end of the winter in New Zealand, Mark Oates and his partners climbed from their boats and immediately experienced a drop in core temperature.

> We were all warm and happy in our boats, but as soon as we jumped out to set up camp, we could barely function. Our hands were shaking so much we struggled to light a stove. Fortunately, a hot, sugary drink seemed almost immediately to solve the problem. We were all glad that we weren't trying to deal with this condition solo.

I have experienced a less-extreme version of this phenomenon. Moving usually generates warmth; what is different in a packraft?

A friend explained it to me this way: While paddling through cold water, the blood in our legs gets cold and doesn't circulate. Our core remains relatively warm because our upper body moves and the blood recirculates. When we get out of the boat, the cold blood in our legs circulates through the rest of our body, lowering our core temperature.

Carry a spare set: Keep a set of clothing in a dry bag. You don't need two of everything, but switching from wet to dry base layers makes a big difference when you get wet.

Hats and gloves: These are very effective at trapping heat and can make a big difference in comfort. A neoprene helmet-liner is worthwhile during cold days on the water. Cold-weather paddling is much more comfortable in neoprene gloves, mittens, or pogies.

Glove options:

- **Gloves:** Gloves are dexterous, to a degree, but usually have to be removed for finger work.
- **Mittens:** Mittens are warmer and easier to remove.
- **Pogies:** Pogies are sleeves that attach to the paddle. Pogies are surprisingly effective at keeping your hands warm and allowing you to quickly do tactile work, like using a throw bag.

PRO TIP!

One-gallon plastic bags make for effective makeshift expedition pogies. Cut off the two bottom corners of the bag and split the paddle to feed the bag onto the paddle shaft. Even using one bag is helpful, switching hands throughout the day.

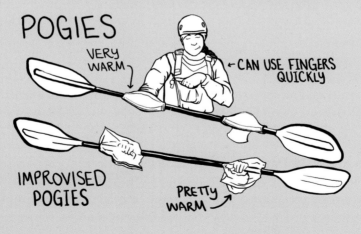

Footwear: Packrafting footwear should be lightweight, drain well, have good traction, and provide full coverage to protect your feet from rocks. If minimal hiking is involved, specific river footwear and neoprene booties are generally warmer and more comfortable. If you are hiking, trail-running shoes are preferable to hiking boots because boots are heavy, bulky, and less likely to dry. The bulk of hiking boots could contribute to foot entrapment.

Open-toed shoes, like sandals, are not a good choice because they don't protect your feet during swims and portages, and will likely be ripped from your feet while swimming.

Tuck shoelaces away as best as possible as they can present an entanglement hazard.

OUTERWEAR: DRYSUIT AND RAINGEAR

The most common outerwear options are drysuits and rain gear. Rain gear is light and often sufficiently warm while paddling, but jackets can be dangerous during a swim. When you use rain gear, acknowledge that you are more vulnerable and more at risk.

When friends in Alaska ask for advice regarding a packraft purchase, I recommend that they include drysuit cost in their budgeting. Many packrafters (like me) start in rain gear instead of a drysuit. But in addition to not being as safe, packrafting is not as fun when you are cold.

Depending on your location, other outerwear options might be preferable. Outerwear options include:

- **Splash jackets and rain gear:** Rain gear is the most affordable outerwear option. Rain gear may be suitable for easy water, but swimming in rain gear can be dangerous. Besides getting soaked and cold, moving your arms is difficult when the jacket sleeves fill with water. Be sure to wear your life vest over your outerwear to limit the jacket's ability to fill with water. Rain gear is not appropriate on cold and challenging whitewater.

- **Drysuits:** Drysuits are fully waterproof, one-piece layers that have latex gaskets at every opening. Latex gaskets can be uncomfortably tight, especially when they are new, and during long days on the water.

- **Dry tops:** Dry tops keep your upper body dry and are appropriate in moderate climates.

- **Semi-drysuits:** Semi-drysuits feature neoprene gaskets instead of latex. The neoprene gaskets are more comfortable but do not keep you as dry during a swim.

- **Wetsuits:** Wetsuits are less popular than drysuits in the packraft community because they are bulky and can't accommodate clothing layering.

- **Waders:** Do not wear waders on moving water. Waders (waterproof pants with permanently attached booties) can fill with water. The trapped water increases your lower body mass to hundreds of pounds; you can't use your legs to swim when they weigh that much.

Drysuits

Drysuits are a significant investment but well worth the price if you are paddling cold water. Drysuit considerations include:

- **Cost and materials:** Drysuits range from 500 to 1,200 USD. Breathable suits may use GORE-TEX (most expensive) or other waterproof/breathable fabrics (less expensive). Some guiding companies use non-breathable materials since they are more affordable, but these suits are not popular with recreational boaters because trapped moisture (sweat, condensation from body heat) can lead to cold body temperatures.

- **Fit:** An appropriate fit allows a full range of motion without excess loose material. Standard-size gaskets (e.g., a large suit will come with large wrist gaskets) might not fit you. You can either order a suit with specific gaskets or replace the gaskets yourself (see *Chapter 10: Equipment Repair and Modification*).

- **Entry:** Drysuits come with various entry options, with either metal or plastic-toothed zippers. Drysuits will have an entry zipper between the shoulder blades, across the chest, or around the waist. Entry style is a matter of personal preference.

- **Relief zippers:** Drysuits typically have no relief zipper, a front relief zipper, or a full drop-seat. Your preference will be based on ease of peeing, comfort, and cost.

- **Feet:** Drysuits are available with different foot configurations. Options include latex gaskets at the ankles, integrated latex socks, or integrated waterproof socks. Latex socks are less durable than GORE-TEX but are easier to repair. Both materials will wear out with any significant hiking.

- **Gaskets:** Gaskets come in several sizes. Neck gaskets that are too tight can be stretched, either on a cylindrical object or by multiple hours of wear. You can also trim neck gaskets. Trim and test the gasket in small intervals (⅛ inch, 2 millimeter) so that you don't risk making it too loose. Wrist gaskets are not meant to be trimmed. Consider including an extra neck and wrist gasket in your repair kit for major expeditions. Refer to *Chapter 10: Equipment Repair and Modification* for gasket repair instructions.

- **Durability:** As a general rule, lighter suits are less durable. And despite their price tags, drysuits do not have a long life expectancy. Anticipate replacing wrist and neck gaskets every one to two years and the full suit after four or five years of moderate recreational use.

Swiftwater Rescue Technician training. Eagle River, Alaska.

> ## PRO TIP!
>
> Significant hiking in a drysuit with integrated socks will cause leaks. Thin neoprene socks (0.5 mm) are an inexpensive way to keep your feet warm and protect drysuit socks. Wear the neoprene socks over your drysuit.

Putting on your drysuit:

1. Remove sharp objects from your wrists and neck, such as watches and jewelry.
2. Remove your shoes.
3. Enter the drysuit through the zipper, stepping into each leg.
4. Push your hands and feet through the gaskets (or into the socks).
5. Grab the neck gasket with both hands, stretch the gasket, and pull it over your head in one motion. Do not drag the gasket over your head by pulling on the drysuit fabric, which may damage the gasket.

Maintenance: Gaskets are the weak link on drysuits. Latex degrades naturally with time, but the process will be significantly faster with UV or chemical exposure (mosquito repellent, sunscreen).

New latex is shiny, and the luster will begin to dull with age. Old latex develops a soft tiger-stripe texture when stretched. The tiger stripes are a sure sign that the gasket will fail at the next least-convenient opportunity.

You can extend the life of a latex gasket with the regular application of 303 Aerospace Protectant (UV protection). Drysuit brands recommend monthly applications. Spray the protectant on to the gasket material and remove the excess with a rag.

Keep your suit zipper clean of dirt and never force it open or closed. Use soap and water to clean the zipper. Lubricate metal zippers with paraffin or beeswax and store the suit with the zipper sealed except for the last two inches (5-cm). Lubricate plastic zippers with semi-solid zipper lubricant (Gear Aid, McNett, etc.) and store the suit with the zipper entirely closed.

> ## *PRO TIP!*
>
> Only apply 303 Protectant to latex drysuit gaskets, not to packrafts. It will make your packraft look new and shiny, but the coating can make a field repair less likely to adhere.

COMMUNICATION

For trips without cell service, carry a satellite communication device. Keep your device protected from the water, and wear it on your body (inside your drysuit) so that you don't risk losing it during a swim.

Communication devices:

- **Phone or satellite phone**: Rescue professionals want to hear your voice. Even with frequently dropped calls, satellite phones are the most efficient way to transfer critical information. Store your phone in a waterproof case.

- **Two-way text messengers (SPOT X, Garmin inReach, and similar):** These devices are more affordable than satellite phones and work well for everything except an urgent evacuation.

- **Personal Location Beacons (PLBs) and one-way messengers (SPOT):** SOS messengers are only suitable for an outgoing SOS call, which, depending on your situation, might not be as helpful as you hope.

ADDITIONAL PACKRAFTING EQUIPMENT

In addition to standard overnight and outdoor equipment, these items are also worth adding to your kit.

Throw bag: Throw bags are used to quickly deploy rope to a swimmer in the water. Throw bags are discussed in detail in *Chapter 9: River Rescue From Shore*.

Whistle: Attach the whistle to your life vest so that it is easily accessible. *Do not attach a whistle to the zipper-pull* (refer to the *Life Vest* section earlier). Whistles intended for water don't have a cork ball inside because the cork deteriorates when exposed to water.

Carabiners: Locking carabiners are handy in many applications. Don't use or carry a non-locking carabiner anywhere that it might get inadvertently clipped—this is an entrapment hazard.

River knife: River knives are specifically designed for water-related activities. River knives feature a sheath designed to mount on a life vest, a blunt nose, and one cutting and one blunt edge. The flat nose prevents accidental punctures and the dull edge provides a thumb-stop for applying cutting power.

Mount the knife on your life vest. Note that most attachment plates place the knife in a position that can snag during wet re-entry. Review the *Life Vest* section above.

Practice quickly accessing the knife and placing your thumb on the blunt edge. You want to have the muscle memory to retrieve your knife with eyes closed and in turbulent water.

Extra paddle: Large groups and remote destinations justify carrying a spare 4-piece paddle.

Sails: The sea kayak community uses lightweight and compact sails (less than 1 lb, 0.5 kg) that work well with packrafts. The sail can be managed with one hand, freeing up your other hand to drag the paddle behind you as a keel. These sails are rated for winds of 4 to 14 knots (4-15 mph, 2-7 m/s).

Rudders/skegs: Detachable rudders or skegs can improve the packraft's tracking. These accessories can easily earn their weight by improving efficiency.

Firestarter: Carry a firestarter in an inner pocket in case you get separated from your boat.

First aid kit: Carry a standard first aid kit: pain-killer, anti-inflammatory, wound care, etc. Refer to *Chapter 11: Medical Emergencies* for first aid kit suggestions.

BRAD'S FACE SMEAR

During the 2014 McCarthy Creek Packraft Race in Alaska, Brad Meiklejohn was paddling sweep (safety boat) to keep a line-of-sight with the last few packrafters. Brad looked over his shoulder to check for packrafts behind him but then broached (drifted sideways) into a rock and capsized.

During the capsize, a non-locking carabiner attaching a throw bag to the back-band clipped onto a drawcord on Brad's drysuit. The entrapment kept Brad from re-entry; he was stuck under his boat until he ground to a stop in shallow water: "I can only describe it as a face-smear." Once he drifted to shallow water, Brad was able to kneel and get his head out of the water. Becky King and Tony Perelli arrived and unclipped the carabiner.

The story of Brad's close call made the rounds, and by the next week, the rest of us had removed all non-locking carabiners from our kits. Of course, the kayakers already knew to do this. It took a close call by "one of our own" to make us recognize the hazard of non-locking 'biners.

Brad Meiklejohn. Meghalaya, India.

Sarah Heck. Willow Creek, Alaska.

CHAPTER 2

BOAT CONTROL AND WET RE-ENTRY

Once you become familiar with your equipment's limitations and safety consid-erations, you'll likely be eager to get in the water. This book's common theme is anticipating what can go wrong and practicing how to respond when it does. The most likely thing to go wrong while packrafting is capsizing and coming out of the boat. Therefore, your priority is to experiment with recovering from a capsize. We call this technique a **wet re-entry**. Wet re-entries are not possible for all paddlers and all packrafts, so it is important to determine your options ahead of time. Start in a lake or other controlled setting, and stay close to shore until you perfect your technique.

After gaining confidence when recovering from a capsize, turn your focus to boat control. Boat control involves using different paddle strokes to maneuver your packraft, and shifting your body position to influence how the packraft's edges interact with the water. **Edging** involves pushing one side of the packraft deeper into the water to give the river something more substantial to grab. These techniques allow you to use the river's force to play, explore, and manage hazards. These boat control techniques should be practiced in a controlled setting (ideally a lake or pool) before venturing far from shore or down a river.

WHAT YOU NEED TO KNOW

This chapter presents how we would spend our first hours in the water during an in-person class:

- Start by ensuring that you can get out of the boat if you capsize. If the packraft has a spray skirt, practice pulling it free.
- Practice wet re-entries, assisted and alone. Train yourself not to push off the bottom, which could result in foot entrapment.
- Experiment with different paddle strokes. Paddling will be most effective with a well-fitting boat, proper paddling position, and suitable paddle length.
- Experiment with edging by shifting your weight from side to side to balance the boat on edge. Try to prevent capsizing with a low brace (discussed below), and when you do capsize, practice your wet re-entry.

GETTING IN AND OUT OF THE BOAT

Entering and exiting your packraft sounds like the easy part, but I'm not the only packrafter who has taken an embarrassing swim at the take-out.

Spray skirt: If your packraft has a spray skirt, you will generally want to put it on before entering the water.

To put on the spray skirt:

1. Start by putting the skirt's back over the back of the cockpit coaming behind you.
2. Work the skirt up the sides to your hips, ensuring that it stays secured under the coaming.
3. When the skirt is in place up to your hips or farther forward, use both hands to pull the skirt forward and tight.
4. Make sure the grab loop is visible and on top of the skirt.
5. Stretch the elastic of the skirt until you can secure it over the front of the coaming.
6. Run your hands around the coaming to make sure that the skirt is in place.

MR. COOL GUY

One of my first packraft trips was through the Bob Marshall Wilderness in Montana in 2008. I was a confident hiker and novice packrafter, which helps explain why I thought it was okay to travel alone. I borrowed a bike in Missoula, chained it to a tree at a Bob Marshall trailhead, and felt proud of my route as I hiked and packrafted through the impressive wilderness.

I saw a large raft party camped on the South Fork of the Flathead River and paddled over to say hello. The group had never seen a packraft and was impressed when I explained that I was midway from Missoula to Great Falls (250 miles, 400 km), alone and under my own power.

I enjoyed the attention—I was proud of this creative and ambitious trip. But in classic Mr. Cool Guy form, when I stepped out of the packraft, I immediately slipped and fell in the mud. The rafters' demeanor changed from impressed to concerned, despite my claim that I was okay and knew what I was doing. Obviously.

Pulling the grab loop: It is important to keep the spray skirt's grab loop exposed—not folded under the deck—when putting on the skirt. Packraft skirts are generally eager to pop off, but if not, you will need to pull the skirt by the grab loop to exit the boat. Practice finding the grab loop with your eyes closed, like you might need to do while underwater. To find the grab loop, place your hands on the coaming at the 10 and 2 o'clock positions, then slide them together to the 12 o'clock position. If the grab loop is caught under the deck, drive a knee through the center of the skirt to break it free.

PRO TIP!

- If your skirt is difficult to stretch over the coaming, get it wet. The skirt fabric is more willing to stretch when wet.
- A wiffle golf ball attached to the grab loop makes it easier to find and pull when you are underwater.

Entering the water: Getting in your packraft is easiest in shallow water that is not swift. For our purposes, "swift" implies that you can't fully control your movement. It is generally appropriate to wade into shallow water until it gets swift.

Getting in a packraft in shallow water:

1. Wade into the water until you are ankle- to knee-deep.
2. If you can place one foot in the packraft and depress the floor to the river bottom, straddle the side tube and climb in; the packraft will stay in place.
3. If you can't push the floor to the river bottom, straddle the stern, sit, then swing one leg at a time into the cockpit.
4. Lift your hips and push off with your paddle to scoot into deeper water.

Getting in a packraft in deep water that is not swift:

1. Lay the paddle across the packraft as a brace, one blade on the packraft and one blade on the bank.
2. Place your hands on the paddle shaft and press down, lowering your butt onto the side tube or stern.
3. When you are balanced, slide one leg into the cockpit, then the other leg.
4. Slide into the seat.

Seal launch: If the shore is steep and smooth (nothing that could tear the floor), you can perform a seal launch by sitting in the boat and then sliding down the bank into the water. Be careful not to use this technique on sharp ground.

Swiftwater: Entering swiftwater along a steep and rocky bank is the most challenging scenario. It is usually worth the effort of searching for an eddy, even a small one, as an entry point. Eddies are zones of slower water that often form behind rocks or protrusions in the bank. We can use eddies as on- or off-ramps into the main current rather than merging directly into traffic. Catching and exiting eddies are discussed in *Part II: Rivers and Open Water*.

Getting in a packraft in swiftwater:

1. Place your boat in a position where it is barely secure on land, but be wary of sharp rocks. It is usually easier to have the bow facing upstream.
2. Enter the boat and slide into the water with an aggressive downstream lean.
3. Use the paddle as a stabilizing lever arm on the shore and then grab the downstream current by plunging the blade into deep water (refer to the principles of river-running in *Chapter 5: The Principles of River-running*).

Having a partner to hold your boat is a huge help. Note that installing perimeter lines makes it much easier for a partner to stabilize your boat.

Exiting the packraft: Exiting the boat is the reverse process of entering. The trick is trying to get the boat stuck on the bank, which is easiest in calm water.

1. Release your thigh straps and spray skirt.
2. Approach the shore with speed and try to catch the bow high on the bank at the last possible moment.
3. Use the paddle as a stabilizing brace between the hull and the shore.
4. Swing a leg out of the cockpit and into the water. Scoot your butt onto the side tube or stern and then stand up, keeping a hand on your boat. Again, having a partner hold your packraft is a huge help.

Exiting the packraft in swiftwater: Getting out of the boat in fast and continuous water can be especially challenging. One trick is to take advantage of the slower water along the inside bank of a **riverbend**. Note that river dynamics get more complicated at high water levels; refer to *Chapter 6: Navigating River Features* for more information.

Exiting the packraft in swiftwater:

1. Paddle toward the inside of the riverbend and rotate your boat so that the bow points upstream.

2. Use forward strokes to paddle upstream and slow your downstream drift.

3. When you are near the bank, use a powerful forward stroke to scoot the bow up onto the bank. Hopefully, the bow will stick to the bank long enough for you to swing a leg onto shore.

Dry exit: Sometimes, especially when making an urgent exit, you have limited choices. An option in these scenarios is a dry exit, which involves climbing directly onto rocks or wood. Position your packraft next to the object you want to climb on. Use the same principles as a standard exit, possibly transitioning to a seated straddle on the side tube or stern, or using the paddle as a brace to push out of the cockpit. Leave one foot in the cockpit holding the boat in place while you secure your other foot on land.

SELF-RESCUE: WET RE-ENTRY

A wet re-entry should be second nature for all packrafters. Develop re-entry skills in a controlled environment before paddling swiftwater or attempting open-water crossings. This is our capsize recovery technique, our version of the kayak roll.

There are two techniques for re-entry: horizontal and vertical. Practice them both to determine which is best for you. Some paddlers will need help; practice assisted re-entries.

Considerations when attempting wet re-entries:

■ Don't allow yourself to push off the bottom. Standing on the riverbed in swiftwater can result in foot entrapment. Managing foot entrapment is covered in *Chapter 9: River Rescue From Shore.*

■ Re-entry is more challenging with bulky life vests and more difficult for smaller and shorter paddlers.

■ I prefer not having perimeter lines along the sides of my boat since they can snag a life vest, especially the knife handle. Review the discussion in *Chapter 1: Packrafting Equipment.*

Overturning the Boat

Before you can re-enter your packraft, you need to restore it to the upright position. Overturning the boat can be challenging, especially when loaded with cargo. Overturning a boat with a heavy pack or bike might not be possible.

An empty boat can usually be flipped from the side. Try to push the nearest tube up and away. If the boat is sideways to the current, pushing the downstream tube up out of the water allows the current to grab the upstream tube and help rotate the boat. You might be able to grab the far tube (deck or thigh strap) from under the water and pull it toward you.

Loaded boats are easier to flip from the bow or stern. If there is a pack on the bow, grab the pack itself, with both hands, and twist it. The boat should follow. If there is no pack, use the same twisting motion with the perimeter lines at the bow or stern.

PRO TIP!

During Erin McKittrick and Bretwood "Hig" Higman's 4,000-mile expedition from Seattle to False Point (Aleutian Peninsula, Alaska), they devised a cargo release system to quickly release their packs from the bow so that the boats were easier to overturn. The pack was leashed to the boat so that they could retrieve it after their wet re-entry.

Refer to *Chapter 7: Open-water Crossings* for more discussion about leashes.

Wet re-entry practice. Margaret Williams and Tony Perelli, Willow Creek, Alaska.

Horizontal Re-entry: The Sneak

Most paddlers find a horizontal 'sneak' wet re-entry technique to be easiest. With the boat in the upright position, hold the near tube with one arm and brace the paddle over the cockpit with your other arm. While holding onto the packraft, bring your legs to the surface of the water and kick hard, effectively swimming directly at the packraft. Build momentum toward the boat, then push the nearest tube down with your arms and torso so that you can slide your torso over the tube. An aggressive kick is critical here. I think of this as a sneak because you can effectively pull the boat under your torso, like pulling a tablecloth out from under dinnerware.

You will reach a balance point where the boat will either flip back on top of you or stay upright so you can kick your way into the cockpit. Get your butt in the cockpit and swing your legs into the boat, checking downriver for the next hazard.

Vertical Re-entry: The Dunk

In this technique, set up holding the boat as described above, but now position your body upright in the water. Dunk your body straight down, and then use the life vest's buoyancy along with hard kicks to launch yourself up out of the water as high as possible (like a dolphin or water polo player). Kick! At your highest position, push the nearest tube down and fold your torso into the cockpit. Kick and squirm to get your butt on the seat and legs in the boat.

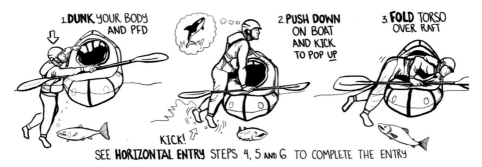

SEE **HORIZONTAL ENTRY** STEPS 4, 5 AND 6 TO COMPLETE THE ENTRY

Angled Approach Technique

Some swimmers struggle with re-entries because the packraft flips back upside down as soon as they put any weight on the side tube. The problem is that the packraft is least stable in this orientation—the same orientation that caused it to capsize in the first place. Try approaching the boat at a 45-degree angle from the stern. Placing some of your weight on the stern instead of the side tube can make the boat more stable.

Wet re-entry practice. Sarah Histand, Lowe River, Alaska. © Jessica Young, PWSC

Assisted Wet Re-entry

Even if you know a swimmer is capable of a solo wet re-entry, get in position to assist. Helping as a safety boat is discussed in *Chapter 8: River Rescue From the Water*.

Steps to assist a wet re-entry:

1. Paddle to the loose boat and flip it upright.
2. Drag or bump the boat to the swimmer.
3. Move into position to hold the far side of the packraft as the swimmer climbs in. If you don't have a free hand, brace your paddle across their boat and apply downward pressure.
4. A tired swimmer might need more help—reach across the cockpit and grab the swimmer by their life vest lapel to help pull them into the cockpit.

PARTNER-ASSISTED RE-ENTRY

PADDLE STROKES

Boat control—getting your boat to go where you want—is fundamental to making a plan and executing it. Boat control involves grabbing, or being grabbed by, the river. We have two ways to grab the river: using the paddle and using the bottom of the packraft. This section describes using paddle strokes to grab the river, and the following section describes edging, which involves pushing one side of the floor deeper into the water.

Boat control is a full-body activity. Adjust your outfitting to support a proper paddling position as much as possible, and use your core muscles for stability and power. Keep your elbows low to protect your shoulders from injury. Use or install thigh straps for even more control.

An effective way to learn different paddle strokes is to play games on flat water. Options include tag, passing a ball around, chasing a (beach) ball downriver, or bumper boats (try to tap opponents' sterns with your bow).

Develop your boat control skills in a safe setting before venturing out to more committing locations. Applying these principles to rivers and open water is discussed in *Part II*.

Athletic Stance

Crossover athletes are likely familiar with the concept of an athletic stance. The athletic stance puts you in a position to move quickly with power—on the court or in the mountains. The athletic stance equivalent in paddlesports is proper paddling position.

Adjust fit and position: An athletic paddling position involves sitting tall (good posture) with a slightly relaxed spine. Depending on your flexibility and leg positions, sitting tall can be taxing on your core muscles. The boat can help—every point of contact provides support to hold you upright. Adjust your seat and backband, and consider installing thigh straps and a foot brace to maximize contact.

Relax your spine: A slight spine relaxation serves two purposes: it is exhausting to hold tension in the spine, and relaxation provides shock absorption. You will need a relaxed spine to change positions as your paddle: a forward lean (hinging from your hips) when using power strokes, leaning to a side for edge control and to make a draw stroke, etc.

Use your core: Arm muscles are significantly smaller and weaker than torso muscles. Effective paddling comes from the core, with arms used for placement rather than power. If you notice that your arms are doing the power work, re-engage your core. To convince yourself that your torso can do all of the work, hold the paddle in front of you with arms straight and elbows locked. Notice that you can make paddle strokes by rotating your torso, even if your elbows stay locked.

Protect your shoulders: To protect your shoulders from injury, keep your elbows low and in front of your torso. Arm extensions, especially reaching overhead, put your shoulder in an injury-prone position. Shoulder injuries are discussed in *Chapter 11: Medical Emergencies.*

Grip and Orientation

The paddle should be gripped with spacing similar to doing push-ups or pull-ups. Grab the paddle shaft with both hands and raise it to a resting position on top of your head. Slide your hands along the paddle until each elbow is at a right angle (90-degrees between the forearm and upper arm).

Paddle index: Some paddle shafts have an index, which is a slightly ellipsoidal section in the grip positions. The indexes can help you identify where to hold the paddle.

Dominant hand: Hold your paddle with one fixed grip (dominant hand) and one pivoting grip (off-hand). Left-handed paddlers might be able to find custom paddles, but most use a right-hand paddle. Note that a loose grip is usually sufficient; holding the shaft too firmly results in forearm fatigue.

Power face: Most paddle blades have a concave and asymmetrical shape. Orient the paddle so that its concave part—the power face—faces the stern. You get more power when the power face scoops water. If your blade is asymmetrical, the shorter edge of the blade should be on the bottom.

Power Strokes

Power strokes are used for propulsion—to move faster or slower than the current. When you passively float in a river, the boat goes where the river wants you to go. Power strokes provide the propulsion to move the packraft to where *you* want it to be. If you need to avoid a hazard and only have time for a few strokes, make them count by using power strokes.

It is fairly common for novice paddlers to make forward strokes that barely catch the surface of the water. This "**lily-dipping**" technique does not effectively propel the boat. A few strong power strokes are much more effective than a whirlwind of lily-dipping strokes.

Forward stroke: Power comes from your core, and the easiest way to transfer that power to the water is with a forward stroke and torso rotation.

- **Catch:** Lean forward by hinging from your hips. Plunge the entire blade into the water, as near to upright as possible—think of the water as wet cement. The blade should be at your knees or farther forward for maximum power.

- **Power:** Rotate your torso to pull the boat through the water. Visualize pulling the boat through the water as opposed to pulling the paddle toward the boat.

- **Release:** Withdraw the blade from the water when it is in line with your hips. You might need to rotate the blade's angle so that it can slice up and out of the water with the least resistance.

PRO TIP!

Extending the stroke past your hips doesn't add power; it pulls your boat down into the water and leaves you in an unstable position. When the paddle is behind your hips, in line with the side tubes, you lose the ability to brace for stability.

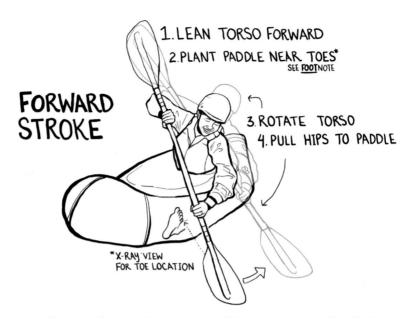

FORWARD STROKE

1. LEAN TORSO FORWARD
2. PLANT PADDLE NEAR TOES*
SEE **FOOT**NOTE

3. ROTATE TORSO
4. PULL HIPS TO PADDLE

*X-RAY VIEW
FOR TOE LOCATION

Back stroke: Back strokes are the opposite of forward strokes. Catch the water near your hips and use your torso to push the boat away from the paddle. Back strokes are beneficial when you want to keep facing downstream but need to slow your downstream motion (to scan downriver for hazards, allow other paddlers to catch up, etc.). Aggressive back strokes can feel unstable; you might be better off spinning the packraft to face upstream and using forward strokes.

Boof stroke: A boof is an advanced power stroke used to propel your packraft over **sticky** features. Boofs are discussed in *Chapter 6: Navigating River Features*.

PRO TIP!

All of the paddle strokes can be blended. See how many you can do without taking your paddle out of the water.

Sweep Strokes

Packrafts are inclined to turn, whether we like it or not. For intentional turning, try a sweep. A sweep is like a power stroke turned on its side. Instead of digging vertically into the water, you will sweep horizontally, keeping the paddle shaft as close to horizontal as possible. The blade should remain in the upper six inches (15 cm) of water during the entire stroke. Sweeps can either be slow and passive or quick and powerful. The farther you can reach the paddle, the more effective the turn.

Steps to make a forward sweep:

1. Reach toward the bow and place the blade at the surface of the water, with the power face oriented vertically to catch the upper six inches (15 cm) of water.
2. Twist your torso to provide the power that will sweep the blade in a broad arc at the top of the water column. Finish at a position in line with your hips.
3. The boat will rotate away from the sweep.

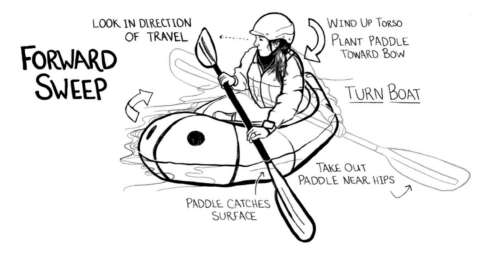

Reverse sweep: A reverse sweep is similar in principle. Start the stroke by placing the paddle toward the stern (45 degrees from the stern is a good target) and then sweep it forward to finish in line with your hips.

Draws

Draw strokes are very effective in packrafts and are a valuable addition to your quiver—especially if you intend to paddle more challenging water. Draw strokes are practical because packrafts sit shallowly in the water and spin easily. A draw stroke allows us to "grab" deeper water. These strokes are used to slide the boat laterally, make rudder-like rotational adjustments, or catch the river's current like an anchor. Draw strokes are recognizable by their distinct near-vertical paddle orientation.

Paddle dexterity: Draws and braces (discussed below) involve paddle dexterity, or wrist manipulation, to control the blade's angle in the water. By bending your wrists, you can change the blade's angle in the water by 180 degrees.

Practice paddle dexterity with this exercise:
1. Hold the paddle level in a ready-to-paddle horizontal position.
2. Bend both hands down at the wrist so that your palms face toward your body (flexion) and the blade's power faces orient upward.
3. Bend both hands back so your palms face away from your body (extension). Note that the power faces of the blades rotate down, toward the water.

Paddle dexterity during a draw stroke allows you to change the force of the current on the blade, similar to playing with the air current when you reach your hand out the window of a fast-moving car. Adjusting the blade angle allows you to capture more or less of the river's force to suit your needs.

Side draw: A side draw can be used to move sideways or turn. This stroke can help maneuver your boat to shore in calm water or anchor into a **tongue** of well-behaving water when running rapids.

1. Rotate your torso toward the side tube. An engaged torso is critical; it provides power and stability.
2. Plant the paddle in an upright orientation, blade parallel to the boat, at a position in line with your hips.
3. The blade's distance from the boat will depend on the boat's width, your arm length, and what you are trying to accomplish. My side draws are commonly within a foot (30 cm) of the tube.
4. Keep your elbows below shoulder height and the upper hand below head height to protect your shoulders from injury. Holding the paddle in an upright position requires you to bring your upper arm across your torso such that your upper hand stacks above the lower hand. A nice form-check is to imagine looking at a watch on your upper wrist. If your imaginary watch is too high to read, you are at risk of a shoulder injury.
5. With the blade fully submerged in the water, power face toward the boat, draw your hip toward the paddle to move sideways. If using the draw to anchor into the river's current, lean against the paddle to put the boat on edge.

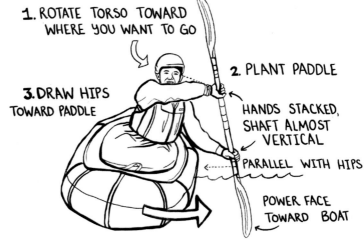

SIDE DRAW

1. ROTATE TORSO TOWARD WHERE YOU WANT TO GO

2. PLANT PADDLE

3. DRAW HIPS TOWARD PADDLE

HANDS STACKED, SHAFT ALMOST VERTICAL

PARALLEL WITH HIPS

POWER FACE TOWARD BOAT

Sculling draw: A side draw with active paddle dexterity can move your boat sideways in the water. This technique is called a sculling draw. Instead of pulling the blade out of the water to make multiple draw strokes, leave the blade in the water and trace figure eights on their side (like the infinity symbol, or spreading frosting). The straight segments of each "eight" slice the blade away from the boat diagonally. The other parts of the "eight" are the draws that pull your boat toward the paddle.

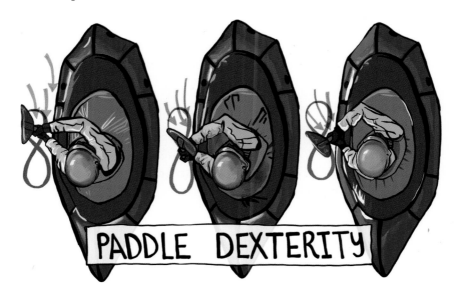

PADDLE DEXTERITY

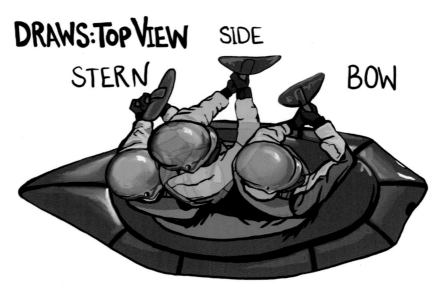

DRAWS: TOP VIEW   SIDE
STERN   BOW

Bow draw: A bow draw functions similarly to the side draw, but with the paddle nearer to the bow. The bow draw is useful for making sharp turns, especially catching and peeling out from eddies, as discussed in *Chapter 6: Navigating River Features.*

With hands stacked on a near-upright paddle, place the paddle at a position approximately 45 degrees from the bow. Submerge the entire blade. The angle of the blade relative to the current will depend on your application. In general, you want to catch the current with the power face of the blade. Use paddle dexterity to adjust the angle of the blade during the stroke.

The bow draw turn can be gradual, by holding the draw in a stationary position, or quick, by pulling the boat toward the paddle. Bow draws are more effective with forward momentum because the blade's power face can catch more current and do more work.

A bow draw can transition to a forward stroke, a great combination when you want to turn and then propel away.

Stern draw: A stern or rudder draw is very similar to a bow draw, but the paddle is placed in the water behind your hips at approximately 45-degrees from the stern. A slight stern draw can be used at the end of a forward stroke to help the packraft track in a straight line.

Braces

Braces are recovery and stability strokes. Braces can be anticipated ("I expect to get pushed to the left by that wave") or reactive, like reaching out to catch a fall. Low and high braces share the same strategy: slap a paddle blade flat against the surface of the water to generate leverage and restore the packraft to an upright position.

A good brace can prevent you from capsizing, but bracing is difficult in packrafts. Our boats have poor secondary stability (stability on edge); by the time we need to brace, it is often too late. Even so, these techniques are worth practicing and will help keep you upright in whitewater, the surf, or choppy open water.

Bracing to stay upright. Shasta Hood, Kings River, Alaska.

Braces work because of torque. Torque depends on the length of a lever arm, the arm's angle relative to the rotation axis, and the force at the end of the arm. You can generate the most torque when each variable is optimized:

- **Force:** Large paddle blades generate more force on the surface of the water.

- **Length:** Reaching away from the boat makes the lever arm longer. Bracing is easier with longer paddles.

- **Angle:** Place the paddle as close to perpendicular as possible; ideally, in line with the hips.

Low brace: Low braces are my default response to any instability. I prefer a low brace to a high brace because low braces are safer for my shoulders. Unfortunately, low braces can be challenging in packrafts due to the tube height. Having the right boat fit, especially sitting tall enough, is critical to developing a low brace in a packraft. But this technique might not be possible in all models.

How to low brace:

1. Hold the paddle horizontal in a neutral paddling position. Use paddle dexterity—don't change your grip—to position the back of the blade toward the water. Part of why the low brace is so useful is that you can quickly get into position without changing your grip.
2. With the paddle held low and the back of the blades facing the water's surface, raise your elbows to a height near your armpits, keeping a 90-degree angle between your torso and upper arms. One of my mentors calls this the "Donkey Kong" or "angry boss" position.
3. Reach the paddle to the falling side. Keep the paddle horizontal, low, and as close to the water as possible. The leading elbow should be bent at approximately 120-degrees; the following elbow will be bent tight, and held near your stomach.
4. Punch your leading fist downward to slap the surface of the water. The slap is important—you lose the brace's power as soon as the blade sinks into the water.
5. Drop your head toward the water and snap your hips away from your head—pushing your hips away from the brace.
6. Use paddle dexterity to rotate the blade for an easy slice up to the surface. If you don't make this correction, pulling the blade upward can catch water and cause you to fall back toward the water.

The hip snap: Dropping your head toward the water (from step 5 in the preceding list) is not intuitive and takes time to perfect. Your brain anticipates capsizing and naturally reacts by pulling your head away from the water. The problem is that a high head raises your center of gravity, which makes you less stable and prevents your hips from rotating the boat back to upright. The solution is to decouple your upper body from your hips; a hip snap actively pushes the boat to an upright position while the upper body is passive.

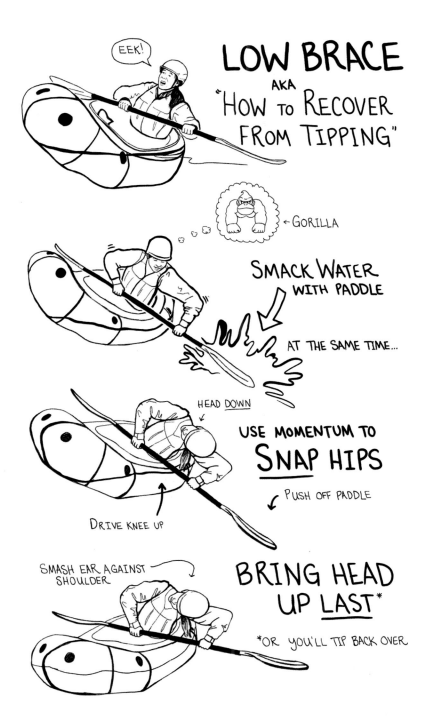

One trick to help keep your head low in the water is to watch the leading blade, the one that slaps the surface. Keeping your eyes on the blade prevents you from lifting your head prematurely.

DIG DEEPER

This exercise can help you learn to decouple your upper body and hips to build muscle memory for hip snaps.

Decoupling your hips (try this now!):

1. From a seated position, shift your torso to the left. This simulates tipping, falling to the left. In the water, you would brace on the left side of the packraft.
2. Notice your hips' rotation as you shift left—more weight goes on your left sitz bone and your right hip raises slightly.
3. Lean farther left and tip your head to the right, away from the imaginary water. Exaggerate this position by placing your right ear on your shoulder. This crunches your right obliques, trying to make your lower rib touch your hip. Notice that your torso is in a "(" shaped arc and that your weight is on your left sitz bone. Here is the important part: if you were in a boat, the angle of your hips would push the boat into the water leading to capsizing.
4. Return to the starting position.
5. Lean left again and this time, try to place your left ear on your left shoulder. Crunch your left obliques to make a ")" arc with your torso. Notice that dropping your head and crunching your obliques allows you to roll (snap) your hips to the right, putting more weight on your right sitz bone. This is the key. Once you put weight on the right sitz bone, your hips rotate the boat to a stable position. Your torso and head will follow the lead of your hips.

LEADS To TIPPING

STABILIZES BOAT

High brace: The high brace is more powerful than the low brace and will feel easier in some packrafts because the paddle will be held above the side tubes. However, high braces pose a severe risk for shoulder dislocations. In preparing this text, I reviewed packraft videos and noticed that nearly all high braces were done with one or both hands overhead, the exact position we need to avoid. Some instructors only teach the low brace, but since our packrafts' tubes stand tall above the water, some prefer the high brace. High bracing is a great option; you just need to use proper technique.

The high brace technique is very similar to the low brace. The difference is that the paddle's power face is placed against the water.

How to high brace:
1. Hold the paddle level in a neutral paddling position. Use paddle dexterity to position the blade's power face toward the water. Your elbows will drop to a level below your hands.
2. Reach to the falling side, keeping your elbows (and the paddle) close to the water. Bend the leading elbow at about a 90-degree angle. The other elbow will be fully bent and held near your stomach, with the wrist near your chin in the "reading a watch" position. Both elbows should be lower than your wrists and shoulders. Bent elbows are essential; refer to the inset below for why extended arms lead to shoulder injuries.
3. Slap the water's surface with the blade's power face.
4. As with the low brace, the stabilization needs to originate with a hip snap. Plunge your head down toward the water and snap your hips away from your head. Watch the blade to keep your head low and let your hips lead your torso and head back to an upright position.

The critical part is keeping your elbows and hands below your head. One way to lock this policy into your muscle memory is to focus on keeping the paddle low. A low paddle and bent elbows ensure that your arms have enough shock absorption to withstand a surprise. Experiment with leaning over the side tube and toward the stern as you brace; leaning back allows you to maintain a high brace without putting your shoulders at risk.

DIG DEEPER

Improper bracing causes shoulder injuries because our arms are placed in a position that doesn't absorb shock. In a low brace or proper high brace, bent elbows allow for shock absorption: force on the paddle blade is accommodated by straightening your bent arms. The more bend in your elbows, the more shock you can absorb.

High braces with improper technique (hand overhead) lead to shoulder injuries because your arm is already extended and can't absorb shock. Unexpected force on the paddle blade stretches the arm beyond its limit and forces the humeral head out of the shoulder socket. Common sources of unexpected force are powerful hydraulics, contact with a rock, or the boat pulling your torso underwater or downriver. Refer to *Chapter 11: Medical Emergencies* for how to reduce a dislocated shoulder.

EDGING: GIVING THE RIVER SOMETHING TO GRAB

Edging is the technique of using your hips and oblique abdominal muscles to press one side of the packraft into the water. Edging becomes more important as you progress into turbulent water because it allows you to influence how the boat responds to the current. When you cross the current, as when ferrying or catching eddies, edging gives the river something more substantial to grab than a smooth boat bottom. Pressing a tube into the water also changes the frictional drag on the boat's bottom. When used correctly, this technique helps keep you upright, as discussed in *Chapter 6: Navigating River Features*.

Edging is challenging in packrafts due to the boat's width and primary stability. It will help to outfit the packraft and install thigh straps for a proper paddling position. Getting the packraft on edge will feel unstable at first, but can become a subconscious effort with practice. Edging might not be possible, or effective, in all packrafts.

Edging versus leaning: Ideally, edging is done while your head stays centered over the boat. The hips and body make a "J" shape (tilted hips and upright torso), and edging is sometimes described as a J-lean. But an actual lean—shifting your weight to the side—is required for smaller paddlers and wide packrafts, especially those without thigh straps or a supportive backband. Leaning is less preferable than edging because shifting your weight off-center is less stable.

Edging requires functionally separating your lower body (hips), upper body (torso), and head. Start by practicing in flat water, on the ground, or even seated in a chair.

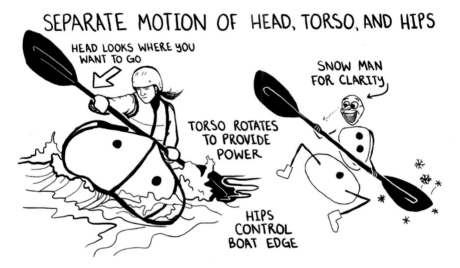

SEPARATE MOTION OF HEAD, TORSO, AND HIPS

HEAD LOOKS WHERE YOU WANT TO GO

SNOW MAN FOR CLARITY

TORSO ROTATES TO PROVIDE POWER

HIPS CONTROL BOAT EDGE

Edging while upright:

1. Shift your torso to the left while keeping your hips centered. Put more weight on the left sitz bone and crunch your right obliques (try to make your lower rib touch your hip). Crunching your obliques puts your torso in a "(" shape rather than a "\" lean. The arc keeps your weight centered over the boat.
2. Repeat this process on the right side: shift your torso to the right while crunching your left obliques.
3. In the water, practice getting on edge to expose as much of one side tube as possible. While on edge, maintain an upright torso and hold your paddle in a low brace paddling position. If you tip too far, try to recover by bracing.

DIG DEEPER

Edging gives the river something to grab. Without an edge, the boat's bottom smears along the surface of the water—you don't have much say in where you go. A depressed edge catches the current and allows you to *carve through the water* rather than *spin on the water*. When combined with speed, the more you edge, the more the water grabs you. But if you let the upstream tube get grabbed, the river's force can capsize the boat.

Giving the river something to grab also changes the frictional drag on the bottom of the boat. Drag force is a function of area and velocity. When you push a tube deeper into the water, you provide more boat area and increase the underwater drag on that tube.

Once you have spent some time edging in flat water, move your practice to slow currents—paddle across the current, directly toward the opposite bank. Shift your weight to push the downstream tube deeper into the water. In this orientation, the current can grab the downstream tube and pull it along. The additional friction on the tube works to rotate the packraft into a flat (stable) position. If you want to go for a swim, switch your lean to the upstream side. This orientation allows the river to grab the upstream tube, and the additional frictional drag on the tube will pull it under you, capsizing the boat.

Edging with a strong lean: Some edging maneuvers require a strong lean, moving your center of gravity to an unstable position unless you brace against a paddle stroke. This technique allows you to make sharp turns—like riding banked corners on a bike—and is incredibly fun.

You can build muscle memory for aggressive leaning by bracing against a sculling draw. Increase the pressure on the blade and see how deeply you can edge into the water. When you reach the tipping point, snap your hips to rotate the boat back into a stable position.

Maintaining a strong lean against a draw stroke requires proper outfitting with three points of contact: your butt against the seat and backband, your feet against the bow, and your knees against the side tubes.

Edge toward your attention: A general rule while river-running is to tilt downstream because this lifts the upstream edge, reducing the drag that works to capsize the boat: "Upstream up! Downstream down!" But this guideline gets confusing when the current doesn't flow downstream, such as in eddies. A better rule-of-thumb is to lean toward your attention—your objective. Shifting your weight toward your objective conveniently places weight on the tube that should be pressed deeper into the water.

Edging with a lean. Casey Fulton, Grand Canyon section of the Colorado River.

Examples of edging toward your attention:

- **Turning**: Direct your gaze toward the turn's center and put weight on your inside hip.
- **Pushed against a rock**: Lean into the rock to reduce the drag on the upstream tube, helping to stabilize the boat.
- **Front-ferrying**: Edging toward the destination shore pushes the downstream tube into the water, stabilizing the packraft.

JAMES SMITH: "THIS IS NOT SHIT!"

I joined UK kayakers Dan Rea-Dickins and James Smith for a ski and packraft traverse of Iceland in 2015. I led the glacier crossing, and Dan and James held my hand through the Class IV big water rapids of Jökulsá á Fjöllum.

James, a sponsored kayaker, had never seen a packraft before. Like every other kayaker's first time in a packraft, James' first act was to pull the thigh straps as tight as possible and then rock back and forth to get a feel for the boat's edging. James looked up with a surprised grin and announced, "This is not shit!"

James was so good at edging with a sculling draw that he bailed water from the cockpit mid-river, leaning past the tipping point to drain water over the coaming.

James Smith walking braided channels. Iceland.

John Pekar. Headwaters of the glacial Tana River, Alaska.

Dan Rea-Dickins and James Smith. Jökulsá á Fjöllum, Iceland.

CHAPTER 3

RISK

Most of our goals are only achieved after taking risks. Some of these goals are part of our survival: food, shelter, and security. Packrafting can have real benefits, but it is important to recognize that *we choose to put ourselves at risk*, usually to have fun. All packrafters expose themselves to some level of risk for these rewards, so risk assessment is more about management than avoidance.

Risk assessment involves these three questions:
- What can happen?
- How likely is it to happen?
- If it does happen, what are the consequences?

Our ability to work through these questions depends on the setting. I find it useful to think about risk in two settings: the before and after (planning and debriefing), versus on-the-fly decision-making (on the water or scouting). Risk assessment before and after an outing can be driven by logic. In these settings, I evaluate risk in terms of hazard, exposure, and vulnerability, as discussed below. A familiarity with **heuristics** (common mental mistakes) can help identify what went wrong after an incident, and help you recognize similar decision-making mistakes in the future.

On-the-fly decisions are often governed more by emotion than logic—most of our brains can't evaluate exposure, vulnerability, and heuristics while scouting a rapid. In these settings, we are better off with a simplified assessment:

- Can I stay upright?
- What will happen to me if I capsize?

The good news is, we can always portage. Our boats are built to be portaged. It turns out that the Culture of Safety is also a culture of portaging.

WHAT YOU NEED TO KNOW

The risk assessment community (natural disasters, avalanches, etc.) uses specific terminology to talk about risk. We benefit from adopting this terminology as well. This is especially true during the planning phases of a trip when it is easier to use the logical part of the brain.

Risk is the likelihood of harm due to exposure to a hazard. The degree of risk depends on hazard, exposure, and vulnerability.

- **Hazard:** Hazards are environmental dangers, the things *we can't control.* Open-water hazards include waves, currents, wind, temperature, etc. River hazards include holes, waves, strainers, precipitation (water level), landslides, etc.
- **Exposure:** Exposure refers to the people and possessions that the hazards can influence. Choosing to run a rapid or cross open water exposes you to hazards.
- **Vulnerability:** Vulnerability is the likelihood that exposure to a hazard will have harmful consequences.

We can't control river hazards, but we can influence exposure and vulnerability by selecting appropriate destinations, deciding to portage, and building a safety net through proper use of equipment and training.

> ## DIG DEEPER
>
> The real and perceived risks of an activity aren't always the same. In packrafting, two of the most likely *perceived* risks identified by expert paddlers and swift-water rescue instructors are strainers (objects that let water pass through but not bodies) and foot entrapment (getting a foot stuck on the river bottom while standing in swift water). However, there has only been one fatality clearly due to these risks. Statistically, the most significant *real* risks involved with the fourteen known packraft fatalities are cold water and paddling alone.

RISK ASSESSMENT

Risk assessment is the process of identifying hazards and their associated consequences. Water systems are complicated, and the hardest part of risk assessment is recognizing what you don't know. We can use the hazard/exposure/vulnerability framework to manage risk in the planning phase of packrafting.

River Hazards

Hazards are environmental dangers that we can't control. River hazards include holes, waves, strainers, and environmental factors like cold air, water, precipitation (water level), landslides, etc. These hazards are equally *dangerous* for all paddlers regardless of skill level. But the *likelihood* of a hazard being harmful to a paddler depends on their exposure and vulnerability.

Factors that influence river hazards include:

- **River features:** Try to get a specific description of river hazards from guidebooks and other boaters. Are there any undercuts? Sieves? Log jams?
- **Water level:** Water levels change the danger of a river. At low levels, rocks are more exposed. At high levels, holes are stickier, and then at even higher levels, holes might get flushed out and turn into waves.
- **Weather:** Wind and rain can turn a smooth lake surface into a dangerous crossing.
- **Temperature:** A swim in cold water is more dangerous than a swim in warm water.

Exposure

Exposure refers to the people and possessions that hazards can influence. In packrafting, exposure includes ourselves, our partners, and our equipment.

I think of exposure as on/off switches along a spectrum of decisions. At the largest scale, you can choose to go to the river or not, based on current conditions. Once you are on the river, you can choose to paddle or portage a rapid. Within the rapid, your boat-control skills—your ability to place the boat where you want—determines if you will be exposed to a hazard or not.

The important part to remember is that you usually have control over your exposure and that it isn't a one-time decision—you will want to evaluate your exposure throughout the day or week.

Vulnerability

Vulnerability is the likelihood that exposure to a hazard will have harmful consequences. We don't have any control over hazards other than choosing appropriate destinations, and our influence on exposure is a series of on/off switches. The factor that we can really adjust is vulnerability. An experienced and competent boater in Class IV water is less vulnerable than a novice boater with improper outfitting on a Class II river. The difference is that the experienced boater is less likely to be exposed to the hazard due to their training.

Reducing vulnerability (building a safety net) includes:

- **Partners**: Your partners' experience and training determines how well they can respond to an incident. Are your partners alert, trained, and able to help?
- **Equipment**: Appropriate safety gear and knowing how to use it decreases your vulnerability.
- **Location**: Some rivers are closer to help than others.
- **Training and practice:** Having formal training helps reduce your vulnerability. Regularly practicing that training is even more beneficial.

SAY IT ANYWAY

Regardless of your experience level, you might feel uncomfortable bringing up concerns and fears. Say it anyway. We all benefit from a new perspective.

Dan Rea-Dickins and Banjop lawphniaw assessing risk. Meghalaya, India.

A DATE WITH ERICA

In 2010, after several months of wooing, I convinced Erica Madison to go on a packrafting date. Erica was an athletic bird biologist that could fix engines. In other words, an Alaskan dream.

At the Resurrection River put-in, I noticed Erica had a leash connecting her paddle to her boat. I told her we needed to remove the leash because it was an entanglement hazard. Erica resisted and said that she was sure to lose the paddle without the leash. I persisted.

We got in our boats, paddled 50 yards (45 m), and then Erica capsized and let go of her paddle. We weren't able to find it. I felt responsible for the loss, but was confident that removing the leash was the safe decision.

This sounds like a story about me improving Erica's safety net by removing the leash. But the more important lesson is that Erica knew her vulnerability, and I disregarded it. After looking at the water and predicting that she would swim and let go of the paddle, we should have recognized that the river was an inappropriate destination for a date!

Probability and Consequence

I like the hazard/exposure/vulnerability framework for big-picture decision-making: where to go and what to bring. But when we are actually on the river, a simpler assessment is preferable. The on-the-fly mitigation strategy is to minimize both components of vulnerability: minimize the likelihood that things will go wrong and minimize the consequences when they do. Can I stay upright? Yes, I'm pretty sure that I can. What will happen to me if I capsize? I can swim into that pool and Tony can recover my equipment. This discussion involves assessing the group's skill, the water level, nature of the river, and so on. We will revisit on-the-fly risk assessment in *Chapter 5: The Principles of River-running* and *Part III: When Things Go Wrong.*

Probability and consequence are handled differently in the water environment compared to avalanches and other natural hazards. In those cases, probability and consequence are part of the hazard, the things we can't control (e.g., how likely it is that an avalanche will be triggered and how large it will be). Except for floods and other dynamic hazards (e.g., floating logs), river hazards are relatively static. We have much more control over the probability and consequence of things going wrong while packrafting.

High-probability incidents: High-probability incidents are predictable. Knowing that they are likely, we can train to respond appropriately.

High-probability incidents can have low or high consequences. Our willingness to expose ourselves to these hazards is largely a question of risk tolerance (discussed later in this chapter). More people are willing to expose themselves to low-consequence hazards—these are the little things that go wrong all the time—you get pushed against a rock and capsize, flipped by converging channels, etc. You can train for these incidents by practicing wet re-entries and swimming.

High-probability and high-consequence incidents are even more predictable: Class V rapids would likely severely harm a novice boater. The boater should spend years training for this water, but their decision to run it is ultimately based on their tolerance: what level of risk is acceptable. You get to choose.

Low-probability incidents: Low-probability incidents are hard to prepare for and anticipate. Low-probability incidents might be unforeseeable events—or they might involve several low-consequence hazards lining up perfectly wrong. These are the events that give us the greatest grief: the time you forgot to zip your drysuit, didn't bother to attach a paddle leash because the sun was setting, and underestimated the wind and length of an open-water crossing.

SAFETY DRIFT

Another lesson we can borrow from the avalanche community (who borrowed it from safety science) is that incidents are often the products of a series of decisions rather than a single major mistake. Each small decision might even be "correct" given the data we have collected. Safety drift describes the cumulative effect of decisions that gradually increases your exposure or vulnerability. The final "mistake" might be a minor decision. Try to keep a big-picture perspective and recognize if the additive effect of your decisions is leading to safety drift.

PRO TIP!

Risk assessment is more difficult when we are physically and mentally fatigued. Monitor your team for a sense of urgency (a rush to get off the river before dark) or exhaustion (not engaging in decision-making).

Brad Meiklejohn. Metal Creek, Alaska.

RISK TOLERANCE

Our willingness to expose ourselves to hazards boils down to risk tolerance. Risk tolerance is your consent to accept that something might go wrong. It varies from person to person and is governed by age, experience, upbringing, fitness, etc. Risk tolerance varies throughout our lifetimes too. While our actual ability gradually increases during intentional practice, our confidence (deserved or not) changes with training, success, failure, near-misses, and loss.

A healthy attitude creates healthy risk tolerance. My Denali mountain ranger friends say that they can generally spot the climbing teams that will get into trouble by their attitude (have inappropriately high risk tolerance). A false sense of security, overconfidence in their abilities, and underestimating risk lead to greater tolerance than groups that acknowledge risks, fears, and concerns.

The best way to determine your risk tolerance is to practice paddling and rescue scenarios. Once you know your tolerance, stay safe by not exceeding it. For many of us, this is easier said than done.

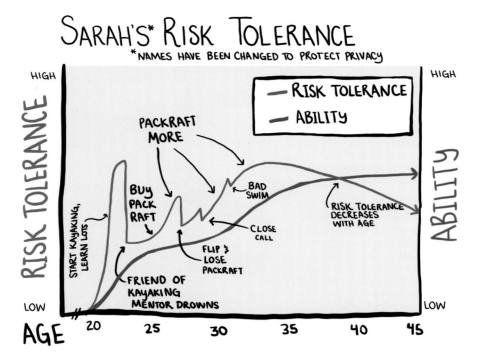

DIG DEEPER

Avalanche professionals have identified several common mental mistakes that lead to avalanche fatalities. These heuristic traps—subconscious rules of thumb—are also relevant to packrafting (and pretty much everything else that we do). In my experience, these concepts are most valuable when trying to understand a scary situation or close call after the fact.

Our brains rely on rules of thumb as shortcuts in day-to-day life. We would be overwhelmed with options if we didn't adopt these mental shortcuts. This decision-making process works well . . . until it doesn't. Awareness of these traps might help you make good decisions on the water.

- **Familiarity**: Familiarity with a section of water leads us to assume that we know its risks. But rivers are dynamic, and hazards change. A rapid that was unobstructed last weekend might now have a log across it.
- **Confirmation bias:** We tend to seek and receive data that confirms our existing beliefs. If we believe it will be the perfect day to complete an open-water crossing, we may fail to acknowledge the signs of deteriorating weather.
- **Consistency**: Once we make a decision, we tend to stick with that decision. The problem is that we stay consistent even when the conditions change, such as a rock shifting in a rapid after a high-water event.
- **Acceptance**: It is human nature to seek approval from those we like or respect. Evaluate why you want to run a rapid. Acceptance by your peers is a strong motivator but a weak excuse.
- **The expert halo**: Many groups default to engaging a leader, either formally or informally, especially in high-stress scenarios. The leadership role might be granted based on experience, but age, vocal volume, gender, or assertiveness can also be factors. The expert halo refers to the group's willingness to defer to the leader's decisions, whether justified or not.
- **Social facilitation**: Social facilitation has a magnification effect. A paddler's risk tolerance will be boosted or diminished based on their confidence in their risk assessment. When other people are seen on the river, a confident paddler is *more* likely to take high risks, and an insecure paddler is *less* likely to take risks.
- **Scarcity**: The scarcity trap is the willingness to ignore risks due to a sense of limited opportunity. "I only get this one chance, so let's make it worth it."

GOALS AND REWARDS

Spend time evaluating your goals. Is being outside enough? Or do you seek the blast of dopamine, adrenaline, and endorphins that you get from running rapids? At what cost? The tricky part is to determine when achieving your goals is worth the risk. The situation is complicated by paddling with partners who have different goals than yours and who can't help but try to influence you.

For paddlers whose goals include focused concentration, the sweet spot is the mental state of "flow." Flow is the "in-the-zone" experience when your focus overpowers other senses, and you perform at your peak capacity. Paddlers experience flow when the difficulty of the activity matches their skillset. Note that all paddlers can achieve flow, not just the experts; the point is that skill and difficulty are matched.

I appreciate the flow model because of how well it explains some of the other mental states I've experienced on the learning curve: anxiety when the water is more difficult than my skill, relaxed when the water is easier than my skill. What I don't like about the model is the possible interpretation that you have to keep paddling harder water as your skills develop to maintain the mental state of flow. I now recognize that I can find greater challenge by focusing on perfect technique, not that I need to run harder rapids.

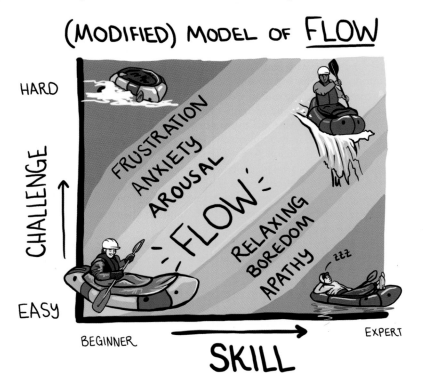

Sarah Histand finds a state of flow. Pelorus River, New Zealand.

PART II

RIVERS AND OPEN WATER

The equipment and boat control techniques in *Part I* are relevant to both river-running and open-water crossings. Our next step is to apply these skills to more complicated settings: moving and open water. Each of these environments presents a unique suite of hazards.

River hazards are generally easy to identify (hole! wave! rock!). Open-water hazards are often underestimated because conditions can become hazardous during the crossing (for example, wind-generated waves). Applying the risk assessment frameworks to your river and open-water trips will help you make good decisions.

Okpilak River, Brooks Range, Alaska.

A collapsing permafrost bank on the Okpilak River, Brooks Range, Alaska.

CHAPTER 4

HOW RIVERS WORK

An understanding of how rivers work will help you choose appropriate destinations and anticipate river features. River hydrology is complicated, so we will focus on the characteristics that are helpful when picking your paddling destination.

Hydrology relevant to packrafting:

- **Character:** A river's character provides an overall sense of what to seek and expect. Is the river braided, a single meandering channel, whitewater?

- **Gradient:** Gradient is a quantitative measure of steepness. A river's feel and difficulty are related to its gradient and whether the gradient is consistent or not.

- **Water level (discharge or stage):** Your paddling experience will vary according to how much water is flowing in the river.

This chapter finishes with a hydrologic explanation of common river features, such as holes, waves, and eddies. I find that understanding why a river feature exists helps me figure out how best to avoid or use the feature.

WHAT YOU NEED TO KNOW

Of the above three factors, the amount of water is the only one that can change hourly, daily, or seasonally. Safe boating necessitates anticipating water level changes due to weather (storm response and seasonal variations) and how different water levels change the feel of the river (**pushiness**). This knowledge pays off when you do river research and check gauges before heading out to the water.

RIVER CHARACTER

Different rivers offer different challenges and rewards. Rivers are sophisticated systems characterized in terms of geology, topography, weather, vegetation, biota, etc. A simplified understanding is appropriate for our needs. We can describe river character in terms of the bed surface (substrate) and shape (morphology). Additional whitewater descriptors are included for people focusing on whitewater packrafting.

River Substrate

The river substrate is the bed surface at the bottom of the river. We can simplify the substrate into two categories:

- **Bedrock:** When more sediment is eroded than deposited, water can strip the substrate down to bedrock. Bedrock rivers are most often found in steep headwaters where fast-flowing water has the energy to erode and transport sediment.

- **Sediment:** A river that deposits more than it erodes will form a sediment substrate (also known as alluvium). The energy of the river system governs the sediment size. Steep gradients and high energies near the mountains deposit boulders on the river bottom. Shallow gradients and low energies deposit fine silt.

Bedrock sections are a real aesthetic treat, but the rapids can be hard to understand. Part of the issue is that each bedrock rapid is unique, whereas sediment beds on different rivers share predictable characteristics. When I first notice bedrock sticking out from the banks, I instantly perk up and pay more attention. The presence of bedrock sometimes indicates unusual rapids or a constriction downriver.

Morphology

River morphology describes the shape of the river. Most rivers will include a mix of both braids and meanders along their length.

Braids: Braided rivers form where there is energy and source material to transport a significant sediment load. Braided rivers continuously erode and deposit sediments, changing the course of the river.

Paddling braided rivers often involves choosing between diverging channels and managing converging currents. Strategies for navigating braided channels are discussed in *Chapter 6: Navigating River Features.*

BRAIDED RIVERS AND A HEADWIND

Sarah Histand likes to tease me by sharing a photo of me scowling during a float of the Kavik River in Arctic Alaska. I don't often scowl, but the Kavik had barely enough water to float and not enough gradient to make forward progress against the daily headwind. We recognized that the diurnal (infernal!) wind let up in the evenings, so we spent three "days" paddling from 9 p.m. to 9 a.m. to reach the Arctic Ocean. We were rewarded with a view of hundreds of caribou in the early hours of our final day on the water.

Grumpy Luc, 3 a.m. Kavik River, Coastal Plain, Alaska. © *Will Koeppen*

Meanders: If a river can't support a high sediment load, it forms a sinuous meandering channel. Meandering channels are common at low elevations and low gradients.

Meanders develop because any irregularity in a channel deflects the current, which creates pockets of high and low velocity that promote erosion and deposition, respectively. The erosion and deposition transform straight channels into sinuous curves.

Riverbanks apply friction to the water, slowing the current at each edge. The current is fastest near the center of the channel, offset to each bend's outside edge. The difference in velocity along the inside and outside of each bend forms paired cutbanks and point bars.

Meandering river features:

- **Cutbanks and undercuts:** The fast river current along the outside of each bend pushes into the outer bank and erodes bank material. Cutbanks are steep faces of eroded banks. Undercuts are more deeply eroded at or under water-level.

- **Point bars:** Point bars are formed where slow currents deposit sediments at the insides of bends. Bars grow with time and can make ideal campsites.

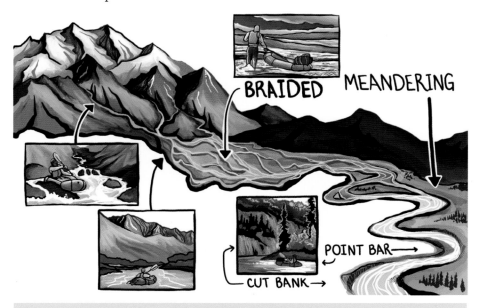

PRO TIP!

I love camping on gravel bars and point bars because of how easy it is to wash campfire ashes into the river—one of the Leave No Trace guidelines. I think of Leave No Trace as a bit of a game, challenging myself to see how effectively we can hide signs of our passage.

My preferred camping surface has pea-sized pebbles. Larger rocks can be uncomfortable, and smaller particles can get in our zippers.

A NIGHT ON BIG RIVER WITH JOE AND CATHY

In 2008 I joined Joe Stock and Cathy Flanagan for a ski, hike, and packraft traverse through the Alaska Range to the Kuskokwim, the river I grew up on. Many things went wrong—we caught the mountains in an avalanche shed cycle, and I accidentally brought a cookbook for my reading material, and then ran out of food.

The Big River was braided and fast for 70 river miles (110 km), but then the gradient decreased and the river transitioned to slow meanders for the remaining 40 miles (65 km) to the Kuskokwim.

Meanders are beautiful from the air, but slow to paddle. We decided to take turns paddling through the night to avoid spending an extra day on the numbingly slow water. After tying our three packrafts together, Cathy and I wrapped up in our sleeping bags in our boats, and Joe kept us from drifting into the bank. Joe ended up paddling all night, never asking us to swap roles.

Before settling in to sleep in our boats, we discussed a large river island we had noticed on the map. The channel on the right was four miles long (6.5 km), and the channel on the left was six miles long (10 km). We wanted to take the shorter channel. In the morning, I asked Joe if the right channel had been easy to identify. Joe looked at me sheepishly and said, "Hmmm, the right channel . . . I don't remember seeing that. I think I was asleep!"

We finished our float at the Blackwater fish camp, where Dichinanek' Hwt'ana (Upper Kuskokwim Athabascan) elder Philip Esai scolded us for getting blisters and running out of food, and then promptly caught us a pike and fried it in Crisco.

Luc Mehl asleep on the Big River, Alaska. © Joe Stock

Glacial rivers: Glacial rivers are found in arctic and alpine environments where glacial melt contributes to the waterways.

Glacial river morphology often includes fast and violent flow at the glacier snout, followed by an abrupt transition to braided channels peppered with large rocks or erratics. Throw in some driftwood when you reach the treeline, and you've got a full suite of hazards.

Glacial rivers carry a remarkable sediment load, both in the form of fine silt that clouds the water, as well as large boulders that bound along the river bottom ("saltation"). You can often hear the sediment load. Suspended sediment hisses as silt particles bounce off the boat, and rocks bouncing on the river bottom make loud clunks. I've mistaken the hiss of suspended sediment for a slow leak in my packraft.

Paddling glacial rivers introduces new hazards, such as cold water, steep gradients, and limited visibility. Another challenge when paddling glacial whitewater is that the large rocks on the riverbed are often the same color as the water. Glacial water's poor visibility makes it more likely to broach sideways into rocks or unexpected holes. You can reduce your vulnerability by paddling with appropriate clothing and a drysuit.

Whitewater Character

Whitewater has many flavors, and a single river might feature multiple styles along its length. One challenge for the river rating system (see *Chapter 5: The Principles of River-running*) is that Class III big water and Class III creeks are equally difficult, but for very different reasons. Describing the character of whitewater sections makes it easier to visualize the hazards you are most likely to encounter.

These categories describe distinct types of whitewater; many rivers will feature a blend of categories.

Big water: Big water refers to large and deep rivers with high volume, such as the Grand Canyon section of the Colorado River. Some high-volume rivers are not difficult to navigate; others feature intense rapids that require considerable skill. High-volume rivers are likely to flush swimmers and boats out of holes, and the water is generally deep enough that collisions with rocks are less likely. But swimming to shore might be difficult or impossible.

Creeking: Navigating steep and low-volume whitewater is referred to as creeking. Creeking may require quick and subtle boat control to navigate complicated rapids. These sections are more likely to be found in the headwaters and tributaries of a river system. Creeks merge to become bigger creeks and eventually rivers—the feel of the water transitions as the characteristics of the riverbed and topography change. Swimming in creeks poses a greater risk of blunt force trauma; impact is likely.

Rock gardens: Rapids that feature numerous rocks are called rock (or boulder) gardens. The interaction between water and rock is an aesthetic treat and a paddling delight when conditions are right. Rock gardens can be playful at low water levels and terrifying at high water levels. Rock gardens are beneficial for practicing quick maneuvers, like catching and peeling out of eddies. Knowing proper swimming technique around rocks is critical before paddling rock gardens.

Rock garden heaven. Meghalaya, India.

Erosion and landslides feed rocks into rivers, and high-water events like storms and spring melt can transport and rearrange rocks into dangerous configurations. You can often anticipate where rocks will be in a river: steep banks and side drainages are logical sources of new rocks. Any incoming side drainage should alert the paddler to the possibility of a constricted channel—the reduced channel area results in greater river velocity and an increased ability to move rocks.

Bedrock rapids: Bedrock rapids don't seem to play by the same rules as other rapids. Even at low water, a bedrock rapid might involve powerful boils or unexpected hydraulics. Depending on the geological setting, a river might flow through sieves, and undercuts may be significantly more pronounced. Bedrock rapids are obvious—indicated by exposed rock walls—and should trigger an alert in your brain: *the rules just changed.*

WHITEWATER VERSUS SWIFTWATER

You can get training in *swiftwater* rescue or *whitewater* boating. What's the difference?

Whitewater refers to a creek or river with a number of rapids. Rapids cause **aeration** of the water, which makes it appear white.

Swiftwater is more nebulous. In the safety context, swiftwater is water in which you can't fully control your movement. By this definition, slow, deep water and fast, shallow water can both be swift, and what is swift to you might not be swift to the person next to you. Swiftwater might not be white, and whitewater might not be swift.

RIVER GRADIENT

River gradient describes the average elevation drop of a river. Gradients are described in feet per mile (fpm) or meters per kilometer. River gradient is an important attribute that can tell you about a river's character and help you to anticipate river hazards. Developing a sense for gradients will help you understand and anticipate the feel of a river.

Gradient is commonly included in guidebooks. I recommend using Google Earth if you need to measure a river's gradient, as outlined in *Chapter 13: Research and Trip Planning.*

The important aspects of the gradient include:

- **Steepness:** Is the gradient steep or shallow?
- **Continuity:** Is the gradient uniform or does it alternate between steep and shallow sections?
- **Scale:** Does the gradient value represent a long or short river length?

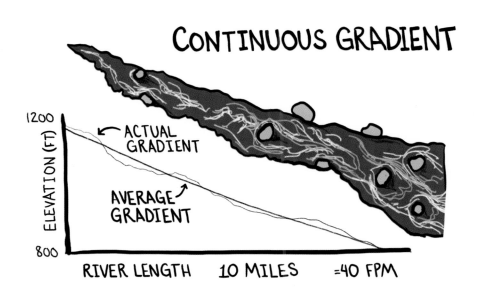

POOL-DROP GRADIENT

POOL   DROP

1200

ELEVATION (FT)

AVERAGE
GRADIENT

ACTUAL
GRADIENT

800

RIVER LENGTH   10 MILES   =40 FPM

CONTINUOUS GRADIENT

1200

ELEVATION (FT)

ACTUAL
GRADIENT

AVERAGE
GRADIENT

800

RIVER LENGTH   10 MILES   =40 FPM

Steep gradients: Rivers with steep gradients are typically found in headwaters, steep terrain, or as a result of discrete geologic features. Steep rivers in headwaters generally have low volumes, but even a low volume can produce high-energy flow. Steep sections of water are typically assigned difficult ratings, and mistakes have high consequences.

Shallow gradients: Rivers with shallow gradients are usually found farther from the river source. Shallow gradients are associated with greater volume, deeper water, and can have high velocities.

Continuity: We can describe river gradients as continuous or pool-drop. A river with a relatively constant gradient will be continuously fast, with few opportunities to catch eddies or recover from a swim. These conditions make it difficult to manage a group descent.

Some rivers erode into a series of alternating steep and shallow gradients. The shallow areas feature calmer water (pools), and the steep sections feature rapids (drops). These **pool-drop** rivers are popular with paddlers because the drops are exciting and the pools provide **recovery zones** to regroup.

Knowing the continuity of a river's gradient helps you anticipate the run. For example, a gradient of 150 fpm (25 m/km) and continuous nature could feature ongoing Class III rapids and no recovery zones. But if the gradient has pool-drop continuity, the creek might alternate between Class IV rapids and pools.

Scale: Gradient is an average value. The gradient might be reported for an entire river section or individual miles. These scales fail to capture the actual steepness of individual drops. For example, the Grand Canyon section of the Colorado River features dozens of world-famous steep rapids and has a low average gradient of 8 fpm (1.5 m/km). Other rivers with that gradient don't feature any rapids.

Unfortunately, given these considerations, there is no direct relationship between gradient and difficulty. To choose appropriate destinations and anticipate hazards, we also need to know the water level.

MEASURING THE AMOUNT OF WATER IN A RIVER

Unlike character and gradient, the amount of water in a river can vary by hour, day, and month. Different amounts of water correspond to different conditions, both in terms of fun and hazards. High water levels have been a significant factor in boating incidents worldwide.

The amount of water flowing in the river is quantified in two ways:

- **Stage:** The height of water relative to an arbitrary reference.
- **Discharge:** The volume of water that moves through the river in a unit of time.

River discharge is particularly useful to paddlers because we can develop a sense of a river's "feel" and hazards at different levels. Monitoring discharge trends (increasing, decreasing, or constant) informs us about how the river responds to rain or seasonal patterns.

Discharge is monitored and reported for many rivers around the world. Unfortunately, it can be difficult to relate a gauge's value to the section of the river you want to paddle. The gauge's value can differ from what you experience due to the presence of tributaries, and your distance from the gauge. The point is to collect as much information as possible before planning an outing. Note that some gauges will only report stage, not discharge.

Stage

Stage is the height of the water surface above an arbitrary reference (a "datum"). Stage is useful as a proxy for discharge for that specific river.

For example, a stage of 10.0 feet (3 m) on Sixmile River indicates that there is more water than a stage of 9.6 feet (2.92 m). Paddlers familiar with the run will anticipate the different feel of the river at those levels. But a stage of 10.0 at Sixmile doesn't relate to a stage of 10.0 on a different river.

Stage is an arbitrary value. A stage of 10.0 feet (3 m) might mean that the water is ten feet above a bridge foundation (the datum), not that the water is ten feet (3 m) deep. This sounds more complicated than it is—measuring the stage can be as simple as placing a stick in the mud at the waterline and watching how the water level changes overnight.

Federal or state/provincial agencies record stage and discharge for many rivers. In the United States, check websites for the U.S. Geological Survey and NOAA for online data access.

PRO TIP!

Collect "free" river data whenever possible. Place a rock or pole at the waterline when camping or taking long breaks on a river. Changes in the water level help you decide when to boat and what hazards to expect. For example:

- If the river felt uncomfortably high today and the water moves up the stick overnight, you might choose to spend an extra day in camp waiting for the level to drop.
- If there is wet dirt or rocks on the bank above the water's height, you know that the river level has already peaked. Monitor the waterline to identify when the stage is highest and lowest, then time your descent accordingly (e.g., paddle braided rivers at high water to avoid getting stuck on gravel bars).

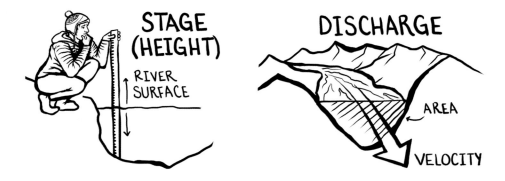

Discharge

Discharge describes the volume of water that moves through a cross-section of the river during a unit of time. Standard units of discharge are cubic feet per second (cfs) and cubic meters per second (cumec: 1 cumec = 35 cfs). River discharge is recorded and reported for many rivers globally and is included in guidebooks whenever available.

Unlike stage, you can compare discharge values on different rivers. Rivers with similar characters and gradients will have similar feels and hazards at the same discharge. As a very rough guideline, "small" rivers have discharges below 500 cfs (14 cumecs), and "large" rivers have discharges above 1500 cfs (42 cumecs).

DIG DEEPER

Discharge is calculated by measuring the stream's cross-sectional area with survey poles, sonar, GPS, or other means and multiplying the area by the stream velocity.

discharge = area x velocity

Discharge is too labor-intensive to measure frequently, so hydrologists develop a formula to calculate discharge as a function of the stage, which is easier to measure. To determine the "rating curve," hydrologists measure the discharge at multiple stages and plot discharge versus stage. A best-fit line through the data points can be used to calculate discharge at any stage. The rating curve is recalculated when the cross-sectional area changes by deposition or erosion, perhaps after a significant storm.

Fluctuating River Levels

A river's water level can change in response to the weather, climate, and the physical environment. Those changes might be rapid, such as a sudden rain storm; cyclical, following the melting of glacial ice in the midday heat; or seasonal, when a water source such as snowmelt phases in and out of significance. Each water level introduces different hazards and influences the time available to maneuver ("pushiness"). Understanding the factors that change water levels helps you choose appropriate destinations and anticipate hazards.

We are most interested in these water level trends:

- **Storm response:** "Flashy" or not. **Flashy** rivers rise rapidly in response to precipitation. You might need to get off the river and wait for levels to drop.

- **Daily fluctuation:** Time your outings to match the preferred river conditions in dam-release, glacial, and snow-melt basins.

- **Seasonal trends:** Plan your boating ventures to catch the water conditions you want. For example, I love paddling glacial rivers late in the autumn when they lose volume and silt.

Pushiness: As a paddler, different water levels are felt as varying degrees of pushiness. When there is more water in a river, the river flows at higher velocities and exerts more force on stationary objects and boats. Pushiness is power; it's the amount of work that the river can do. Rivers do work by converting potential energy—the energy due to storage at higher elevations—into kinetic energy. A river's power depends on the potential energy and how much water is available to do work (discharge). Hydroelectric dams use this kinetic energy to generate electricity.

The most effective way to develop a sense of pushiness is to revisit the same river at different water levels. For example, low water levels on a Class III creek might feature large setup and recovery zones with rocky rapids that can easily tip a boat. The rapids can be more cushioned at higher water levels, but the river's pushiness limits the time available to maneuver or recover.

Response to precipitation: Understanding how a river responds to rain helps you make smart decisions about your objectives: when to squeeze in an exciting run after work or spend an extra day in the tent waiting for levels to drop. Flashy responses can be dangerous, catching you off guard in the water or camped too low.

A basin's response to rain is hard to predict. Your best resources are other boaters, locals, rangers, pilots, and other people familiar with the area. You don't need a comprehensive understanding; knowing the regional reputation can be enough. As a general rule, steep, rocky, unvegetated basins are flashy because the soil and reservoirs can't store much water. Flat, vegetated, silty basins with low relief are less likely to be flashy.

During periods without precipitation, discharge in rivers decreases, and groundwater reservoirs drain by **groundwater runoff**. Storm precipitation will initially be absorbed by the soil, then refill groundwater reservoirs. Once the soil is saturated and reservoirs are full, the excess stormwater will flow as **surface runoff** into the waterways. The rate of increased discharge (flashy or not), and recovery after the storm, depends on many factors: catchment area and topography; surface geology; soil depth, composition, storage capacity, and saturation; vegetation; weather patterns; etc.

A detailed understanding of these factors is beyond the scope of this text, but these examples convey how different basins might respond to rain:

- A large catchment area will have a larger flood flow and more storage capacity in soils, lakes, etc. For this reason, a smaller basin will be more likely to flash flood, and a large basin will take longer to flood.

- The soil's capacity to absorb water depends on its composition. Sandy soils promote absorption; clay-rich soils do not.
- In the arctic, permafrost and shallow soils limit absorption, and the rivers can be very flashy.
- Boreal regions tend to have slower vegetation decomposition, producing peat and other organic matter that act like sponges and store significant amounts of water.

Regional trends in water levels are discussed in *Chapter 13: Research and Trip Planning.*

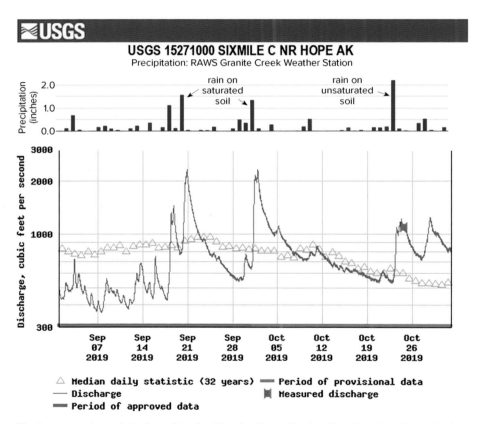

Discharge and precipitation plots for Sixmile River, Alaska. Top: Precipitation in inches from the Granite Creek gauge, 11 miles (18 km) up river from the Sixmile discharge gauge. 2 inches = 51 mm. Bottom: Discharge in cfs. 2000 cfs = 57 cumecs. Note the influence of soil saturation on discharge. Rain on saturated soil results in higher water levels than rain on unsaturated soils. Data sources are provided in the Appendix.

WALKING A THREE-DAY RIVER

Sarah Histand and I walked ten miles (16 km) of Dry Tok Creek during a trip through the eastern Alaska Range. We had optimistically expected to packraft those miles, despite the creek's name.

We visited a hunting camp where two hunters were butchering a moose. One of the hunters had been visiting the area for 30 years and described times when the creek was completely dry and others when water extended from bank-to-bank—a width of several hundred feet (60 m). The old-timer told us that the Dry Tok was a three-day creek.

> *You know what I mean by that, right? If it rains for three days straight, it floods. Then it takes three days to go back to normal.*

We filled up on hot cocoa and continued our walk down the river.

Sarah Histand, Tok River, Alaska.

RIVER FEATURES AND HYDROLOGY

You can enjoy paddling through river features without understanding how and why they form. This section provides a basic hydrologic explanation of river features, which may expand your grasp on the river environment and help you anticipate and avoid hazards.

Many river features can be explained by two hydrologic concepts: fluid flow type and the equation of continuity.

Fluid flow type: Fluid flow has two forms, laminar and turbulent, that are primarily governed by velocity and indicated by the fluid's **pathlines** (the path an object travels in the water).

- **Laminar flow:** Laminar flow describes the linear movement of particles along straight or curved pathlines; it is neat and orderly.
- **Turbulent flow:** Turbulent flow describes unsteady flow with water particles following random or chaotic pathlines. Laminar flow turns turbulent with increased velocity (turbulence dissipates some of the increased kinetic energy of fast-flowing water).

In rivers, true laminar flow is rare, and we are more likely to see and feel something along a spectrum of gently turbulent to chaotically turbulent. But functionally, we can consider flow to be laminar when we can see orderly pathlines.

The equation of continuity: This is a form of the law of conservation of mass. Water flowing in a channel must maintain a constant mass. The equation of continuity indicates that the flow remains constant regardless of riverbends, constrictions, passage over obstacles, etc. We can use the equation of continuity to explain several river features.

Rapids: Where the riverbed constricts (less area), the water must flow faster (higher velocity). With a sufficient increase in velocity, the fluid flow will transition from laminar to turbulent. Turbulent flow is indicated by splashing water in constricted areas; in other words, rapids!

Rapids can also form where a river transitions from deep to shallow. In this setting, a gravel bar or rocks can cause a decrease in area and an increase in velocity.

DIG DEEPER

Discharge is the product of area and velocity. When the river's cross-sectional area changes, the velocity must also change. A familiar example is partially blocking the end of a garden hose with your thumb to increase the water velocity. By decreasing the area, you cause the water velocity to increase.

The continuity relationship between area and velocity is described mathematically as: $A_1v_1 = A_2v_2$ (the equation of continuity). That is to say, the product of area and velocity in one position must match the product of area and velocity in a second position.

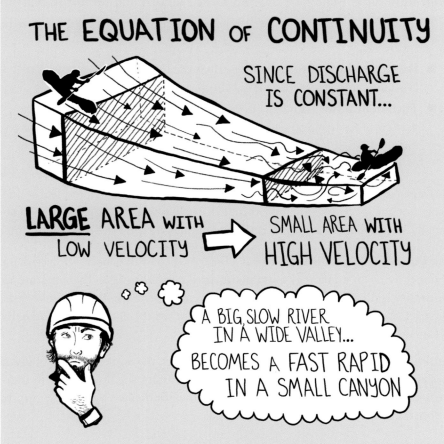

Eddies: When the channel area decreases, due to a rock or protrusion along the bank, the river's velocity must increase. If the channel area quickly returns to the original area immediately below the obstacle, the velocity must also return to the original velocity. But since the downstream current has momentum, it can't slow soon enough to meet the requirements of the equation of continuity. Instead, the water immediately behind the protrusion compensates for the primary current by flowing very slowly, or even upstream.

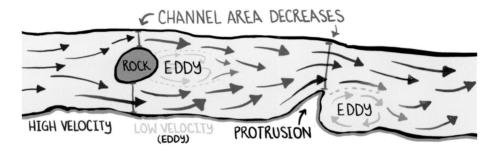

Holes: The river water accelerates when it flows around or over a rock—the rock decreases the cross-sectional area of the channel and, per the equation of continuity, the velocity must increase.

The channel's cross-sectional area recovers immediately after the rock. The fast current over the rock must stall out to maintain continuity. The fast water volume flowing downstream along the hole's bottom and edges is compensated by a volume of water with a negative current (backwash). If this sounds familiar, it's because we just used the same explanation for eddies. Holes are kind of like eddies on their sides.

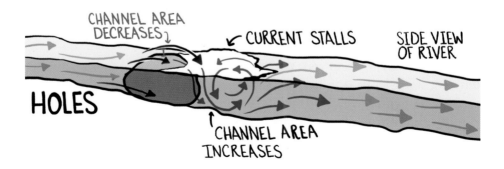

This relationship helps explain why holes "drown out" or form waves at higher water levels. As the discharge increases, the area over and around the rock increases. The current might still speed up, but not nearly as much as at lower water levels. In turn, a wave might form instead of a hole.

Waves: As outlined above, a horizontal or vertical constriction produces an increased river velocity. At the other end of the constriction, the area increases, and the water slows. The transition from fast to slow velocity is marked by a pile up of water, which forms a wave. A small velocity reduction might result in a single wave, but a large drop will likely create a **wave train**: a series of waves dissipating the water's energy.

Casey Fulton in a wave train. Grand Canyon section of the Colorado River.

RIVER DIARY

An effective way to build your understanding of how rivers work and feel at different water levels is to keep a river diary. Recording river conditions after each of your outings will help build a baseline when planning new adventures. If researching a new river indicates a lower gradient and similar discharges to a familiar run, it is probably an excellent destination for you. Details to record in a river diary include the river's character, gradient, discharge, and a sense for pushiness or general feel.

TONY'S RIVER DIARY

Artist, craftsman, and educator Tony Perelli keeps a river diary that I admire. Here is his reasoning and an excerpt from one of our days together.

A river's character and difficulty are usually directly related to a river's volume, which is continually changing. As a paddler, my skills and goals are fluid as well.

By keeping some simple river notes, I can understand what to expect at higher or lower water levels, different seasons, and different skills. Notes also encourage me to pay closer attention; it seems easy to remember how much fun I had but challenging to recall some of the details. Taking notes helps deepen my relationship with the river.

Six Mile Creek Beta, 8/16/2020
Neil, Shasta, Timmy, Luc, Sam, Tony
8.83 ft - 8.85 ft, 511 - 522 cfs
⌐ *Gauge height*   *Flow* ⌐

Sunny, hot, and perfect. 4hrs on the water, all three canyons. For me, this is a water level to look for, dreamy fun. Active and challenging but not scary, not pushy.

- *This refers to the 1st and 2nd canyons* — 1st and 2nd were more defined than at higher levels but less push. When lazy at the bottom of a couple of rapids, they did want to pull boat back.
- Several surf waves were in good shape.
- *Tony is talking about himself* — Staircase (most intimidating for me) seemed at its best behavior at this level. We read & ran. I wanted to rerun it but eddied out too low to motivate the walk back up. ⌐ *Left to right*
- *Named rapids* — Staircase: Top chute, L to R. Middle squeeze down the tongue but ready to head R. Let speed drop and set up to run final stairs from R to L.
- Marry-go-round: Looked fun catching eddy on L just above main rapid.
- Middle to R line on Jaws, just L past rock, then paddle hard R just behind it to an abrupt drop! Remember there is a following abrupt drop shortly downstream, catch a very steep chute R of C. ⌐ *Right of center*

Thor Tingey, Becky King, Tony Perelli, and friends on the Grand Canyon.

CHAPTER 5

THE PRINCIPLES OF RIVER-RUNNING

It is not unusual for packrafters to feel the allure of river-running regardless of their initial intent. I suspect the appeal of rivers is partly due to the three-dimensional nature of the water. I love the geographic aesthetics of rolling hills and valleys; rivers can have a similar character, in the hydrologic sense: waves and holes. Reading rivers is like reading the landscape.

The principles of river-running involve managing hazards so that you can keep paddling into old age. Recall from *Chapter 3: Risk* that our on-the-fly risk mitigation can be split into two efforts: minimize the likelihood that things will go wrong and minimize the consequences when they do. In river parlance, this translates into: "Can I stay upright? What will happen to me if I capsize?"

WHAT YOU NEED TO KNOW

Methods to minimize the consequences of a swim include boat control (*Chapter 2: Boat Control and Wet Re-entry*) and setting safety with throw ropes or safety boats (*Chapter 8: River Rescue From the Water* and *Chapter 9: River Rescue From Shore*).

Methods to reduce the likelihood of a swim are covered here; they include:

- **Difficulty rating:** Use river ratings to choose appropriate destinations.
- **Read the river and pick a line:** Read the river and choose a path that allows you to use the river's force to move to and from safe positions.
- **Scout:** The point of scouting is to ensure that you are not surprised by hazards. Shore scouting is a more fundamental and safer practice; boat scouting is introduced as you gain experience.
- **Portage:** Walk around features that you choose not to paddle.

- **Group size:** Choose an appropriate group size and space yourselves correctly.
- **Maneuvering:** Work with the river's force to put your boat where you want it to be.

Paddling techniques for running specific river features (rocks, waves, etc.) are discussed in the next chapter. Your ability to perform these maneuvers will improve with practice.

RIVER DIFFICULTY: CHOOSING WHERE TO PADDLE

Rivers are rated by difficulty. The right difficulty for you depends on your ability to execute an appropriate sequence of maneuvers. Since capsizing is likely when you paddle difficult water, you also need to be confident in your ability to swim to safety. In other words, a Class III boater should be able to maintain control while paddling and swimming Class III rapids.

Difficulty and danger are two different problems. A rapid can be one, both, or neither. The scariest hazards are both difficult and dangerous. Understanding this distinction will help you use the difficulty scale to choose where to paddle and when to portage.

Any given river or open water hazard has the same difficulty (rating) regardless of who is paddling. Danger depends on you: your skillset, training, equipment, as well as your partners' ability to help. When exposed to the same rapid, a novice is more likely to experience harmful consequences than an expert.

This section presents the International Scale of River Difficulty and caveats for interpreting the rating system. A list of applicable skills accompanies each river rating (pgs. 144-145). You can use these lists to evaluate gaps in your skillset.

The International Scale of River Difficulty: This is a collaborative creation from expert paddlers from around the world. The difficulty scale has been adopted by paddlers, guidebook writers, and government agencies. The scale attempts to convey the risks associated with a specific class of water, where higher class ratings correspond to increasing difficulty. The system is not perfect, but it allows the global community to plan and prepare for river trips using a common language.

Class I: Easy. Moving water with few or no obstacles. The obstacles can easily be avoided without previous training.

Class II: Novice. Faster moving water with more obstacles. Obstacles are easily avoided by trained paddlers.

Class III: Intermediate. Class III rivers feature rapids and waves that can be difficult to avoid. Technical boat-handling skills are required to navigate through obstacles. Scouting skills are required.

Class IV: Advanced. Class IV rivers have powerful holes and waves. Their rapids are generally predictable, with established routes; the routes require fast reactions and excellent boat control. Rescue generally requires group assistance.

Class V: Expert. Class V rapids are long and violent, with limited eddying opportunities. Scouting may be difficult, and swims are dangerous.

Class VI: Extreme. Class VI rapids are extremely difficult; consequences are likely to be fatal.

There are several caveats when using the difficulty scale:

- **Difficulty along a river is not constant:** A Class III section might contain a notable Class V rapid that is routinely portaged. Some guidebooks assign the single hardest rapid rating to the entire section, and others will indicate the general difficulty followed by the difficulty of the hardest rapid in parentheses: Class III (V).

- **Initial perception:** The person that first rated the rapid might have under- or overestimated the difficulty due to their expertise.

- **Ratings have regional variation:** Ratings can differ by region; start paddling easier grades in a new region to determine their equivalence. For example, the Pacific Northwest of the United States, British Columbia, and New Zealand have a reputation for ratings that underestimate difficulty.

- **Published ratings can change:** High-discharge events might change the rapids.

- **Word-of-mouth ratings:** Not all rivers have published ratings, and when ratings are spread by word-of-mouth, they fall prey to the whims of personal opinion. A popular river that gets run by many experienced paddlers is likely to get verbally downgraded.

WHEN DANGER DOESN'T MATCH DIFFICULTY

Campground rapid, Eagle River: Campground rapid, close to my home, features a particularly persistent log jam (see photo on pages 220-221). The water directly above the log jam is Class II in difficulty at normal water levels but the consequences of a swim are severe. The *danger* of this feature far exceeds the *difficulty* of the river rating. The Eagle River log jam feels like Class II water with Class V consequences.

Veracruz: When Todd Tumolo and I took a packrafting vacation to Mexico, I was shocked at what a difference the warm water made. I told Todd, "This feels like Class IV water with Class III consequences!" It was still Class IV water in *difficulty*, but the warmth made it feel less *dangerous*. Alaska's cold, glacial rivers would probably feel more dangerous to our Mexican partners.

Luc Mehl. Cascadas Micos, Mexico. © Todd Tumolo

THESE ARE NOT CLASS III RAPIDS BACK HOME!

I experienced downgrading on the heavily visited Green River Narrows in North Carolina. Our guide described the first several rapids as Class III, and when we turned the corner, Roman Dial and I thought, "Uh oh, these are not Class III rapids back home!" The guide's familiarity with the rapids made them feel Class III to him, even though the guidebook lists them as Class IV.

Roman Dial. Bald River Falls, Tennessee.

Progressing up the difficulty scale: The river classification scale can be used as a guide to monitor your skill progression. I've made an effort to associate each rating with a skillset. While this table is not definitive, you can use it to identify gaps in your skillset.

If you are working to improve your boating skills, "paddle up a level" by applying the skills from a rating above that which you are on. For example, use the strokes from the Class III list when you are paddling Class II water.

Each rating includes a list of hazards that you might encounter. This list is not all-inclusive! The list of hazards is included as a reminder that a strainer might be around the next bend, even in Class I water.

	Class I: Easy	Class II: Novice	Class III: Intermediate	Class IV: Advanced
Description	Moving water with few or no obstacles. The obstacles can easily be avoided without previous training.	Faster moving water with more obstacles. Obstacles are easily avoided by trained paddlers.	Class III rivers feature rapids and waves that can be difficult to avoid. Technical boat-handling skills are required to navigate through obstacles. Scouting skills are required.	Class IV rivers have powerful holes and waves. Their rapids are generally predictable, with established routes that require fast reactions and excellent boat control. Rescue generally requires group assistance.
Risk assessment	Recognize that even Class I can be hazardous.	Identify your limitations and be willing to portage rapids.	• Identify when you need to scout or portage, and do it safely • Assist another boater when they swim	• Expert judgment regarding lines and portages for the entire group • Able to scout from boat and shore • Able to assist team members and provide leadership during scouting and rescue
Outfitting	Ensure that there are no entanglement hazards on the boat, with other equipment, and in the water.	Able to adjust the seat and backband to paddle in a proper position.	Able to safely rig your packraft and recognize entanglement hazards: thigh straps, perimeter lines, cargo attachment, tail, etc.	Aware of entanglement hazards and comfortable discussing hazards with other boaters you meet on the river.
Boat control	• Forward strokes • Back strokes • Gradual turns • Sweep strokes	• Intentionally use different strokes for different movements, such as sweeps to turn and back strokes to paddle against the current • Pick a target and get the boat there • Catch large eddies and ferry at a high angle (relaxed ferry)	• Use draw strokes to grab the current • Use fewer and more intentional strokes • Quickly maneuver the boat in high-stress scenarios using paddle technique and edging • Catch medium and small eddies • Ferry at moderate angles (with a sense of urgency) • Move horizontally in the river even when in a wave train	• Able to brace to keep the boat upright • Highly effective at using draw strokes to grab the current • Precision boat control with intentional strokes and timing • Able to catch small eddies mid-rapid and keep track of other boaters

River-reading	Able to read conditions such as deep versus shallow, fast versus slow, etc.	Able to identify when the water goes where you want to go and when it doesn't.	Able to quickly read fast-moving water and pick a line through rapids that uses the principles of river-running (grab the current or paddle across it).	Able to quickly read fast water while boat scouting.
Rescue skills	• Able to intentionally exit the boat while in the water (wet exit) and get to shore • Able to tread water	• Able to recover equipment after capsizing • Able to perform a wet re-entry • Competent swimmer	• Swim in offensive and defensive positions • Able to prioritize yourself over equipment and manage equipment during a swim • Very confident with solo wet re-entry • Able to assist partners with re-entry • Know when, where, and how to use throw ropes	• Able to swim continuous rapids and transition to the offensive mode when approaching holes and other sticky hazards • Able to manage a group rescue from boat or shore, with and without ropes
Hazard recognition	• Wood • Cold • Wind • Waves • Seams where channels converge	• Wood • Getting swept into bends and cutbanks • Rapids approaching Class III difficulty • Seams at confluent channels	• Wood • Holes • Waves • Rocks • Sieves • Undercuts • Lateral waves	• Wood • Holes • Waves • Rocks • Sieves (more common, harder to avoid) • Undercuts • Lateral waves

SCOUTING

Scouting is a "know before you go" strategy that can reduce the likelihood of a swim. Scouting involves identifying river features and choosing whether to portage or paddle. You can either scout from shore, which is less exposed, or from your boat, which requires more experience and better boat-control skills.

You will want to pick a line through the hazards if you aren't going to portage. Picking a line is the same if you are in your boat or swimming: identify what to avoid and how to avoid it. In playful water, the line ends up feeling like a series of rock climbing moves—intentional maneuvers up, down, left, and right, that carry you through the rapids. I love this aspect of running rivers, and it doesn't have to be Class IV rapids to warrant a high level of intention. The difference between Class II and Class IV rapids is that being off your line has higher consequences when in Class IV rapids.

Reading the River

Reading the river involves scanning the water to identify hazards and features, and get a sense of where the water flows. This process is similar to the overall strategy in this book: identify what can go wrong and make a plan to stay safe if it does.

River perspective: When discussing river features with your partners, the perspective is always described as looking downriver. If you want to distinguish your perspective when looking upriver, you can clarify with "looker's right" and "looker's left."

River perspective:

- **River right:** The right side of the river while looking downriver.
- **River left:** The left side of the river looking downriver.

Picking a line: Your ability to read rivers, pick lines, and put your boat where you want will improve with practice. Novices should identify the "good water" that steers clear of hazards and pick a line that places the packraft in that water. Intermediate and advanced paddlers will choose a more dynamic line, grabbing the current when it goes where they want and cutting across the current when it doesn't.

Pathlines and conveyor belts: I find it helpful to visualize the river as a series of pathlines and conveyor belts, as illustrated later in this chapter. Pathlines are the paths that water particles follow down the river. Throwing wood into the river is a timeless exercise in observing pathlines. A series of parallel pathlines can be represented as a conveyor belt. Picking a line consists of identifying the pathlines and conveyor belts that go where you want to go. If you detect pathlines on the other side of the river that avoid the hazards below you, you will pick a line that places your boat (or swimming body) in those pathlines.

Markers: River markers can help you remember your line while you are paddling. If you are on the shore, lower your perspective (bring your eyes closer to the water level) so that what you presently see is similar to what you will see from the water. Use rocks, distinct waves, boils, and other features as markers.

I usually need to repeat a verbal recap to help me remember my line: "Center. Left below the pyramid rock. Left to right at the pile-up."

Scouting From the Shore

Scouting from the shore involves getting out of your packraft, securing the boat, and walking to a vantage point. Shore scouting is less exposed than boat scouting and, therefore, a less risky option.

Shasta Hood scouting Kings River, Alaska.

It is generally a good idea to carry your throw bag and paddle while scouting. If someone chooses to run the rapid, you are already in a position to set safety. Having the rope on-hand allows you to set up safety while the paddlers walk back to their boats. The paddle can be used in extension rescues (reaching out to a swimmer), as an aid when wading into the water, or as a replacement if a boater breaks their paddle mid-run. Paddles are also great for signaling "ready" and pointing which way to go.

When efficiency matters, or there is limited space to scout, experienced groups might send one person to scout while the others stay in their boats. The scout evaluates the rapid and signals the group whether—and where—they should paddle, portage, or if they should look for themselves. The scout can set up safety and watch everyone as they paddle through.

Boat Scouting

Boat scouting involves adjusting boat speed and position to get a clear view downriver. Boat scouting is only appropriate when your understanding of rivers and boat control exceeds the river's difficulty level. Scout from the shore if you are intimidated by what you see. Expert paddlers in steep and convoluted drainages might only be able to scout from the water, but the rest of us usually have the option of going to shore.

Key factors of boat scouting include:

- **Hazards:** Identify the river hazards.
- **Noise:** Listen for rapids.
- **Swim plan:** Develop and continually update a swim plan.
- **Eddies:** Use eddies to regroup and scout.
- **Group management:** Pay attention to boat order. Some rapids should be run one at a time; others are better suited for a read-and-run succession.

Eddy-hopping: Boat scouting is often referred to as eddy-hopping. The leader scans the river for hazards from an eddy (or other safe zone), signals to the group (all clear, no-go, or portage), and then continues to the next eddy. The group continues working their way down the river with this follow-the-leader strategy, usually trading the lead role on-the-fly. Ideally, eddy-hopping only exposes one boater at a time and never beyond the scouted section.

Read-and-run: Some river conditions make stopping to scout either challenging or unnecessary, depending on the skill level of the paddlers. Read-and-run describes the strategy of picking your line on-the-fly. You might choose to read-and-run because you and your partners don't need to scout from eddies. Or, river sections with a continuous gradient and few eddies might require you to make snap decisions about your line. Scan the river for the next rapid and then focus on the maneuvers needed to clear the current rapid. Always plan one move ahead.

SETTING SAFETY

Setting safety minimizes the consequences of capsizing in the river. If anyone is going to run a rapid, the next step is to make a safety plan. You might conclude that you don't need to post anyone in a safety role. Or, you might set up people with throw bags, safety boats, or both. Throw bags and safety boats are to river runners what ropes and anchors are to rock climbers. As with rock climbing, we want redundancy in our system. What if the first throw misses the mark? What if we need to recover a swimmer and gear on opposite sides of the channel?

Techniques for setting safety from the water and shore require training and practice and are presented in *Chapter 8: River Rescue From the Water* and *Chapter 9: River Rescue From Shore*.

The basic concepts of staged safety are:

- **Priorities**: Everyone playing a safety role has to remember the rescue priorities: yourself, the other rescuers, the swimmer, and finally, equipment.

- **Safety from shore:** People on shore can help a swimmer with an extension rescue (reaching an arm or paddle to the swimmer) or throw rope.

- **Safety boats:** Safety boats are boats that wait downstream to help a swimmer get to shore or collect gear lost during the swim. The safety boats might have portaged or paddled into position.

You can use a single whistle blast, paddle, or hand signal to let the paddlers know when the safety team is in position and ready. The first boater responds with the same signal. After a boater gets through the rapid, they can join or swap with the safety team, either climbing to shore or serving as another safety boat.

PRO TIP!

Setting safety is hard to do right. Take the time to pre-brief before getting in the water:

- Is this the right group of people for the run? Discuss the water level, river hazards, and Plan B.
- Do the people with throw ropes know how to use them? Does the swimmer? Are the throwers in positions to swing swimmers to safety?
- Can the safety boat portage into position or are we counting on them to paddle through the rapid? Is the safety boater competent and capable?
- What lies around the next riverbend?
- Does everyone have appropriate safety equipment: life vest, helmet, drysuit? Are drysuit zippers zipped?
- Are the boats rigged properly: no long tails or straps, no loose cord, no non-locking carabiners, etc.?
- What are the group resources? Rescue supplies, first aid kit, communication devices, maps, etc.

PORTAGING

Portaging is walking around a section of the river instead of paddling it. Portaging is an excellent option to reduce your exposure and, therefore, risk. You should never feel guilty or regretful for choosing to portage.

LOVE THE PORTAGE

The decision to portage follows your on-the-fly risk assessment: "Can I stay upright? What will happen to me if I capsize?"

The inconvenience of the portage shouldn't be a factor, but it often is. Portaging can be cumbersome: get to shore, get out of the boat, carry your boat over slippery rocks, find a put-in, and so on. But the decision to portage should be based on the river features, not convenience.

There are many reasons to portage, not just because a rapid is deemed too difficult.

- You've run this rapid before, but aren't paddling at your best today.
- You misjudged your layering and aren't appropriately dressed to swim.
- Your boat has a slow leak and can't maintain full pressure.
- You are in a remote setting, and losing gear isn't an option.
- The group is too tired to handle a swim and gear recovery.

Groups with mixed skill levels might split up so that portagers can set safety for people that want to paddle. If the boats are heavy or the portage is challenging, a more experienced group member could paddle their boat and then return to paddle a second boat, enabling the portagers to walk without carrying their packrafts. Challenging portages can be made safer by passing equipment along a chain or using throw ropes as a hand-line or to lower equipment.

PRO TIP!

Keep your safety gear on while scouting and portaging, especially your helmet. Slipping on wet rocks and rockfall in canyons have caused several injuries to paddlers who assumed they were safe once they were out of the water. My worst packrafting injury was a broken toe while scouting.

GROUP SIZE AND SPACING

The appropriate group size depends on your objectives and experience. Choose objectives that are appropriate for the least experienced member of your group. Paddling with partners is fun and, if they are competent partners, reduces the likelihood of an incident. Incompetent partners and large groups can make your outing riskier. Large groups are inconvenient in difficult water because there are often a limited number of eddies to use as safety zones.

Many paddlers prefer a group size of three or four. With a group of three, one person could seek help while another stays with a patient. I prefer a group of four so that someone is available for each of me, my boat, and my paddle. I also like the added safety of sending a pair of people to seek help so that everyone is partnered up.

If you absolutely must paddle alone, recognize that you are much more vulnerable and that minor hazards can quickly turn into severe incidents.

PRO TIP!

Paddling alone significantly increases your vulnerability. Recognize that if you choose to paddle alone, you are your only safety net. Half of the known packraft fatalities were solo paddlers.

If you absolutely *must* paddle alone, consider these recommendations:

- **Scale it back:** Solo paddlers should choose objectives with fewer hazards and less exposure (willing to portage) to accommodate their increased vulnerability. It is a good idea to "paddle down" several levels—below your skill level.
- **Portage:** Walk when there is any doubt. Really. Packrafts are literally made for this.
- **Dial in your kit:** Solo paddlers can't afford the additional vulnerability of sloppy outfitting or partial safety equipment.

- **Leave a trip plan:** Let friends know your itinerary. Be honest with yourself that a rescue effort could be a body recovery.
- **Carry a communication device:** Carry an inReach or similar satellite communication device inside your drysuit. Check in at the start, end, and any crux or decision points.
- **Consider a leash:** For open-water crossings, use a leash to keep track of your gear after capsizing. Do not use a leash in moving water.

Spacing: In calm and easy water, boats can be feet apart or even tied together. In fast and challenging water, you want to be close enough to help but not so tight that you might bump someone off their line. I prefer to follow at a distance that allows me to watch the boater's line in front of me. This vantage lets me watch them complete their line and gives me time to either follow or choose a different line based on how hard theirs looked.

> ## *PRO TIP!*
>
> My paddle partner and co-instructor Tony Perelli advises: If you are in a leadership or instructor role, keep people close enough so that you can see their eyes. Eyes convey a lot about how comfortable people are as they look downriver and evaluate upcoming maneuvers.
>
> This concept is similar to rescue professionals wanting to talk to patients on satellite phones. Rescue professionals can evaluate details of the incident by your tone of voice.

Line-of-sight: Maintain a line-of-sight with the paddler in front *and* behind you. If you lose sight of the paddler behind you, stop and wait for them to catch up. The paddlers in front of you should stop once they notice that you are not following, triggering a cascading effect.

Maintaining a line-of-sight ensures that you can communicate with hand or paddle signals. Signals should be passed up and down the line so that the entire group understands the situation.

If you lose sight of the person behind you, catch an eddy to allow them to catch up, or get out of your boat and hike upriver until you regain eye contact and can communicate with a whistle, hand, or paddle signals.

Designate lead and sweep paddlers: For groups with mixed skill levels, it is best if the most experienced boater leads. Another experienced boater sweeps (comes last) and less experienced paddlers are positioned in the middle. Keep the group compact. Groups with similar paddling skills and familiarity will want to change the lead and sweep roles dynamically. Hogging the lead role might make you unpopular.

Limit exposure: Only expose one paddler at a time to a hazard. In other words, position yourself such that you can paddle to safety when you see someone else in trouble. You should never have more than one swimmer in the water. This strategy is equivalent to skiers descending one at a time in avalanche terrain; it makes it more likely that someone is available to assist in the case of an incident.

A LONELY SWIM

In 2009, Roman Dial and Brad Meiklejohn invited me on what was certain to be my most challenging river trip yet: a fly-in to the Talkeetna River. *Fast & Cold: A Guide to Alaska Whitewater* mentions that the Talkeetna is possibly "the best all-around whitewater river in Alaska" due to sustained rapids and gorgeous scenery. I was excited, but also intimidated.

After a few hours on the water, Becky King was the only group member that hadn't swam. But we had done well at scouting, setting safety, and supporting each other.

After setting safety at one of the larger Class IV rapids, I took the lead position. Unfortunately, I didn't realize we were entering the "Sluice Box," several miles of sustained Class III and IV rapids. My limited ability to catch eddies kept me in front of the group, and once out of sight, I capsized. I managed to hold onto my gear but went for a very long swim with no one available to help. I finally kicked my way to shore, intact.

It was another lesson I only needed to learn once: designate a lead paddler and maintain a line-of-sight. I should also have learned not to paddle rivers that were more difficult than my skillset. Unfortunately, that lesson didn't arrive until Rob's drowning several years later.

MANEUVERING

We can't control the river, but we can influence how the packraft responds to the river. Your approach to maneuvering will depend on your experience and objectives. At the most basic level, maneuvering involves paddling directly away from hazards. More advanced maneuvering combines your power with the river's, using the dynamics of the river to lead you to safety. Maneuvering comes down to three principle concepts. Some of the river terminology in this section might not be familiar yet—refer to the glossary and the following chapter.

Principles of maneuvering:

- **Lead with your head**: Focus your gaze on your objective. Shift your weight toward your attention by pivoting from your hips and rotating your torso. This athletic positioning sets you up for proper edge control.

- **Keep an active blade in the water:** An active blade provides a connection to the river that allows you to turn, brace, and prepare for the next move.

- **Respond to the river's force:** Engaging with the river's force (rather than opposing it) allows the river to do the work.

Lead With Your Head

As with other aspects of life, the key to success is to focus on your goals. Your body will follow your gaze . . . so don't focus on obstacles! Look to where you want to go.

Leading with your head involves decoupling your lower body, torso, and head. Extend your spine and allow your torso and head to shift toward your objective. Lead with your gaze, and the boat will follow.

A focused gaze should feel familiar to athletes crossing over from other sports— mountain bikers keep their focus down the trail, and their bike and body adjust to the terrain. Skiers and snowboarders have active lower bodies that accommodate the slope, but their torsos and heads seemingly float down the fall line.

Leading with your head. Kate Fitzgerald, Willow Creek, Alaska.

> ## PRO TIP!
>
> You won't be able to effectively lead with your head unless you have a proper paddling position, which allows for full torso rotation and increased power. The key to proper paddling position is adjusting your seat and backband. Refer to *Chapter 1: Packrafting Equipment.*

Keep an Active Blade in the Water

An active blade in the water helps maintain your connection to the river. The "active" part refers to constant movement—even if it is subtle. I remember watching a mentor make a slow-motion sculling draw stroke while riding down a tongue and thinking, "What in the world is he doing?" But it looked cool, so I asked about his technique.

Micro-adjustments keep the paddle active, constantly exerting a force on the water and sensing changes in the current. A feel for the current allows you to quickly position the blade for turning, propulsion, or bracing. An inactive blade in the water is along for the ride; it doesn't allow you to change anything.

The concept of an active blade is similar to playing with your hand's aerodynamics out the window of a moving car. Changing your hand's position increases or decreases the drag forces on it. The more data your brain collects, the better your ability to make a controlled and intentional adjustment, to understand the relationship between action and reaction. The same is true for a blade "collecting data" in the water.

An active blade serves many purposes:

- **Maintaining momentum:** An active blade engages deeper currents than the boat's hull. Deeper water is often denser and follows more orderly pathlines compared to surface water. This effect is particularly evident when paddling against a headwind; grabbing the deeper current helps pull the boat against the wind.

- **Stabilization:** Turbulent water in waves, holes, and other river features can push the boat on edge and lead to capsizing. An active blade provides a mobile outrigger that you can use to keep the packraft upright.

- **Turning:** The same forces that can capsize a boat can also be used to turn it. An active blade—leveraging and twisting—can orient the boat for the next maneuver.

PRO TIP!

Common advice for new river runners is "paddle hard and lean forward!" or "paddle hard and brace like hell!" Paddling hard involves quickly transferring between each paddle blade; in other words, one of the blades is almost always active in the water. The "brace like hell" addition accomplishes the same thing: bracing involves placing the blade against the water—another way to maintain active contact.

Respond to the River's Force

As a novice paddler, I thought of the river as a two-dimensional surface (like a lake), and paddled my packraft in straight-line segments to avoid obstacles. I realized that there was more art to river-running after watching more experienced paddlers. The big difference with the experienced paddlers was that they used the river's force to their advantage, working with the river to finesse their position and speed.

Responding to the river's force is a complicated concept. The idea is to respond to an external force rather than oppose it, to balance your input (paddle strokes and edge control) with what the river wants to do. This interaction can take the form of grabbing currents that go where you want to go and transferring across, or punching through, those that don't. In both cases, you need to move faster or slower than the current to change your position; otherwise, you are just along for the ride.

Conveyor belts: Picturing sections of mostly parallel pathlines as conveyor belts will be helpful in the next chapter. Masses of water behaving uniformly suggests laminar flow. The behavior of laminar flow is more predictable than turbulent flow, and laminar flow generally offers safe passage. Picture the river as a series of separate conveyor belts and then search for a line that connects the belts. Running the river consists of using boat control to grab and transfer across conveyor belts.

Grab the river: When the river is going where you want to go, grab it (or be grabbed by it). Packrafts sit shallowly in the water, so grabbing the river with

THE RIVER AS A SERIES OF CONVEYOR BELTS

FULLY PLANT BLADE FOR STRONG CONNECTION TO RIVER

a paddle stroke and boat edge makes a huge difference in maneuvering. This technique is most apparent when using a draw stroke to catch or "peel-out" of an eddy, as described later. The idea is that you want to paddle hard toward an eddy and then grab the calm or opposing eddy water to come to a stop. Or, you want to paddle hard out of an eddy and grab the main current to be pulled downstream. In both cases, you work with the river's force rather than oppose it.

The two ways to grab the river are by placing a blade in the water, and edging. Fully planting the blade and orienting it to catch the current provides a strong connection to the river. Edging, pushing one side of the boat deeper into the water, presents a section of the hull for the river to grab, as opposed to the flat bottom. Edging the correct side matters because the depressed tube will feel increased frictional drag. You can generally rely on the "lead with your head" principle to edge correctly. The combination of these two techniques gives the river the most grip on your packraft.

Powering on and off: When the river goes where you want to go, there is no need to propel yourself downstream. When being along for the ride is safe, you can "power-off," catch your breath while maintaining an active blade, or even back-paddling. Take this time to read the river, assess your line, and prepare for a "power-on" pulse. Other useful times to power-off include at the crest of a wave or when you want to slow down and reset or redirect your momentum. Maintaining an active blade while powered-off keeps you prepared for your

Shasta Hood "powering on" to clear a drop on the Kings River, Alaska.

next move, which might be paddling across the current in a ferry, or building momentum to punch through a sticky feature.

Paddling across the current: When the current, or conveyor belt, doesn't go where you want to go, you will want to move across it. You might cross the current in a ferry, pointing the bow at an upstream angle and moving slower than the current, or you might charge down and across, moving faster than the river. In both cases, powerful paddle strokes will build the boat's momentum across the current. The river's force will govern the boat's angle and your paddling speed.

Building momentum: Conveyor belts often end in features that we don't want to drift into, such as sticky holes. If traveling across the belt isn't an option, you will likely want to add your force to the river's, using five or six strong forward strokes to build momentum and drive through the sticky feature. Lead with your head and aim to grab the water on the other side of the sticky feature.

> ### PRO TIP!
>
> Packrafts usually reach maximum speed with five or six power strokes. Trying to maintain power for more extended periods can deplete your reserves and leave you unprepared for a critical sprint. It is always a good idea to leave some energy in the bank. This applies to capsizing, too: save some energy for the swim.

Let's use an extreme waterfall rapid to illustrate responding to the river's force. These concepts apply just as well to a friendly Class II rapid, but waterfalls are more fun for Sarah to illustrate.

Responding to the river's force:

1. Our friend in the little yellow boat grabs a tongue with a draw stroke and keeps an active blade in the water.
2. The tongue feeds into a turbulent mess and then down the waterfall, so the paddler makes a few hard strokes to transfer off the tongue and grab the eddy in (3).
3. The paddler keeps an active blade in the water while pausing (power off) to pick a line. The active blade helps the paddler prepare for a quick move to (4).
4. A few forward strokes bring the paddler onto a new tongue, which they grab with the paddle blade and boat edging. The tongue feeds into a hole, so the paddler makes powerful strokes to build momentum down the tongue.
5. A boof stroke on the fall's lip disconnects the paddler from the river.
6. The paddler's momentum drives them clear of the sticky part of the hole. They set up in a low brace position to get a blade in the water as soon as possible.
7. The paddler grabs the water in the pool and thanks the river gods.

RESPONDING TO THE RIVER'S FORCE

PRO TIP!

A useful way to practice working with the river's force is to count your paddle strokes. By keeping an active blade in the water and using fewer and more intentional strokes, you learn to respond to the river's force. It takes time to develop boat control and river-reading skills, and most novice packrafters default to using their own force (more strokes) when they could be using the river's force (fewer strokes).

Advanced paddlers can be seen making just enough forward strokes to move slightly faster than the current, and then using an active blade to orient the boat. With this approach, it only takes one or two quick and powerful strokes to reach top hull speed and maneuver through river features.

Ferrying

Ferrying is a maneuver to transport your boat across the current when it doesn't go where you want to go. Ferrying requires moving slower than the current. Most packrafters prefer a front ferry, facing upstream and using forward strokes to paddle against the current.

The front ferry is a fundamental maneuver and should be one of your practice priorities if you are new to river-running. A fun and effective way to practice ferrying is to work your way as far upstream as possible in Class II water. Paddling upstream forces you to use river features to your advantage, catching eddies and gaining ground wherever the current is weakest.

Front ferry: Because ferries are often done with limited space or time (e.g., above a series of rapids), it is common to turn the boat to an upstream angle and paddle while facing upstream. This technique, the front ferry, allows you to use powerful forward strokes to slow your downriver progress and travel across the current. The boat's angle will depend on the water's speed and the downstream distance you are willing to drift.

Ferrying across the river exposes your side tubes to the current. Lead with your head, weighing your downstream edge, and reducing the drag force on the upstream tube.

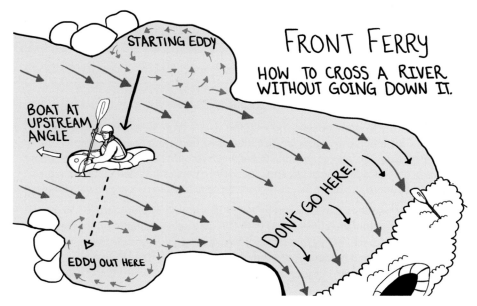

Back ferry: You can also back ferry by facing downstream and making back strokes. I struggle with this. It is hard to identify the best ferry angle when facing downstream, and it is difficult to hold an edge while making back strokes. Packrafts spin so quickly that I default to turning the boat around and using a front ferry.

Catching Eddies

Eddies are among the most important and useful river features, providing opportunities to regroup, scout, or get to shore. Catching eddies is very rewarding; no maneuver incorporates the principles of boat control and river-running so gracefully. Your ability to catch eddies will largely govern your progression to more difficult water.

Catching and exiting eddies reinforces the maneuvering principle of grabbing the river when it goes where you want to go. Learning to catch eddies provided an "Aha!" moment for me: the discovery of how to use a draw stroke to grab the river and use the river's force to my advantage. Learning to catch eddies is self-critiquing; you will know when your technique is right.

Eddies: When current moving downstream encounters an obstacle, such as a rock or protrusion, the current is deflected and compressed against the object. Zones of slow current offset these zones of compressed and fast current to maintain the river's constant overall flow. The slow-current zones are called eddies, and the offset can be so strong that the current flows upstream. Eddies are essentially low-pressure pockets or shadows.

Eddy lines: The boundary between the main current and the eddy current is called an **eddy line**, **eddy fence**, or **seam**. Eddy lines can be so strong that they prevent boats from crossing.

Catching eddies:

1. Visualize your objective: the main current is a conveyor belt, and you want to paddle across it and then grab the water in the eddy. You will need momentum to drive across the eddy line and then use a draw stroke to anchor into the still water in the eddy.
2. Focus your gaze on the top of the eddy and lead with your head as you approach.
3. Enter the eddy as far upriver as possible. The eddy line is the sharpest (narrowest) at the eddy's source (upriver end). Aim for this high point.

The eddy line gets wider downstream, which makes it harder for the boat to punch through. It can help to visualize tapping your paddle against the eddy's source.

4. Approach the eddy line at a 45-degree angle. Approaching at an angle ensures the momentum you need to punch across the eddy line. 45-degrees is a good rule of thumb, but anything from 30 to 90 degrees might be appropriate depending on the velocity difference across the eddy line.

5. Time your strokes so that you can make five or six power strokes to build momentum just before crossing the eddy line. Your last stroke in the main current should be on the outside of the turn. This final stroke helps initiate the turn into the eddy.

6. Keep your head directed at the turn's center to ensure that you are leaning into the turn, which will place your boat on the proper edge and give the river something to grab and hold in place.

7. When the packraft has crossed the eddy line past your knees, reach toward your feet to plant a draw stroke—grabbing the water in the eddy. This stroke needs to be placed in the calm eddy water, not in the messy water along the eddy line. Use paddle dexterity (bend your wrists) so that the blade's power face catches the eddy's upstream current—this allows you to grab the calm eddy water most effectively.

8. Leave the draw stroke in the eddy as an anchor.

9. Let your momentum naturally pivot the boat around the anchored draw stroke. Try not to pull the paddle through the water.

There are several common mistakes when learning to catch eddies:

■ **Sneaking**: It is tempting to move your boat into a pathline that flows right next to the eddy and then try to sneak into the eddy. Sneaking doesn't work because your momentum is downstream; you are at the mercy of the river's current, going where it wants you to go. To catch the eddy, you need to cut across the current and build momentum to punch across the eddy line. If you are positioned directly upstream of an eddy, you will need to paddle away from it and then come back at a 45-degree angle.

■ **Draw stroke too early:** You need the draw stroke to catch the water in the eddy. An early draw stroke catches the fast conveyor belt's edge, not the eddy's calm water.

CATCHING EDDIES

■ **Wrong blade orientation:** You want to use paddle dexterity to orient the blade's power face so that it catches the water in the eddy. Even when the eddy current is negligible, imagine that it is flowing upstream. Orient the blade to catch an upstream current.

Eddy practice is fun and arguably the most important skill to accompany your progression into more playful paddling. Look for opportunities to practice. Ideal practice eddies are large and feature sharp eddy lines. You can practice peeling out and turning into the same eddy or, my favorite, if there are paired eddies on both banks, peel out of one and into the other, in a figure-eight pattern.

> ## *PRO TIP!*
>
> With sufficient momentum and aggressive edging, you can give the river enough to grab without using the paddle blade (draw stroke as an anchor).
>
> Find a strong eddy line to practice, bring a lot of momentum into your eddy line crossing, and then tilt your hips to drive the boat's inside edge deep into the water. Hold your paddle out of the water in preparation for a low brace.

Peeling Out

The process of exiting an eddy to catch the main current is called "peeling out." This maneuver is useful anytime you want to cross seams between different currents, such as at tributaries and merging channels.

The maneuver to peel out of an eddy is similar to catching an eddy: build momentum to punch through an eddy line and then grab the main current with a draw stroke as an anchor. The tricky part is that the current changes from virtually zero in the eddy to several miles (km) per hour in the river. The eddy line separating these currents can be wide and diffuse or narrow and sharp. A boat sitting half in the eddy and half in the main current will feel complex forces trying to drag and shear the boat's bottom, especially if you don't have proper edge control.

Peeling out of eddies:

1. Visualize your objective: you want to paddle out of the eddy, quickly cross over the eddy line, and then allow the main current to grab your boat and carry it downriver.

PEELING OUT OF EDDIES

EXIT AT TOP

~45° ANGLE

EDDY LINE

LEAN DOWNSTREAM

GRAB THE MAIN CURRENT WITH DRAW STROKE

2. Exit the eddy as far upriver as possible. Eddy lines are shear zones, and the shear zone is narrowest at the top (upriver). Crossing the eddy line high allows you to get the boat into the main current quickly. Crossing the eddy line low leaves the packraft in a wide and chaotic shear zone.

3. Cross the eddy line at an appropriate angle. Forty-five degrees is a good rule of thumb, but anything from 30 to 90 degrees might be suitable depending on the velocity change across the eddy line. If crossing into a slow current, you can afford to exit at 90 degrees because the current won't produce a significant drag force on the hull. If there is a significant current differential across the eddy line, you will want to exit oriented more upstream, say 30 degrees, which presents the (stable) bow of your boat to the main current, rather than the (unstable) side.

4. Use five or six powerful forward strokes to build momentum and punch through the eddy line. No lily-dipping here!

5. Lead with your head and push the downstream edge of the boat deeper into the water. Edging gives the river more boat to grab, and by leaning

downstream, you reduce the frictional force working to capsize the boat—more aggressive edging results in a sharper turn.

6. At the same time, place a draw stroke on the boat's downstream side to grab the main current. Use paddle dexterity (bend your wrists) to orient the blade's power face so that it catches the downstream current.

7. Plunge the draw stroke deep *and leave it there*, anchored in the water. The paddle blade is your connection to the water. Use your core strength to keep the paddle in this position. You will initially feel a significant force on the blade as it catches the fast-moving water and drags you and the packraft downstream. The force on the blade will decrease to zero as the boat's speed increases to match the current.

Common challenges to peel-outs and crossing currents are:

■ **Exiting low:** It is common for novice packrafters to avoid peeling out by entering the main current at the bottom of the eddy, where the eddy line is most diffuse. This is usually safe, but it doesn't help you develop boat control skills and you can't always count on sneaking out from an eddy.

■ **Draw stroke too early:** As with catching eddies, the draw stroke needs to be across the eddy line. An early stroke catches the messy eddy line at the edge of the conveyor belt.

■ **Wrong blade orientation:** You want the blade's power face to catch the downstream current. Other orientations result in weakly grabbing the river.

■ **Edging:** If you accidentally lean upstream (away from where your head should be leading you), you will press the upstream tube into the current. In this orientation, the current can catch and drag the tube under, leading to a capsize.

Brad Meiklejohn, Roman Dial, and Russell DeVries. Honolulu Creek, Alaska.

Dan Rea-Dickins. Meghalaya, India.

CHAPTER 6

NAVIGATING RIVER FEATURES

This chapter takes the principles of river-running and applies them to maneuvering through features commonly found in rivers. The principles of river-running apply to rivers of all difficulties.

All packrafters will benefit from reviewing the braided, single channel, and strainers and wood sections because everyone is likely to encounter those features. Whitewater packrafters will want to study the remaining features, all of which might be found in a section with rapids. In my experience, the techniques in this chapter will make the most sense after you have encountered river features and realized you don't have as much control as you had hoped. The best way to get better at running rapids is to dedicate time to intentional practice.

WHAT YOU NEED TO KNOW

Whether you expect to or not, knowing how to maneuver your boat through river features can be fun, rewarding, and required to keep you out of harm. The techniques in this chapter are the culmination of everything we've covered so far: knowing your equipment's limitations, practicing paddle strokes and wet re-entries, evaluating risk, understanding how rivers work, and practicing the principles of river-running.

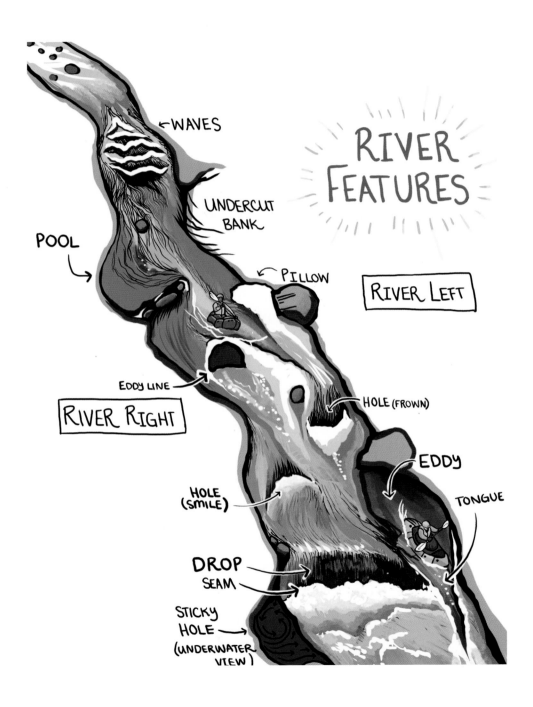

RIVER FEATURES

WAVES

UNDERCUT BANK

POOL

PILLOW

RIVER LEFT

EDDY LINE

RIVER RIGHT

HOLE (FROWN)

EDDY

HOLE (SMILE)

TONGUE

DROP

SEAM

STICKY HOLE (UNDERWATER VIEW)

BRAIDED CHANNELS

Braided rivers are popular packrafting destinations because there are generally fewer river hazards. The things that go wrong in braided channels are grounding out on island bars, running into wood, getting divided into separate channels, and capsizing in the turbulent water where channels converge.

Choosing the Deepest Channel

Despite your best efforts, you are likely to ground out at some point. Identifying the deepest channel can be difficult, but the consequences are minor—get out of the boat and portage to a different channel.

Methods to manage shallow water:

- **Starfishing**: One trick to sneak through shallow water is to shift your weight to the tubes instead of the seat. Lay back on the stern and push down onto the side tubes with your arms (and legs if possible).

- **Crutches**: Split the paddle into two halves and use them as crutches to help scoot the boat over the gravel. This isn't great for the paddle or your boat, but sometimes it is worth the morale boost not to have to get out of the boat (yet again).

- **Walking the dog**: In long shallow sections, use a tail or accessory strap to walk the boat like a dog on a leash.

Luc and Sarah Histand "walking the dog." Canning River, Alaska. © W. Koeppen

PRO TIP!

When confronted with multiple channels to choose from while paddling down a braided river, John Schauer's advice is: "Take the first channel that drops quickly." John is an Alaska river guide with decades of experience dragging his boat back upstream to look for a larger channel. John's advice is based on the idea that a lower-elevation channel will only gain water, whereas a higher-elevation channel will continue to lose it. The "first channel that drops quickly" is often marked by a cutbank—erosion indicating that the water is deep enough to allow a boat through. This approach is kind of a "better the devil you know than the devil you don't" strategy.

John also keeps track of the big picture: where most of the water will end up, according to the map or geography. If he knows one side of the valley will eventually have most of the water, he'll move to that side early.

Keeping the Group Together

Paddling braided rivers often turns into a game of guessing which channel has enough water to keep the boat afloat. It isn't always obvious which channel has the most water, and groups can get separated into different channels that might take miles to merge. Ideally, everyone commits to the same channel. If not, expect to use a whistle and signal with an upright paddle to track one another. In my experience, white blades and helmets are the easiest to spot from a distance.

After having been separated from my partners multiple times, I try to adopt a policy to follow the leader even if I think they aren't going into the best channel. It is better to be in the same crappy channel than to risk losing sight of each other.

Merging Channels

Paddling across converging channels is a common challenge for packrafters. When two channels have different currents, which is almost always the case, the seam between the channels can be a turbulent jumble. The greater the contrast between channel velocities, the messier the boundary where they merge. Large boats hardly notice these turbulent zones, but packrafts are easily thrown.

The seam between channels is best defined where they first meet (farthest upriver). You can cross the seam at this point (using the techniques described in the *Peeling Out* section in the previous chapter), or you can drift downriver and wait until the channels have mixed. Waiting is the easier option when available.

HOWLING AT THE WRONG CHANNEL

Amy Christeson is an instructor for the National Outdoor Leadership School. She shared this story from a personal trip in Arctic Canada.

We had been zigzagging in and out of a shallow, braided section of the upper Firth all day without consequences, so it seemed harmless when Frank Preston chose a different channel.

It was not immediately obvious that this unassuming split would separate us for hours. We continued paddling, keeping an eye on Frank's helmet and trying to work our way toward him through the maze of braids. We lost visual contact and checked our map to confirm that the riverbed was nearly a mile wide (1.6 km) and the channels wouldn't merge for some time.

Scanning the horizon through the binoculars, I was relieved to spot Frank towing his packraft on an aufeis shelf [river ice that can last year-round]. But then I noticed three dots lumbering behind him. There was no way to signal him, so we just hoped for the best and continued our float.

Through a combination of paddling and portaging, we finally united two hours later, with Frank exclaiming, "You'll never believe what was tracking me ... three wolves!"

We were careful to take the same braids from then on!

SINGLE CHANNELS: RIVERBENDS AND CUTBANKS

Braided channels transition into meandering single channels when they can no longer transport a significant sediment load. Single channels are most likely to cause problems for packrafters at the bends, either because erosion swept rocks or trees into the channel or because the current in a bend pushes you into the outer bank. Approach blind bends with the assumption that a hazard is just out of sight. Position the packraft so that you can get to shore until you are certain the bend is clear of hazards.

Riverbends: As the current approaches a bend in the river, its momentum drives the water into the outside bank. Continuous pressure on the outside bank causes erosion, leading to vertical walls and eroded debris, such as rocks and trees. Steep and tall banks sometimes indicate deep channels; undercuts indicate strong currents.

In typical conditions, the safest line through a blind bend is along the inside edge. In slower currents, you might have a better view from the outside of the bend, and plenty of time to get to shore if needed.

Paddling blind riverbends in fast currents:

1. Anticipate how the direction and velocity of the current will change as it goes around the bend.
2. Orient the packraft toward the inside of the bend.
3. Paddle toward the inside of the bend (cutting across pathlines) until you have a clear downstream view. Pointing the bow farther upstream and ferrying toward the inside bend will buy you time to look downstream or get out of the river. It is easier to paddle from the inside to the outside than in the opposite direction, so get to the inside while it is easy.
4. When you have confirmed that the outside of the bend is clear of hazards, you can spin and catch the main current and possibly a wave train. Some bends will have rocks or a strong eddy line along the inside edge, which might force you into the main current sooner than your preference.

If you find yourself on the outside bank, prepare to brace into a pile-up of turbulent water. The water that crashes into the wall has nowhere to go, so it stacks into chaotic piles. It is important to lean into the stacked water, into the wall. This lean helps to reduce the drag force on the bottom of your boat. Leaning away from stacked water gives the current a tube to grab and pull under, almost certainly resulting in a capsize. Note that an absence of stacked water might indicate an undercut, which is even scarier.

The paddling technique to manage cutbanks and rocks is similar. Review the *Rocks: Pillows, Undercuts, Sieves, and Tongues* section below for more discussion.

Riverbends in big water: An exception to the inside-is-safest guideline is in big-water rivers or high water levels. The flow will be chaotic along the inside bend and more laminar along the outside in big water. The laminar flow on the outside of the bends will feature large waves, but these might be preferable to the turbulent flow on the inside. Refer to the *Waves and Big Water* section below.

PRO TIP!

You are likely to experience nervousness as you build your river-running skills. Seizing up is a normal fear response, but it doesn't help you get down the river. The most effective way to manage fear is to gain experience through education, practice, and training, which you are already doing. Good job! These tricks might also help you stay engaged when your brain wants to panic:

Splash water on your face: Preemptively splashing your face takes away some of the shock when you get splashed in a rapid or go for a swim.

Breathe: Take a deep breath. Deep, slow breathing tells your brain that things are okay, even if they aren't.

Use a mantra: Help your brain by simplifying your options with a mantra. My mantras have included:

- *You've got this!*
- *Lead with your head.*
- *Keep a blade in the water.*
- *I've been training for this!*

STRAINERS AND WOOD

Strainers are a major concern for all boaters. Trees, logs, roots, branches, rocks, and other objects pose numerous opportunities to trap and drown people. You should anticipate strainers around every blind riverbend.

Wood enters rivers when trees topple into the water or are washed in during storm events. Eroding banks, headwaters, and steep tributaries are familiar sources of wood. Fallen trees progressively work their way downriver during the rising stage of high-water events, so rivers are most likely to have new wood hazards during storms and spring runoff.

Static strainers (fixed in place) are likely to have moved into downstream alignment with the river flow. Dynamic strainers, such as floating logs, are even less predictable and are very dangerous. Strainers are possible in all rivers. When you see strainers in the river, do everything in your power to steer away.

Most road-side and frequently paddled rivers have communities who actively clear the river of wood hazards. Packrafters are more likely to paddle remote and otherwise unmaintained rivers, so wood is a major concern for us.

Strainers: Strainers are submerged objects that act like pasta colanders—they allow water to pass through, but not people. Strainers don't have to be wood; any object that only lets water through is a strainer.

Sweepers: Sweepers are overhanging trees with branches that sweep the surface of the water. The concern with sweepers is that they can knock the paddler out of the boat. Deeply plunging branches can also snag and trap a swimmer.

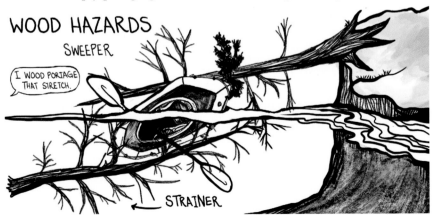

Paddling into strainers: There is no safe way to paddle into a strainer. If you have done everything in your power to avoid a strainer but are still going to hit it, identify your best hope for climbing up onto it. Do everything possible to stay above the wood; this is a life-and-death situation. Pull your skirt, release your thigh straps, and make a plan. Develop as much downstream momentum as possible and fight like hell to get up and over it. You absolutely cannot afford to drift into a strainer—you will capsize and get pulled under, even with a moderate current.

ROCKS: PILLOWS, UNDERCUTS, SIEVES, AND TONGUES

Rocks are both a blessing and a curse for river-runners. Rocks provide fun features to navigate and can be islands of safety, but rocks can also pose high-risk hazards. This section provides terminology followed by techniques to maneuver around and over rocks.

The key techniques to stay safe around rocks are:

- Know how to identify rocks and when to avoid them.
- Lean into the rock (hug it) if you are pushed up against it.
- Grab tongues of **green water** that offer passage between rocks.

Sarah Histand. Buller River, New Zealand.

Pillows and cushions: When water flows into a rock, it either deflects around the rock or stacks on top of it. If all the flow goes around the rock, an eddy will form behind it. If much of the flow stacks on top of the rock, a pillow or cushion will form. When scouting from upriver, pillows appear as anomalous high points on the river.

Undercuts: Water that flows against a rock without forming a pillow indicates an undercut. Undercuts are very dangerous because you don't know where the missing water went. Swimming into an undercut can lead to entrapment and drowning.

Brad Meiklejohn navigating rock hazards. Coffee River, Alaska.

Rock gardens: Rock or boulder gardens are boulder-choked sections of the river. Rock gardens are an excellent way to learn boat control at low water levels, providing multiple tongues and eddies to catch. Typically, many lines work to maneuver through rocks, a "choose your own adventure" treat. Rock gardens at high water levels can be hazardous. Evaluate the recovery options before paddling rock gardens.

Sieves: When boulders are piled on each other in the channel, they can form sieves. Like pasta colanders, sieves let water flow through, but not larger objects such as boats and people.

Part of what makes sieves so scary is that they are in the three-dimensional part of the river flow, which is difficult to detect from the surface. Most of the other river features and hazards have obvious indicators at the surface. Sieves are largely marked by a lack of an indicator—a lack of a pile-up.

Trailing wakes: Rocks and other hazards are often indicated by a trailing wake of water. These waves of diverted water are referred to as an "upstream V," but I dislike this term because "upstream" isn't intuitive (the V's point is upstream of the V's wings). The important part is to recognize that an obstruction diverts the current. You might not be able to see the obstruction, but you should be able to spot the trailing wake (and paddle away from it!).

Tongues: When two rocks or obstacles are near each other in the channel, the water diverted between the rocks forms a tongue. A tongue can also be described as a chute or "downstream V" (the V's point is downstream of its wings). Tongues often provide safe passage.

Paddling Through Rocks

Drifting into rocks: Swift water or lackadaisical paddling can push packrafts into exposed rocks. If your bow or stern hits the rock, you will likely bounce, spin, and continue drifting downriver. If the side tube hits the rock, you may broach, pin, and capsize.

When we drift into a hazard, our intuition is to lean away. But leaning away pushes the upstream tube into the water, which increases the drag force in a way that leads to capsizing. To stay upright, lean into the rock and brace against the pillow. Hugging the rock lifts the side tube that the current is trying to push underwater. Big rafts call this high-siding.

Paddling tongues: Tongues are conveyor belts with concentrated flow that provides deeper water and less likelihood of hitting rocks. The trick can be getting on and off the tongue. Fortunately, the water in the tongue is dense, "green," or "hard," and provides better purchase for paddle strokes compared to the aerated water at the tongue's edges. Grab the tongue with proper edging (lead with your head) and the paddle blade. Keep an active blade in the water while you are on the tongue.

1. Use the paddle blade to grab the current in the tongue—a draw stroke is very effective. Like catching eddies and peeling out, the blade's power

face should catch the tongue's current. Use paddle dexterity (bend your wrists) to keep the power face oriented to grab the current.

2. Keep an active blade in the water and let the current pull you down the length of the tongue. It is an incredible feeling to catch a tongue through complicated hydraulics, watching the gnarly stuff slide by while you are on a magic carpet ride.

3. If the tongue ends in a feature that you want to avoid, paddle hard, forward, to build momentum, and punch through the feature. Reach to grab the river on the other side of the feature.

TONGUES OFFER PATHS THROUGH OBSTACLES

STAY ON THE DARK, GREEN WATER

Boofing: A boof is a boat maneuver that carries you over a steep drop to land flat at the bottom. Boofing is as fun as it sounds. It's a move that requires planning and precision timing—practice in low-consequence settings first. Thigh straps are essential because they allow for lower body control of the packraft.

Water flowing over rocks can be perfect settings for boofing. The boof stroke will lift the bow and provide momentum to punch over and through holes and seams at the bottom—the burst of power can help you land clear of sticky features. But scout the hole below the rock to determine the consequences of missing your boof. A good boof stroke can drive you clear of trouble, but it would be a mistake to count on a boof; the hazard is still there waiting for you.

How to make a boof stroke:

1. Use five or six powerful forward strokes to gain as much speed as possible. **You need to be moving faster than the current.**
2. Lean forward aggressively and adjust your paddle cadence to catch the drop's lip with the blade's power face, all the way forward at your feet.
3. When you plant your paddle on the lip's face, leave it there for a microsecond so that the water pressure builds on the blade. Edge your boat toward the paddle stroke and fully commit to the stroke so that you can apply the most force against the lip. These details will allow you to pull harder on the stroke and produce greater power.
4. Lift your knees to keep the bow high while in the air. Use your abs—a crunch sit-up motion—to bring your body forward and raises the bow.
5. Continue the natural follow-through of the paddle stroke. You want to land flat and immediately ready for a forward stroke or low brace on the side opposite of the boof stroke.

Mark Oates boofing on Collingwood River, Tasmania, Australia. © Todd Blackhall

PRO TIP!

You don't need to have a perfect boof technique to take advantage of the boofing strategy. Whenever you are confronted with a sticky hazard, use your last few strokes to build as much momentum as possible and try to scoot or sneak your boat across.

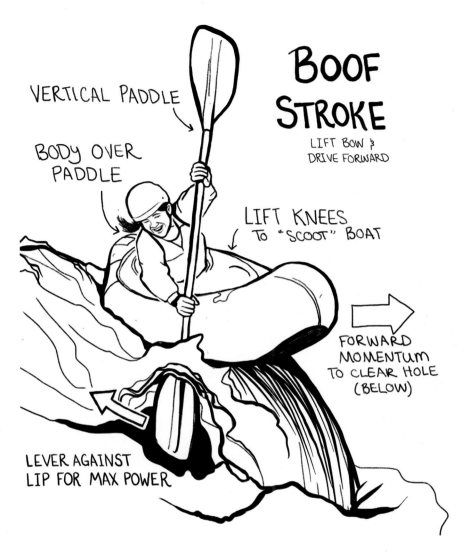

VERTICAL PADDLE

BODY OVER PADDLE

BOOF STROKE
LIFT BOW & DRIVE FORWARD

LIFT KNEES
TO "SCOOT" BOAT

FORWARD MOMENTUM TO CLEAR HOLE (BELOW)

LEVER AGAINST LIP FOR MAX POWER

HOLES

Holes are common features in Class III and more difficult rivers where water falls over an object, typically a large rock or ledge. Holes vary in stickiness and consequence. Studying holes from shore can help you identify which are okay to paddle and which you want to avoid. Using a shared vocabulary for holes will help you assess hole hazards. This section starts with terminology and is followed by paddling techniques.

Hole terminology:

- **Hole or hydraulic:** Any feature where water recirculates on itself.
- **Falls or drop:** The zone where water falls into the hole.
- **Backwash:** The zone where the current recirculates into the hole.
- **Seam:** The line separating the drop from the backwash.
- **Boil line:** The line separating the backwash (upstream flow) from the main current (downstream flow).
- **Kick:** The component of the recirculating water in the hole that flows to the sides.

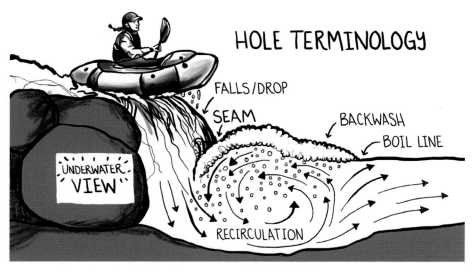

Stickiness: The width of the backwash indicates the hole's stickiness. An object in the backwash zone will get pulled back into the hole and recirculated. Holes with strong recirculation are described as **sticky** or **keepers**.

The size of the backwash zone is a function of the height, angle, and volume of the falls and the shape, width, and depth of the hole. Low-volume flow over a partially exposed rock can create a playful hole on the rock's backside. High-volume flow over a pour-over or waterfall can plunge deeply into the river and create a large backwash zone. Destination **play holes** are generally sticky; they keep the boat in the hole but are safe in that they eventually kick the boat out the side.

Recirculation: The scary aspect of holes is recirculation. The water falling into the river drags backwash water down with it. If there is sufficient drop or flow, the downwelling current creates enough drag to continuously feed the hole. An object downstream of the hole but still within the backwash will get dragged upstream into the hole.

Kick: Recirculating water almost always includes kick—a lateral component of flow. In other words, some of the recirculating water moves sideways within the hole. A hole's kick is the key to reading, running, and escaping the hole, as described in the friendliness section below. If the kick's direction is not obvious, toss a piece of wood into the hole and watch how it recirculates.

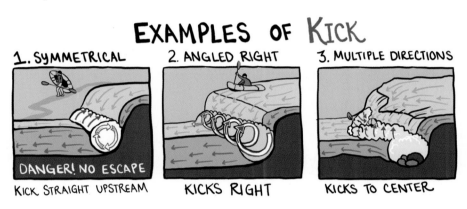

Friendliness: The kick direction determines if a hole is friendly or not. Friendly holes kick you out the sides. From the upriver perspective, the edges of a **smiling** hole are downstream relative to the hole's center. Both sides of a smiling hole kick to the sides, indicating that you would eventually get flushed out. **Frowning** holes kick you back toward the center of the hole, setting you up for recirculation. Frowning holes have edges upstream of the center and can be impossible to escape. I don't use the 'smiling' and 'frowning' descriptors because it can be hard to remember that they require a down-river perspective. The direction of the kick is the key.

Horizontal and diagonal holes: Horizontal or river-wide holes form due to water pouring over a ledge. Horizontal holes can have insufficient kick to flush a packraft or paddler out. This is especially true in the case of low-head dams. **Low-head dams** (weirs) are human-made horizontal holes with a uniform ledge. The smooth ledge produces wide zones of backwash *with no kick*. There have been several tragedies where multiple rescuers were pulled into the backwash zone of low-head dams. Low-head dams are serious trouble; stay away.

Natural ledges that are oriented diagonal to the riverbed (along a geologic layer, for example) create **diagonal holes**. Diagonal holes can have wide zones of backwash, but the downstream kick should eventually flush objects free.

Paddling Through Holes

It takes experience to read the stickiness of a hole. Try to determine the steepness of the drop and the width of the backwash zone when scouting.

The best way to avoid holes is to paddle around them. But if you find yourself approaching a hole, accidentally or intentionally, position your boat perpendicular to the seam and go into power mode. Use five or six forward strokes to gain maximum speed and generate the momentum needed to punch through the backwash into the main current. Grab the main current with a bow draw. Note that you may be better off trying to punch through a hole's narrower edge rather than its middle.

T-boning: Orienting your boat perpendicular to the hole is called T-boning. T-boning aligns the boat with the shortest path across the backwash and ensures that you hit the hole with your bow rather than exposing a less stable side tube. T-boning is a good strategy whenever you are confronted with a sticky river feature.

HOW TO PUNCH THROUGH A SMILEY HOLE

T-BONE

SEAM

KICKS TO EDGES

REACH FOR GREEN WATER

TOP VIEW

KICK

HOLE SMILES WHEN LOOKING DOWN RIVER

If you get stuck in the backwash of a hole, you have two options:

1. **Reach for the green water downriver of the backwash:** A draw stroke used to grab the water moving downriver can drag you out of the hole. Paddle strokes within the backwash are generally ineffective because the water is frothy, aerated, and provides no purchase.

2. **Work toward the hole's edge:** Hopefully the kick is directed toward the edge. But even if it isn't, lean downstream toward the edge (lead with your head). Keep the upstream tube lifted so that the current doesn't grab it, and brace into the pile of water on the downstream side of the hole. Remember to keep your elbows low while bracing!

If you capsize in a hole, ditch your equipment and prepare for a swim. Swimming into holes is covered in *Chapter 8: River Rescue From the Water.*

> ### *PRO TIP!*
> Distinguishing holes from waves can be difficult while in your boat (on the water). Accurately reading water comes from experience, so whoever in your group has seen the most water is probably in the best position to read it. I've followed more experienced leaders on rivers and been shocked at how much better they are in their ability to distinguish holes from waves.

WAVES AND BIG WATER

Waves are stacks of water common in Class III and more difficult water where the river flow piles up abruptly. Waves might be individual or stacked in trains. "Big water" rivers feature long stretches of wave trains.

Waves can be intimidating and enjoyable at the same time. The hardest part of paddling wave trains is often getting to or from the more predictable flow in the channel's center. **Helical** (**cork-screw**) currents along the banks can block access to the shore.

This section starts with terminology followed by paddling techniques.

Waves: Small waves can provide stable surfing playgrounds, whereas large waves can grow tall enough to break on themselves, just like ocean waves (**breaking waves**). Breaking waves can create a wall that packrafts can't punch through.

Big water: The whitewater community describes high-discharge rivers as big water. In big water, most of the water flows down the middle of the channel, creating a series of waves and holes. These features are intimidating, but the flow through the waves can be surprisingly laminar and orderly compared to the flow along the banks. The flow along the banks is strongly sheared, resulting in a turbulent, chaotic mess of **boils** or **upwellings**, **undercurrents**, and helical or cork-screw currents. Helical flow can look less intimidating than the main current because it has lower relief, but the chaotic flow can be very difficult to manage and may prevent swimmers from reaching the shore.

Big water conditions also introduce the hazards of floating debris and strainers. New debris transport is more likely while the river level is rising.

"HEY DIDDLE DIDDLE"

Before heading to Iceland to paddle sustained big water, Trip Kinney gave me a local lesson on big water. Trip is an accomplished kayaker, but what really draws me to him is his academic passion for unraveling risk and play—and his willingness to share his insights, many of which fill the pages of this book.

We scouted the river, and Trip asked me to describe my line. I identified a sneak on river-right that would keep me in lower-relief water and out of the big waves. Trip said, "Nope, right down the middle. The sides are a mess."

In the next eddy, Trip asked me for my line again. I identified another sneak. "Nope, right down the middle." In the third eddy, Trip looked at me expectantly. I sighed, resigned to what I knew I was supposed to do, even though it looked scary. Trip explained that the mantra is, "Hey diddle diddle, straight down the middle." While in Iceland, James Smith told me the Scottish version is "Dinnae fiddle, down the middle!"

Sarah Tingey paddling big water. Grand Canyon section of the Colorado River.

Paddling waves: Time your paddle strokes in each wave trough to build momentum, ride the crest, and prepare for the next trough. When approaching the wave's face, attack it: lead with your head and charge in. Grab the wave's face with a piercing brace, and *keep an active blade in the water* (grab the river) until you stabilize. Staying connected to the current in waves is critical to staying upright.

Paddling big water: Big water conditions are only appropriate for experienced paddlers. Determine whether the water level is rising or falling, and identify a high cutoff level. Keep the boats close together. All paddlers should be strong swimmers.

The hardest part of running big water can be peeling out into the main current. Paddling big water is all about getting in the main current and staying there. Trying to stay upright in the chaotic sides of the channel is asking for trouble. Once you are in the middle, manage the waves as outlined above. If you capsize, try to hold onto your boat while you wait for support. Review the swimming sections in *Chapter 8: River Rescue From the Water*.

SURFING

Standing (stationary) waves provide surfing playgrounds. Intentionally surfing waves and holes is a blast and helps you learn edge control. Because of recirculation in the backwash zone, holes are stickier than waves and are harder to surf. Anticipate swimming and ensure that there are no hazards downstream.

The most convenient play waves are accessible from eddies. Peel out of the eddy and ferry into the wave so that you enter the wave's trough without downstream velocity. Waves that aren't near eddies are harder to catch. Line up above the wave, spin the boat to face upstream, and use forward strokes to reduce your speed as much as possible as you drift into the trough.

Front surfing: The most basic surfing technique is to face directly upstream and maintain your position with rudder strokes. Rudder strokes are like setting up for a reverse sweep, but without much sweeping. The rudder stroke provides leverage to turn your boat from side to side. Rudder strokes don't need a lot of torso engagement; they are for positioning as opposed to power.

More advanced front surfing involves carving within the wave's bounds. Carving is difficult in packrafts because our boats lack distinct edges. But give it a shot anyway! Lead with your head to your destination and depress that edge. Lean back if the bow dives underwater. Lean forward and use forward strokes if you start to lose your position in the trough.

Side surfing: If a hole or wave is long and narrow, it will try to rotate your boat parallel to the feature. This orientation is called side surfing. You will need to keep the boat's upstream edge lifted to reduce the river's grip on it. If you let the upstream tube sink, the current will quickly drag the tube underwater and capsize the boat. Use braces on the downstream side of the wave to maintain your position and edge.

Back surfing: The most challenging surf orientation is facing downstream in a back surf. You will need an aggressive forward lean to keep the stern up out of the trough and back strokes to keep the boat from sliding out of the wave. The easiest way to get in a back surf position is to start with a front surf and spin 180 degrees. Sit flat when you spin; edging can push you out of the wave.

WHEN YOUR BEST SURF IS ACCIDENTAL

I joined Amy Christeson for a day on Willow Creek, Alaska, and was very jealous of her surfing skills. I asked her to share her favorite surfing story.

The consensus scouting Georgie Rapid on the Grand Canyon was predictable: avoid the big frothy hole in the middle. The packrafter in me agreed, but my inner kayaker whispered, "There's a chance this is a world-class surf wave!"

Our group debated whether the feature was a great surf or a packraft-eating hole and then chose a boat descent order: the first few boats would go left, I would paddle middle to check out the hole, and the rest of the group would watch our lines and choose for themselves.

I was barely swept into the main current before I realized that the hole significantly outsized my packraft and that I better start paddling hard.

But then that darn kayaker took over, and I paused to stare in awe at the glassy wave surrounding me. My packrafter regained control in time to get hit by the foam pile above the wave. "Well, here we are," I thought. "This would be a good time to remember how to surf."

Georgie Rapid was a delightful mix of surfing and being surfed. I tried to recall tips from kayaker friends at the playpark in Colorado. "Watch your edge! Stay calm! Stern pry! Keep an eye upstream!" I giggled through effortless flat spins, pretending I was actually in control.

The last few folks in our group, tired of waiting for me (and grateful to know that the left line was the better option), paddled left and waved hello.

Ready to continue downstream, I stopped paddling and expected to simply wash free from the wave. Not so. I panic-paddled to both left and right shoulders, looking for an exit, tensed up, and then caught an edge and flipped.

I floated blissfully, smiling as I enjoyed the moment and waiting for my friends to collect me and my gear. I may be a kayaker at heart, but I can swim like a packrafter.

WATERFALLS

A river feature with vertically falling water is a waterfall. A non-vertical drop is called a **slide**. This discussion pertains to both. Paddling waterfalls can be ridiculously fun, or lethal. Study the launch, landing, and consequences before considering running a waterfall.

Depending on the ledge and riverbed, waterfalls can form river-wide holes, benign deep-water pools, or chaotic boiling pools. Many waterfalls have severely undercut walls due to continual high-impact erosion. Turbulent flow and undercut walls are a dangerous combination.

Before considering running a waterfall, assess the consequence of a swim at the base. If you can imagine jumping into the pool for fun, it might be appropriate to try in a packraft. But review the aeration discussion below—aeration can hide rocks. If you are at all unsure, portage!

Aeration: The aeration at the bottom of a waterfall is the key to reading the landing hazard. Highly aerated water—white, foamy, fizzy—usually indicates a deep-water pool with a hole that doesn't reach the riverbed. Highly aerated pools provide soft landings, but the recirculation can be powerful, and the water is so bubbly that paddle strokes won't find much purchase. If you swim, the best hope is to find green water (not aerated) under the hole. Catch the green water, and you might get pulled out.

Low-aeration water—like boiling glass, few but large bubbles—indicates shallower water and recirculation that extends to the river bottom. The lack of aeration is in part due to green water hitting the river bottom and rebounding to the surface. The landing will be jarring, but the water should take a brace stroke. Swimming would likely involve bouncing along the bottom.

Nonuniform aeration mixed with big boils usually indicates an uneven bed surface containing boulders or other features. These pools are dangerous to swim in.

Launching: When scouting for waterfalls, horizontal holes, and low-head dams, look for a **horizon line,** a line beyond which the river can't be seen. The drop's height can be roughly determined by listening for crashing water and how much of the trees you can see: treetops versus trunks. Study the waterfall to determine if there is a clean line to the lip and time and space to make a boof stroke. You will need to launch off the lip with maximum speed and an aggressive boof stroke. Try to land flat or with the bow slightly elevated.

Landing: Study the landing to ensure that there are no hazards downstream and that your partners can set safety. Anticipate swimming.

Packrafts are too buoyant to nose dive, and the bow is too blunt. Even at maximum pressure, the packraft will fold in the middle rather than dip into the water. Lean forward on the front deck while you are airborne to help protect your spine from compression upon landing. The natural follow-through from the boof stroke should set you up to land ready to make a low brace.

Landing flat can be very jarring on your spine and neck—numerous kayakers have broken their backs on flat landings. Todd Tumolo had a stiff neck for weeks after our trip to Mexico (see inset below). The good news is that aeration makes for a softer landing. Todd and I concluded that a 30-foot (9 m) drop on highly aerated water was as jarring as a 20-foot (6 m) drop on less aerated water. Personally, I wouldn't push the vertical drop beyond those limits in a packraft.

RIO DE ORO

In January of 2013, Todd Tumolo and I went on a waterfall mission in Mexico. Todd was working as a Denali mountain guide and had the winter off. We met friends in Mexico City, bought the cheapest bikes we could, biked to Mexico's tallest mountain (Pico de Orizaba), and packrafted out to the coast. Then we rented a car to chase waterfalls.

When kayakers go off waterfalls, they nose-down and plunge their boat under the surface. That doesn't work in packrafts because we don't have rigid hulls. You can thank Todd Tumolo's face for figuring that out. He and I landed dozens of jarring faceplants in Mexico before concluding that we needed to land flat.

Our trip culminated with a 30-foot (9 m) drop on the Rio de Oro. We had trouble finding the trailhead, but there was no problem hearing the massive falls. I had serious reservations about running the waterfall when we scouted it. We studied the landing for a long time, and then Todd said he was up for it. I set up in the pool as a safety boat.

Todd launched off the lip and started rotating forward in the air. He landed on the bow and instantly capsized. Todd came up laughing, as is his nature; the frothy pool had absorbed the landing. Todd said that it wasn't as bad as it looked and that he would try again.

I don't have a great memory, but the horizon line on the 30-foot waterfall is seared in my mind. Approaching the falls' lip, I could only see the tops of trees—very tall trees! As I approached the ledge, it took forever for the river to come into view, making my stomach churn. I put all of my focus on the timing of my boof stroke . . . and then was airborne. I landed upright, barely, and my first thought was, "Thank God I don't have to do that again!" Todd followed, placed a nice boof stroke, and landed clean.

Todd Tumolo's first attempt on a 30-foot (9-m) waterfall. Rio de Oro, Mexico.

Graham Kraft. Cook Inlet, Alaska.

CHAPTER 7

OPEN-WATER CROSSINGS

Lakes and ponds provide playgrounds for packrafters who prefer tranquil days on the water, perhaps with a fishing pole, bike, or furry friend. Packraft artists have drawn beautiful lines weaving up and down the coast, paddling the ocean, and walking the forests. Open water provides expansive vistas, novel access, and a different pace of life.

The open-water environment introduces a suite of new and dynamic hazards. The key is to avoid complacency and always be ready for change. The good news is that learning about the open-water environment provides access to a huge portion of the planet.

It might sound counter-intuitive, but a great way to prepare for open-water crossings is to paddle turbulent rivers. Learning to paddle turbulent water forces you to acknowledge the inherent risks of being on the water and the importance of a reliable wet re-entry. Whitewater paddle techniques can help you prepare for surprises when wind and waves pick up during an open-water crossing.

This chapter relies heavily on the experience and Packrafting Oceans *guidelines by Bretwood "Hig" Higman and Erin McKittrick. Erin and Hig redefined what was possible with packrafts when they spent a year hiking, skiing, and packrafting 4,000 miles (6,400 km) from Seattle to the Aleutian Islands in 2007 to 2008. They have likely spent more time packrafting open–water environments than anyone.*

WHAT YOU NEED TO KNOW

The hazards of open-water crossings are easily underestimated. Ocean hazards can be sneaky: wind and waves can pick up in the middle of a crossing, hidden currents can impede your progress. I always feel exposed and vulnerable when far from shore during an open-water crossing. Even a small incident can turn into a big deal.

Preparation for open water should include:

- Risk evaluation with attention to rapidly changing environmental conditions, such as winds, waves, and currents.
- Special equipment considerations, especially a strategy to keep your boat if you capsize. You can't count on swimming to shore.
- Practicing **active navigation** with and without electronic devices.
- Devising a strategy for launching and landing in marine settings.

RISK ASSESSMENT

Risk assessment for open-water paddling includes the extra challenge of accounting for environmental hazards that can quickly change. These dynamic hazards make assessment more complicated—the right decision based on the present conditions (calm) can become the wrong decision after the conditions change (windy). We can plan open-water crossings in terms of the risk framework introduced in *Chapter 3: Risk*: hazard, exposure, and vulnerability:

- **Hazard:** Recognize the dynamic environmental hazards that can change during the crossing.

- **Exposure:** You are exposed to hazards whenever you are far from shore.

- **Vulnerability:** The most important strategies to limit the consequences of capsizing are to paddle with capable partners, keep the group compact, and use a leash or other method to ensure that you don't get separated from your boat.

Hazard

Unlike relatively predictable and obvious river hazards (holes, waves, rocks), open-water hazards can change with minimal warning. These dynamic hazards have caught packrafters off-guard, leading to close calls and fatalities. The challenge is recognizing the unseen hazards: temperature, wind, tides, and so on. A crossing might start with the equivalent of Class I difficulty, but wind-generated waves might make it Class II, and breaking through the surf to launch and land might feel like maneuvers familiar in Class III water. Open-water hazards are discussed in detail in their own section below.

Open-water hazards include:

- Cold temperatures
- Wind speed and orientation
- Waves (especially wind-generated waves while far from shore and breaking waves during launching and landing)
- Tidal currents
- Water and air temperature
- Ships

Exposure

You, your partners, and your equipment are exposed to open-water hazards during a crossing. The complicated part of choosing your exposure (when and where to cross) is evaluating the dynamic environmental hazards, especially wind and waves. Time is another factor, because being far from shore increases the duration of your exposure.

Vulnerability

Vulnerability is the likelihood that exposure to an open-water hazard will have harmful consequences. The difficulty of assessing open-water hazards is heightened by the vulnerability of being far from shore. The concerning thing about incidents during open-water crossings is that you can't expect to swim to

Aniakchak Bay, Alaska.

shore, which creates a real likelihood of hypothermia and drowning. All of the open-water packrafting fatalities involved separation from boats and the inability to reach the shore. As with river-running, we can reduce our vulnerability by building a safety net:

- **Partners:** Competent partners can help retrieve loose equipment and get you back into your boat. It is easy to underestimate how hard it is to keep the group together when conditions deteriorate. Keep the group compact and plan what to do if the group gets separated.

- **Equipment:** Wear appropriate safety equipment (life vest, drysuit in cold water, etc.) Follow the outfitting guidelines in *Chapter 1: Packrafting Equipment.*

- **Leash:** If a paddler gets separated from their boat during an open-water crossing, it can be impossible to recover the boat, especially in strong winds. Leashes are a good idea in open-water settings (but should not be used in rivers).

- **Objectives:** Choose less ambitious objectives in remote settings.

- **Time:** Add extra days to your itinerary to accommodate poor weather or paddling conditions.

- **Boat control:** Whitewater skills come in handy when open water gets turbulent. Review the bracing techniques in *Chapter 2: Boat Control and Wet Re-entry.*

- **Training:** Seek training, and practice regularly. Practice the wet re-entry techniques discussed in *Chapter 2: Boat Control and Wet Re-entry.* It is especially important to practice with your anticipated load, whether carrying cargo in the hull or strapped to the bow.

- **Navigation:** Practice active navigation techniques to monitor your progress and position during crossings (presented below). What you need to be attentive to during a large crossing is often miles away.

Risk Assessment Prompts

If this risk assessment discussion is intimidating, that is probably a good thing. Use the hazard, exposure, and vulnerability framework with your partners to prepare for your outings. These prompts can help you keep the big picture in mind. Pause and think when you have the chance, especially before launching.

Open-water risk assessment prompts:

- What is the weather forecast? Always be ready for change—especially in terms of increasing winds.
- What is the tide doing? Will tidal currents or changing depths impact paddling?
- Are conditions questionable? If so, get off or stay off the water.
- Can you complete the crossing without changing layers or checking maps (if conditions deteriorate)?
- Do the conditions allow you to keep a compact group during the crossing? What is the plan if the group gets separated?
- Are there any unusual considerations, like icebergs or large river outlets, that might complicate your crossing?
- Is the group adequately prepared for an incident? Trained, rested, fed, watered, etc.?

MANAGING OPEN-WATER HAZARDS

Environmental factors like winds and tides can change during your time on open water. You can anticipate these changes by monitoring the weather and your position and progress (see *Active Navigation*, below). Anticipate changing conditions, have a response plan, and practice recovery techniques.

Cold Water

Cold water rapidly transfers heat from the body, and any sustained time in cold water will lead to hypothermia. Dress for the swim and wear a drysuit. The body's reaction to cold water is presented in *Chapter 11: Medical Emergencies*.

Luc Mehl and Sarah Histand, Arctic Ocean, Alaska. © Will Koeppen

Wind and Breaking Waves

The wind is our greatest concern when paddling far from shore in a packraft. A good policy is to keep an updated plan for a retreat. Watch for indicators of increasing winds: storm clouds, whitecaps, or a dark line on the water. In an emergency, try to connect multiple boats to build a larger (and more stable) raft.

Waves generally aren't a problem for packrafters unless they are breaking. Waves break when they get too steep due to wind, traveling over shallow depths (shoals), or collision and interference (rips). Breaking waves can dump water into the boat or capsize it.

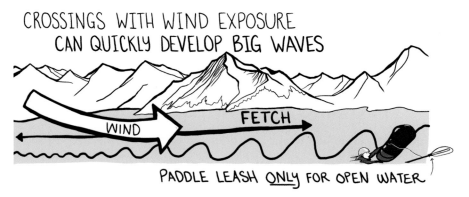

CROSSINGS WITH WIND EXPOSURE CAN QUICKLY DEVELOP BIG WAVES

WIND FETCH

PADDLE LEASH ONLY FOR OPEN WATER

Fetch: Fetch is the distance that wind travels over open water. Long fetch allows wind-driven waves to grow until they reach a state where breaking diminishes their size as quickly as the wind builds it up. Such waves are always near a breaking state. It is unusual to encounter a break large enough to capsize a packraft in open water in winds less than a gale (34-47 knots, 39-54 mph, 17-24 m/s).

If you are caught in waves, quickly reorient the packraft to run with or against the largest breaks. This strategy aligns the more stable bow and stern with the waves rather than the boat's less stable side ("T-boning"). Paddle in the troughs and then attack the faces, driving forward with your head and piercing the face with a paddle stroke. *Keep an active blade in the water!* You want to stay as connected to the water as possible, otherwise the wind and waves will flip you.

It is nearly impossible to make progress against such strong winds and waves. If you capsize, strong winds can make the task of re-entry much more difficult, creating an extremely hazardous situation. Use a leash to prevent the loss of your raft.

CASE STUDY: LAGO NAHUEL HUAPI

In January 2020, a British bikerafter capsized, was separated from his packraft, and lost his life during a 1.25-mile (2 km) lake crossing on Lago Nahuel Huapi, Argentina.

Looking at the map, it is easy to understand why the bikerafters chose this (shortest) crossing. The problem was that the lake's geography includes long arms and, therefore, long wind fetch. Winds blowing from the west had 20 miles (30 km) of fetch to build waves at the paddlers' crossing point.

After two days of ideal paddling conditions further north on the lake, the packrafters were caught off-guard as the wind and waves rapidly picked up during their crossing. Occasional whitecaps were seen, and news agencies reported three-foot (1-m) waves. After capsizing, the packraft was blown away from the swimmer and he was unable to retrieve it. The strong winds also meant that his paddling partner was unable to reach and rescue him.

The victim died of hypothermia, and his body was recovered 15 miles (24 km) from the point of capsize.

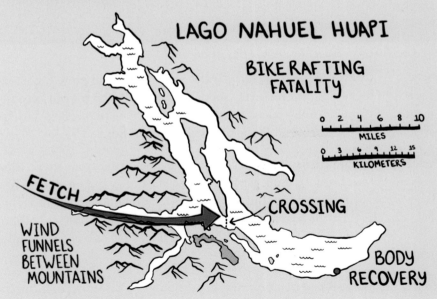

Equipment details:

- Bike strapped to bow
- Warm clothing but no dry suit
- The packraft was equipped with a tail but not a leash
- Inflatable life vest stayed secure and kept the victim's head out of the water

Brad Meiklejohn walking Aniakchak Bay at low tide. Alaska.

Shoals: As waves encounter shallow-water shoals, they will grow higher and steeper. On rocky shores, a relatively subtle 2-foot swell (0.6 m) can become a dangerous 8-foot churning mass of water (2.4 m). On sand or gravel beaches, waves form tall curls that can flip a raft or shove it to shore.

Shoaling waves are particularly hazardous when they're far from shore. Small waves might not break in these settings, so the shoal may not be evident until a large wave abruptly rises and breaks, potentially capsizing the packraft. These breaks can also carry the boat away from the paddler. Examine charts for offshore rocks to anticipate potential shoals. While paddling, keep an eye out for infrequent breaks that might mark shoals.

Rips: If waves travel into a current running the opposite direction, or if currents and shoals cause waves to bend and interfere with each other, they can form rips. Rips are strong localized currents that flow directly away from the shore. Rips commonly form where strong currents (such as a river) flow into open water with large swells. The two currents converge and interfere, building breaking waves even when the ocean seems relatively calm elsewhere. Strong currents can easily pull a packraft into a rip that you expected to paddle around.

Tidal Currents

Tides are caused by the rising and falling of the ocean due to gravitational attraction between the Earth, sun, and moon. Tidal currents, the lateral flow due to rising and falling water levels, can be a blessing or a curse, depending on your timing; do your research if you want blessings.

Global water level gauges and tide predictions are available in print, online, and via satellite communication devices. Tides follow a roughly sinusoidal curve between highs and lows that can be used to plan your outing. Determine the tidal range (the difference between high and low tides) and if the tide is diurnal (one high tide per day), semidiurnal (two high tides per day), or mixed semidiurnal (two high tides with different heights).

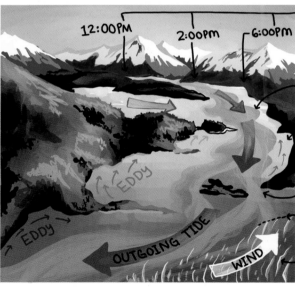

The relationship between tides and tidal currents is complex. Tide tables, which provide the specific times of high and low tides, might be more useful for ensuring you set up camp above the high tide line than indicating when the current will be at your back. To determine when to get on the water, you will want to use tidal current predictions, which aren't as available as tide predictions. If current predictions aren't available, you can use active navigation, as discussed below, to determine currents and timing.

Tidal currents span a spectrum between "progressive" and "standing" wave behavior. Tidal currents in the (deep) open ocean exhibit a progressive wave behavior, with the fastest currents corresponding with high and low tides. As the progressive wave approaches the coast, shallow water and complex geography (islands, bays, inlets, etc.) can drag and reflect the progressive wave to form a standing wave. In standing wave settings, slow currents—known as "slack" water—occur at high and low tides, while fast currents form at each tide's halfway point. The fast current is described as "flood" during rising tides and "ebb" during falling tides. This behavior is most common in the inland portions of large bays and harbors. If you want to paddle with the assistance of the current (you do!), time your outing to catch the rising or falling tide to match your objective.

Unfortunately, most locations display a complicated mix of standing and progressive wave behaviors, and you might be surprised to discover that the fastest currents occur several hours after your prediction. The reality is, unless you have access to tidal current predictions, you will need to collect your own data and validate your assumptions with active navigation.

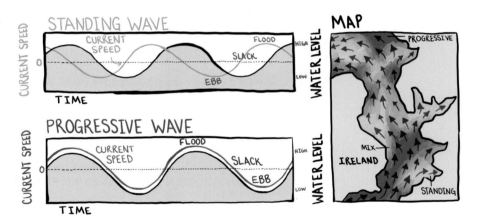

Additional challenges when predicting currents:

- **Eddies:** Eddies often form along the shore between promontories. The eddy current can travel opposite the main current, allowing you to gain ground against a strong current (if you can get around the promontories). Due to the large volumes of water involved, ocean eddy lines are unlikely to be sharp and distinct. Steeper or breaking waves, or a change in the water's color, can mark ocean eddy lines. Crossing an eddy line can change your speed substantially, and eddy lines often identify the edge of hidden channels.

- **Longshore currents:** Waves often approach the shore at a slight angle. The lateral component of the wave can create a longshore current— current parallel to the shore. Significant currents can run along open coasts, sometimes without reversing with the tide at all. These currents are most likely to be found in the surf zone and can be avoided by paddling to shore or deeper water.

- **Lunar cycle:** Currents are stronger when the difference between high and low tide is greatest, near the full and new moons.

- **Surface versus deep currents:** Where rivers bring in abundant fresh- water, or shallow water is influenced by wind, surface currents can differ from deeper currents. Currents are stronger in shallow water.

- **Long passes:** Long fjords or passes between islands can have currents that switch directions well after what you expect. Some passes have no slack current (periods without current). Currents are generally strongest at constrictions.

SPECIAL EQUIPMENT CONSIDERATIONS FOR OPEN-WATER CROSSINGS

Review the safety equipment in *Chapter 1: Packrafting Equipment*, especially life vests, outfitting, and drysuits. The additional considerations in this section pertain to managing equipment during an open-water swim and the added vulnerability of being far from the shore if something goes wrong. You can't afford to get separated from your boat while far from shore, so use a leash to ensure that you can reach and re-enter your boat. Consider a releasable cargo attachment system because it is easier to re-enter an empty packraft.

Quick-release rigging: All equipment should be securely stored so that it isn't lost if you capsize. If you aren't able to keep your cargo inside the hull (cargo zipper), attach your pack to the bow in a way that can be quickly released, but remains tethered to the boat. With a heavy load on the bow, it can be difficult to overturn a capsized boat for re-entry. With quick-release rigging, you can remove the pack, perform a wet re-entry, then recover the pack.

Leashes: The packraft should be rigged so that it can't get blown or carried away after capsizing. A simple leash or lanyard that connects you to the boat can serve this purpose. A more elaborate system involves running a leash from the boat, through a loop on a pack, to the paddle and wrist. *Using a leash violates river safety guidelines because the cord is a significant entanglement hazard in moving water.* Entanglement is still an issue on open-water crossings, but the risk of entanglement is judged to be less than the risk of losing a boat.

Tether: Rafts can easily blow away when unoccupied on the beach. This could be an inconvenience or life-threatening. Always keep your boat tied to an anchor. Don't rely on placing weight (e.g., backpacks or rocks) inside the packraft because strong wind gusts can still flip the boat.

Deck bag: Deck bags mount on the boat's bow or stern and provide easy access to daily essentials: food, water, repair kit, extra clothing, navigation and communication devices, etc. Be sure to use locking attachment hardware on the bag; *don't use non-locking carabiners.*

Packraft chambers: Although there haven't been any fatalities due to the single-chamber design of most packrafts, there have been several incidents on creeks with sharp rocks. The lack of a second chamber makes me nervous about significant time paddling far from the shore. If you have a cargo zipper, store your gear in inflated dry bags inside the tubes; the dry bags function as additional chambers. The long seat in some packrafts (a seat that extends to the knees) also acts as an extra chamber that can keep you afloat.

Valves: Valves should be in good condition and tightly sealed. Check that valve caps are secure after launching—the caps might have become unscrewed accidentally. Valve threads can wear over time, making them more likely to loosen when bumped. A partially deflated packraft is less stable than a fully inflated one.

Paddle: If your paddle has an adjustable feather, increase the feather angle to reduce air resistance. The feather angle becomes increasingly important at higher winds, especially if you need to paddle upwind to reach safety.

Communication: For external communication, review device options in *Chapter 1: Packrafting Equipment*. Consider including a VHF radio for direct contact with nearby vessels and marine weather forecasts.

Clothing: Err on the side of too much insulation since it is easier to cool down (by resting, splashing water on your face, etc.) than it is to warm up. You might not have the opportunity to change layers mid-crossing.

Repair kit: Review *Chapter 10: Equipment Repair and Modification*. In particular, vinyl underwater tape is useful because it can be applied mid-crossing.

Pee bottles: Pee bottles and funnels are handy for long crossings.

ACTIVE NAVIGATION

Active navigation involves monitoring your position and progress while paddling across open water. Active navigation can help you confirm that you are on course to your destination or that dynamic conditions merit changing plans. Techniques for active navigation can include using maps, GPS, smartphones, **dead reckoning** (the process of monitoring your position relative to a fixed marker), and tracking wind or wave orientation. Familiarize yourself with these methods before attempting long crossings.

Maps: Navigation can involve a combination of paper maps or charts. Maps are best for identifying topographic features, and charts are best for identifying coastline features. But either is sufficient for most crossings in decent weather.

Navigating in fair weather: Navigation in fair weather conditions can be straightforward, especially with a GPS or smartphone app. Things get tricky when conditions deteriorate and you can't afford to take your hands off the paddle.

A GPS or smartphone app with maps or charts provides the most precise navigation aid. These devices can display your location on a digital map, chart, or satellite imagery and provide information about your true speed and direction of travel, regardless of visibility. In easy travel conditions, you can pause your forward progress to check your position. However, electronics are susceptible to failure in marine environments, and waterproof cases, touch screens, glare, and batteries can be hard to manage. It would be a mistake to rely on electronics alone.

Navigating in foul weather: When conditions are bad, you might not be able to take your hands off the paddle, prohibiting you from checking a map or GPS. The preferred approach is to carefully review maps and imagery before launching or leaving protected water. Identify landmarks that correspond to important locations on the far end of the crossing. Then, during the crossing, rely almost entirely on dead reckoning. Dead reckoning allows you to estimate your position and speed on-the-fly. Several methods of dead reckoning are discussed below.

Relative Motion of Range Markers (Landmarks)

Dead reckoning involves tracking the relative motion of fixed landmarks to reveal the packraft's position, as well as the current strength and direction. Stationary landmarks can be used as **range markers**. Range markers can be anything distinct that you can keep an eye on, such as trees, rocks, and buildings. Select two range markers that fall on the line that connects you to your destination. Choosing two markers in front is easier for tracking progress, but you could use a target behind you if options are limited. The markers' relative position will indicate the current's direction and speed as you paddle toward your target.

Let's walk through this technique starting with the simplest case, no current, and then add current.

Without current: Choose range markers that form a line connecting your position to where you want to end. As you paddle toward your target, the markers stay lined up and you don't need to adjust your orientation to compensate for a crosscurrent.

With current: Paddle toward the destination, keeping the bow pointed directly at your target. After some progress, you will note that the range markers no longer line up. The current has pushed you off track, and you will have to gradually rotate your boat to keep the bow aimed at the target. Without the range markers, you might not have realized that you were re-orienting the boat during the crossing. The current forces you into a longer crossing, an arc, and you could drift past your objective if the current is strong enough.

HOW TO USE RANGE MARKERS

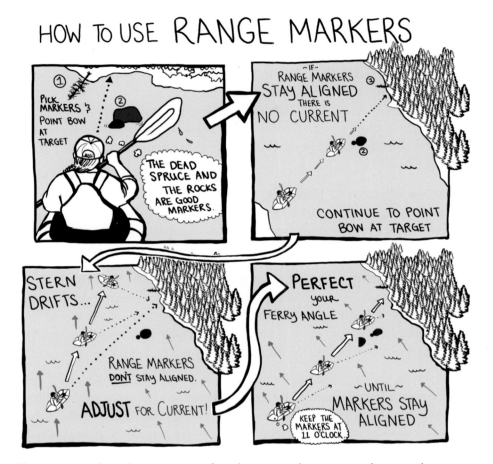

To accommodate the current and make a straight crossing, line up the range markers, and orient the boat at a ferry angle. Determining the right ferry angle will require trial and error. The idea is that your boat orientation, combined with the current's force, propels you directly toward your target.

With your boat oriented at the correct ferry angle, the bow does not point toward your target or range marker, but the range markers remain lined up as you paddle. If the current is pulling you to the left, your bow will point to the target's right. Once you have identified the ferry angle that keeps your range markers lined up, you might be able to use a different landmark, wind or wave direction, or clock position ("keep the markers at 11 o'clock") to keep the boat oriented correctly.

Relative Motion With Limited Markers

You can determine relative motion by sighting with your paddle when there are limited landmarks. Point your paddle toward your destination. Then without moving the paddle, quickly turn your head and sight along the back blade to note the position on the horizon. Make a mental note of the rear position based on distance from shore, location relative to the sun, or any other method that will allow comparison. Continue paddling toward your destination, then repeat the process. A change in the sight's rear position indicates that you are drifting off course.

Relative Motion of Vessels

To avoid a collision course with larger vessels, align the other boat with a range marker behind it, and watch to see if they stay aligned. If they stay aligned, you are on a collision course.

Using Paddling Speed to Determine Current Strength

If you know your typical paddling pace, you can use it to monitor progress and determine the strength of the current. Use a GPS or phone app to record your moving speed in a variety of conditions. A comfortable paddle cadence typically results in a moving speed of 2.5 to 3 miles per hour (4.2-4.8 km/h).

You can use your expected pace to estimate progress. For example, if your expected pace is three mph (4.8 km/h), a one-mile (1.6 km) crossing should take twenty minutes. If you are making more progress than expected, the current or wind is working with you. If you are making less progress, the current or wind is working against you.

You can even use your expected pace to estimate the current speed. Paddle directly into the current and use the range marker technique to monitor progress. If your position doesn't change, the current speed is equal to (and opposite) your expected pace.

Using Waves

In low visibility, waves can provide directional and other information.

Using waves to aid navigation:

- The orientation of waves in open water provides a reference frame to keep yourself oriented (e.g., keep the bow at the 1 o'clock position relative to the waves' orientation).

- Breaking waves offshore indicate shoals that should generally be avoided.
- The sound of waves crashing on a shore can help identify coastlines in low visibility conditions.

LAUNCHING AND LANDING

Sarah Heck landing in Hook Bay, Alaska.

When the water gets scary, you will want to go to shore. When getting to shore is difficult, it is usually due to the threat of breaking waves. Stay beyond the breaking waves while you monitor wave patterns, then pick a suitable landing site and time your approach to match a lull in the waves.

Harbors: Packraft-sized harbors are relatively abundant and provide good launch and land sites. Even a harbor that has a somewhat nasty break at its mouth can be advantageous. Get situated in the boat, wait for the right set of waves, and then shoot through the gap.

Rocky shores: Rocky shores where the waves are not breaking—usually a steep wall—can offer opportunities for launching or landing. In these settings, waves can surge up and down the wall without significant horizontal motion. Launching and landing on rock outcrops is probably prohibitively dangerous with swells more than a few feet high (half a meter). Be sure to pick a site that is not so steep that you can't scramble the rest of the height to a secure position.

Landing on rock outcrops:

1. Identify a site where the waves are not breaking and you can climb the rocks to safety.
2. Find an accessible perch near the wave's highest reach.
3. Bring the packraft in close, broadside to the rock, and as the boat rises toward the high point, reach out and put both hands on the rock.
4. Quickly transfer your weight to the rock.
5. Assuming the waves are not too large, you can stand up from the boat and climb onto the perch.
6. Secure your boat and paddle out of the water's reach.

Open beaches with breaking waves: Open beaches typically have shore breaks that cause continuous waves along their length. To paddle through shore breaks, wait beyond the breaking waves, and then time your paddling to correspond with a small set of waves.

Most waves come in sets due to the interaction of swells and local waves. The largest waves form when the crests of the two wave systems coincide. The timing of the large waves is generally consistent and results in a predictable pattern. For example, each large wave might be followed by four smaller waves.

Once you are inside the breaking zone, surf to shore on a wave that has already broken or is relatively small. If you get caught with a wave breaking directly under you, anticipate capsizing. As a last-ditch effort, you can drive your head and shoulders backward into the breaking wave. If you capsize, keep moving toward the shore in whatever way possible—in or out of your boat.

Todd Tumolo playing in breaking waves. Veracruz, Mexico.

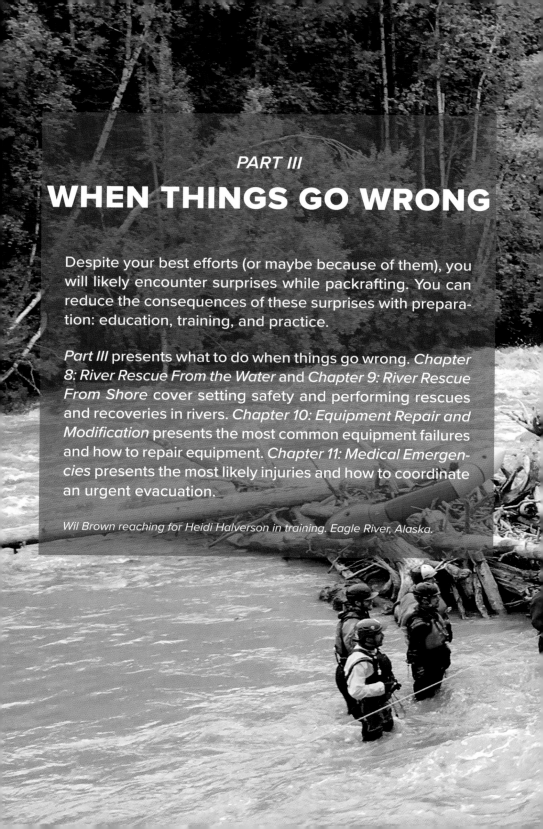

PART III

WHEN THINGS GO WRONG

Despite your best efforts (or maybe because of them), you will likely encounter surprises while packrafting. You can reduce the consequences of these surprises with preparation: education, training, and practice.

Part III presents what to do when things go wrong. *Chapter 8: River Rescue From the Water* and *Chapter 9: River Rescue From Shore* cover setting safety and performing rescues and recoveries in rivers. *Chapter 10: Equipment Repair and Modification* presents the most common equipment failures and how to repair equipment. *Chapter 11: Medical Emergencies* presents the most likely injuries and how to coordinate an urgent evacuation.

Wil Brown reaching for Heidi Halverson in training. Eagle River, Alaska.

Thor Tingey escaping carnage on the Grand Canyon section of the Colorado River.

CHAPTER 8

RIVER RESCUE FROM THE WATER

Setting safety and practicing river rescue techniques help to minimize the consequences when things go wrong in the water. Rivers are dynamic, and so are rescue systems, which fall along spectrums in terms of complexity, urgency, setting, and other variables.

Complexity: Rescue and recovery might be as simple as reaching an arm out to catch a swimmer or as complicated as setting up a zip-line to transfer equipment across the river. The top priority in any rescue effort is your safety. The next priorities are the other group members, the patient, and finally, the equipment. Different rescues expose rescuers to different levels of risk.

Urgency: A rescue may be urgent (e.g., extract a trapped swimmer) or non-urgent (e.g., transport an injured patient across the river). Urgent rescues require quick, and ideally premeditated, planning and implementation. Try very hard to make Plan A work, but anticipate adjusting to the evolving situation. In non-urgent rescues, if Plan A doesn't work, you have time to try Plan B, C, and so on.

Setting: Rescues will often involve people in the water and on the shore. I've split the rescue content into a somewhat arbitrary division of these settings to make the length of the rescue discussion less intimidating. This chapter presents basic principles, communication, and what you can do from the water. The next chapter covers what you can do from the shore.

WHAT YOU NEED TO KNOW

Your ability to help in an emergency will depend on how actively you practice rescue skills. Rescue techniques put rescuers and swimmers at risk and should be practiced as part of a swiftwater rescue course.

Helping from the water is often an immediate response that requires boat control and river-reading and -running skills.

River rescue from the water includes:

- **Communication**: You can't count on verbal communication during a rescue effort. Discuss whistle and signal conventions with your team (before you need to use them!).
- **Swimming**: Swimming rescues can be self-rescues or as a rescue-swimmer. Swimming can involve managing loose equipment.
- **Safety boat**: Capable partners in safety boats can help a swimmer and recover equipment.
- **Rolling**: Rolling your packraft allows you to recover from capsizing without exiting your boat.

PRINCIPLES OF RESCUE

Focus on rescue principles rather than specific steps, as there are many different ways to perform a successful rescue. Water is a dynamic medium, and rigid rules generally don't apply. Keep things simple and flexible.

It is important to prioritize yourself in a rescue effort. Your team, patient, and equipment are lower priorities. Use rescue strategies that limit the risk to rescuers, and recognize concerns when moving to higher-risk techniques.

PRO TIP!

Mistakes and incidents are valuable learning opportunities, so be sure to debrief after any incident.

Debriefing prompts:

- What went wrong?
- What went right?
- What should I/we do differently next time?
- What additional training or practice can I/we seek?

Priorities: People, Boats, and Equipment

The rescue objective is to get the swimmer out of the river. Ideally, one rescuer can take care of the swimmer while others recover equipment, but this will be determined by the group size and capability. It is ideal to keep track of your equipment, but don't recover equipment unless the swimmer's safety is already ensured. There are ways to compensate for lost equipment, even in a remote setting. It is much harder to care for an injured patient.

Ensure that the patients are truly secure before focusing on equipment. Tiredness, cold, and bravado can all contribute to a nearly safe swimmer falling back into the water. A secure patient is on shore and stable.

The swimmer's responsibility: As a swimmer, your concern is to keep yourself safe. Plan A is to hold onto your equipment and perform a wet re-entry, but, in a river setting, immediately abandon your equipment if it compromises your safety. If conditions are appropriate to swim with your equipment, such as a familiar section of water with no known hazards below, be prepared to choose between boat or paddle. Refer to the swimming sections below for a discussion of these options.

Note that in open water—lake, ocean, or wide river—that you should work to stay connected to your equipment since you might not be able to swim to shore.

The rescuers' responsibility: As a rescuer, your priority is to keep yourself from becoming another swimmer. Your second priority is to keep the rest of your party from becoming rescuees. Next is the swimmer, and finally, equipment recovery. Be prepared to extricate yourself and your team members from the rescue, keeping the rescue party safe. If part of your team has to leave a secure patient to recover equipment, make a plan to reconnect. Anticipate losing line-of-sight and communication.

It is common for a rescuer to have the ability to grab a paddle or bump a loose boat on the way to a swimmer. Take these opportunities if they don't endanger the rescuee.

The Rescue System and Risk Hierarchy

All rescue efforts put the rescuers at risk. The level of risk depends on the rescue strategy. While every situation varies and there are no hard rules, rescue systems can be broadly ranked by how risky they are for the rescuer.

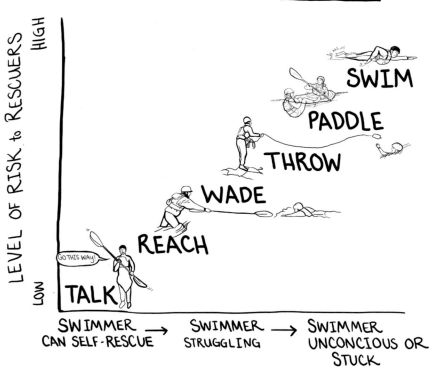

Talk: The least risky option is to direct the swimmer to safety by calling out commands, for example, "Swim left! Hard! Now!" In this scenario, the rescuer is not at risk.

Reach: Reach out, either with your arm or a paddle. Simply extending an arm or paddle to an exhausted swimmer can be enough to pull them to safety. If needed, the rescuer can easily step out of the rescue system, protecting themselves.

EXTENSION RESCUE
CAN HELP A SWIMMER GET TO SHORE

RESCUER

BACK-UP

PADDLE IMPROVES REACH

TIRED SWIMMER

Wade: Wade into the water. This is a higher risk rescue because you can slip, fall, and get caught in the current. Wading is most effective as part of a group, as outlined in the *Shallow Water Crossings* section in *Chapter 9: River Rescue From Shore*.

Throw: A rescuer can stay on shore and throw a rope to a swimmer. However, using ropes in a rescue puts everyone at risk—a loop of loose rope around a limb can trap swimmers or pull rescuers into the river. Refer to the *Throw Ropes* section in *Chapter 9: River Rescue From Shore*. The safety of standing on shore also means that you have limited mobility. Paddling to a swimmer might be the better or only option.

Paddle: Paddle to the swimmer. If you can't make contact with them, you might be able to give directions while floating alongside. Having a boat nearby is a major morale boost for a swimmer. However, many rescuers have lost their lives while trying to reach rescuees from a boat. It is critical to have a good understanding of your boat-handling skills. Assisting from a boat is discussed in the *Safety Boat* section below.

Swim: Our highest risk rescue is to intentionally swim after a swimmer. By entering the water, the rescuer knowingly exposes themselves to river hazards.

The rescuer might come out as a hero or might not come out at all. Rescue swimming techniques are discussed below.

Although our risk hierarchy culminates with a swimming rescue, higher risk rescues are common. These rescues involve rescue professionals and assets such as fire departments, boats, or helicopters. Rescue professionals have to constantly train in preparation for these high-risk rescues.

COMMUNICATION

Communication on the river is often limited to whistle, hand, and paddle signals. Complicated rescue scenarios can be greatly aided by effective communication. Ensure that signals are heard or seen, understood, and acknowledged.

Different paddling communities use different hand signals, so review your signal conventions before getting on the water. The critical signals are whistle conventions, the Universal River Signals, and the eddy out signal.

Whistle
You can hear a whistle blast from as far as a mile away (1.6 km). River whistles are very helpful for signaling.

Whistle signal conventions:

- **One short blast:** Attention. For example, after setting up safety for a rapid, it is common to use a single whistle blast to indicate readiness.
- **Three blasts:** Three short blasts repeated at intervals indicate an emergency or SOS.
- **Other:** Other whistle blast sequences can be pre-defined by your team.

Universal River Signals
Hand and paddle signals can convey much more information than whistle signals. Despite the optimistic label of "Universal River Signals," boating communities might use different signals. The universal signals are limited to: stop, help/emergency, all clear, and "I'm okay." It is important to adopt the universal signals. All other signals (eddy out, strainer, portage, etc.) can vary from group to group. Have a conversation with your paddling partners before starting your day, especially if you are paddling in a new region or country.

Interpret a lack of signals as "stop" or "wait."

UNIVERSAL RIVER SIGNALS

OTHER SIGNALS

OTHER OTHER SIGNALS

Point positive: The convention on rivers is always to point positive, which means indicate the right way to go instead of pointing at the obstacle or feature to avoid. This rule fits well with our "lead with your head" river-running principle—focus on your goals. Use your arm or a paddle to point positive.

There are times when we want to point at an animal or other "Wow, look at that!" features. In these cases, make sure to convey that there is no urgency. I use the two-fingers-to-eyes signal to indicate "look," and once I see that I'm understood, I'll point to the object of interest.

Emergency: In the case of emergency, give three long whistle blasts while waving a paddle, helmet, throw bag, or other equipment overhead.

All clear (go, yes, ready, good): Hold a single arm or paddle upright in the air. Point your arm or the paddle to one side of the river to indicate the preferred course through the rapid: right or left.

Stop (no, not clear, bad): Not making any signal is an assumed negative (no, stop, not ready). "Stop" signals include:

- Extend your arms to the sides, making a horizontal bar
- Hold the paddle horizontally overhead

I'm okay: Repeatedly tapping your head means I'm okay. This signal is used as both a question and an answer, "Are you okay?" "Yes, I'm okay."

Other River Signals

The following hand signals are not part of the Universal River Signal conventions. Keeping signals few and simple helps prevent confusion and miscommunication. However, as soon as something goes wrong or the situation gets complicated, you will need to communicate much more than the Universal signals.

I'm not okay (medical assistance needed): Crossing both arms at the chest to form an X indicates that you are not okay and need help. This signal is sometimes used to mean "no," but, as a community, we should use the stop signal for "no," and reserve the X for "I need help."

Eddy out: An index finger or paddle making circles in the air indicates that you want or need to catch an eddy. It is common to finish the eddy out signal by pointing to the side of the river on which you plan to eddy out.

The eddy out signal is a catch-all that means "let's regroup and check-in." The urgency of the signal conveys how quickly you need to react. A casual signal might mean, "I need a snack." An urgent signal might indicate that there is a strainer in the river.

Need to dump packraft: You could use the eddy-out signal when you need to dump water from the packraft, but we also use the motion of a cupped hand dumping water.

Strainer: There isn't a standard signal for strainer hazards, and the debate mostly revolves around the mental overload of trying to remember too many signals in a moment of urgency. The critical part is to point positive, in the direction of safety, not at the strainer.

Some paddlers will use a "stop" signal and/or an energetic "eddy-out." But there is also an argument for letting the "stop" signal *only* mean "stop." A popular option in North America is a modified "stop" signal: with the paddle held horizontally overhead, slide either hand back and forth along the paddle shaft, like tracing the length of a log. An advantage of this signal is that you don't need to let go of the paddle. Other signals you might see include indicating a tree with splayed fingers as branches pointing up or down from an upright forearm. Discuss hand signals with your team before getting on the water.

Scout or portage: The eddy out signal is a good default for regrouping and discussing scouting or portaging. If one party member is scouting the rapid, they might use a two-fingers-walking signal to indicate "portage" or two-fingers-at-eyes to signal "you should look."

Get creative: Sign language becomes important in rescues because it might be the only available form of communication. Quality communication can lead to a much faster recovery, but it takes planning to effectively signal to your partners. It can be very helpful to return hand signals as an indication that you understand the message. A palms-up shoulder shrug is often used to indicate that a signal wasn't understood.

Examples of other hand signals:

- **Group spacing:** Two hands in a clapping motion (or like playing an accordion) means to pay attention to group spacing. This is typically used to indicate "tighten up" because a rapid is coming.
- **Camp or set anchor:** Two hands overhead in a tent or A-frame shape.
- **Down the middle:** Not pointing to either side is interpreted as a signal to go down the middle. A more definitive signal is to make a karate chop motion (knifehand strike) starting at your forehead and chopping directly in line with your nose.
- **Go right or left:** Point an arm or paddle, or karate chop from the forehead to right or left.
- **Don't go:** A slicing motion at the neck, like decapitation.
- **Boof:** Slide or slap a flat hand over a fist, indicating the boat boofing off a rock.
- **Throw bag:** Mime the use of a throw bag.
- **Swimmer:** Mime an overhead crawl stroke, bending at the waist.
- **Entrapment:** Bend at the waist with arms falling forward as though they are caught in the current.

SWIMMING: SELF-RESCUE

Swimming rivers is just like boating them: grab the water that goes where you want to go and swim across the current when it doesn't. With the proper equipment, team, and a safety net, swimming rivers can be a lot of fun.

There are two modes of swimming: defensive and offensive. Practice offensive and defensive swimming in a controlled setting, ideally as part of a swiftwater safety course. Swimming to avoid hazards will likely involve alternating between modes: using defensive swimming to check for hazards and switching to offensive swimming to avoid them. In both cases, moving at a different speed from the current is critical to influencing where you end up.

Defensive Swimming

Defensive swimming is like playing goalie: you're always alert and watching the entire field of play. Lie on your back with your head upstream. This position is similar to sitting in an innertube or a reclining chair. It is important to keep your feet up on the surface of the water; otherwise, you risk catching a foot on the river bottom (see the *Entrapment* section in *Chapter 9: River Rescue From Shore*). Having your feet on the surface also allows you to push off any rocks that you might drift into.

If you are in a defensive position and watching for hazards, you will be moving at the same speed as the current and at the mercy of the river. This is fine when the current doesn't flow into any hazards—"power-off" to scan the river, catch your breath, and conserve energy.

To move across the current, sweep your arms in large back-paddling circles against the current. These strokes slow your progress downriver, giving you even more time to evaluate upcoming hazards. If you turn your body 45 degrees to the current, you can gradually back ferry with these strokes. Back ferrying is the

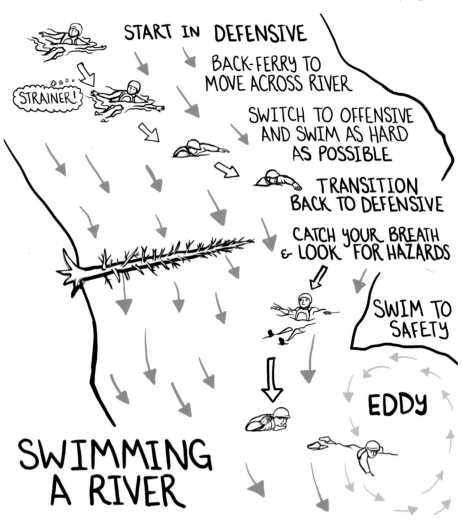

most sustainable swimming position available. You can back ferry all the way to shore if the river is clear of hazards below you.

If the downriver path is not free of hazards, you will need to switch to the offensive swimming position and quickly cut across the current.

"SO . . . NOW WHAT?"

In 2015, I led a corporate team-bonding activity at Portage Lake and River, Alaska. I borrowed packrafts and bikes to supply our group of 16 on a short multi-sport loop. Before we got in the water, I gave a safety talk and emphasized that people should remain calm and in the defensive swimming position if they capsized. During our float, one person capsized into the glacial river, then casually assumed the defensive position, floating patiently, feet up.

I paddled over to the swimmer, and he calmly asked, "So . . . what should I do now?" I looked back with an expression of shock and yelled, "Dude, you need to get out of the water! Start swimming to shore!" I had forgotten to mention that part of the plan. It was an important lesson for me. "Defensive" is not the same as "passive." After capsizing, you need to work to get out of the water.

Axiom Data Science. Portage Lake, Alaska. © Will Koeppen

Offensive Swimming

Offensive swimming is a powerful and aggressive maneuver that can be used to paddle across the current or gain downstream momentum. Offensive swimming while facing upstream is very difficult and quickly tires you out.

Offensive swimming should be performed with a sense of urgency, a quick sprint to get you out of the pathlines that would bring you into a hazard. Unless you are a strong swimmer, you can expect to have the endurance for about ten hard strokes. You will need to transition back to defensive swimming at the end of this exertion, to scan for hazards and catch your breath.

Offensive swimming generally utilizes the overhead crawl stroke. As you fatigue, you might need to revert to a doggy paddle, breaststroke, or sidestroke . . . just do whatever keeps you moving.

Most offensive swimming is directed across the current. However, as with paddling, there are times when you might want to charge downstream to gain momentum and punch through sticky features. Scenarios when you need downstream momentum are described below.

PRO TIP!

Use a barrel-roll motion to transition from defensive to offensive swimming modes so that you never risk placing a foot on the river bottom (an entrapment hazard). Keep your legs and torso at the surface of the water the entire time.

Catching Eddies

Catch eddies and other safe zones to "power-off," catch your breath, or wait for a safety boat. Catching eddies uses the same strategy as when paddling: swim hard to build momentum toward the top of the eddy, cross the eddy line at an angle, and use your hands to grab the still water in the eddy. Don't stop swimming until you are within the eddy—it is easy to underestimate the width of the eddy line and get dragged back into the main current.

Swimming Into Rocks

Approach large rocks in the defensive swimming position and use your feet to push off of them at the water level. Anticipate eddies behind rocks and consider swimming away and then into the eddy as discussed above.

Avoid sieves: Sieves are very hazardous for swimmers. During an unplanned swim, we all seek solid ground. Piles of rock can appear to be a refuge at first, then turn out to be an inescapable sieve. Any significant flow through sieves is very dangerous.

Swimming Through Holes

As with paddling, if you are swimming toward a sticky hole, you will likely want to transition to offensive mode to gain downstream speed and build momentum that can carry you through the backwash zone. Going into a hole without momentum, or even worse, back-ferrying in defensive mode, will make you more likely to get caught and recirculated.

Focus on catching your breath each time you come to the surface. Try to relax as much as possible because fighting against the current will tire you out.

Pull in your limbs: If you are about to swim into a hole, brace your body for impact and relax to conserve energy. Your limbs serve as shock absorbers, but only if they are bent. Tucking into a ball provides shock absorption and protects your core from impact.

Open your eyes: Bubbles indicate that you are in aerated water. Dark water indicates less aeration, which might mean that you are on the edges or below the hole. Dark water is probably moving downstream, and you should try to swim into it. When you are out of the aerated water, swim toward the surface (where the light is).

Embrace change: If you are caught in a recirculating hole, and what you are doing is not helping you escape, try something different. If you've been holding on to your paddle, let it go. If you have held your arms and legs out from your body, try tucking into a ball. Changing your surface area might cause you to get pushed deeper into the hole and allow you to swim out from the bottom.

Use the hole's kick: Try to determine the hole's kick and swim in that direction. Hopefully, the kick will help push you to the side, or enable you to grab green water at the edge of the hole, as you would with an anchoring draw stroke. Reach

EL SALTO

One of my worst swims was in Mexico on the same trip that Todd Tumolo and I trained to boof and, eventually, land waterfalls. We scouted a 15-foot (5-m) drop on El Salto ("The Waterfall") on the Rio Valles. I thought it looked doable, especially after gaining confidence on a 20-foot (7-m) drop earlier that day. However, the landing on this waterfall didn't look nearly as forgiving.

Todd posted as safety at the lip of the waterfall. I charged toward the lip of the fall with maximum speed and placed a boof stroke on the lip. After an exhilarating fraction of a second airborne, I landed in a boiling pool and was instantly pulled out of my boat. I felt an incredible force on my rescue vest and had time underwater to appreciate the snug fit. I had heard of people's vests getting pulled off but had never experienced those forces. I held on to my paddle, which felt like an accomplishment. I congratulated myself: "Good job, Luc!"

The recirculation of the pool brought me back to the surface, only to get dunked again. On my second resurfacing, Todd threw a rope, but I didn't know it. On the third resurfacing, I thought, "I'm stuck in a loop; something needs to change." I let go of my paddle, and on the next circulation, I was kicked out of the hole and able to swim to shore. The lesson has stuck with me: embrace change.

Todd portaged the waterfall.

for any green water you can find, even if it is plunging into the hole. Green water gives you more purchase than aerated water.

When ropes are involved: If there are partners on shore, you might expect a throw bag during one of your surfacings. Adding a rope to a swim introduces a new hazard for the swimmer, but it also might be your escape mechanism. If the swimmer in the hole can hold onto the rope, the belayer should not let go, even if the force is significant. The belayer's priority is to pop the swimmer from the hole and swing them to shore, even if it risks entanglement. If the swimmer lets go of the rope, the belayer needs to immediately pull the rope from the water to prevent it from wrapping around the swimmer.

Entanglement is much more likely if multiple ropes have been deployed. Having multiple ropes in the water is a common and serious mistake, usually due to poor communication between rescuers.

Swimming Through Waves and Big Water

You will likely want to stay in defensive mode while swimming through wave trains, monitoring the troughs and peaks of the wave and timing your breathing accordingly. Inhale in the troughs because you will be pushed through wave faces, not over the crests. Use the crests to scan the river for upcoming features.

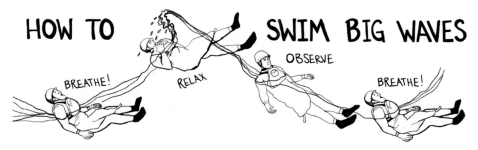

HOW TO SWIM BIG WAVES

BREATHE!   RELAX   OBSERVE   BREATHE!

Swimming big water can be very intimidating because you might be far from shore and have limited visibility. Helical currents against the banks can prevent escaping the main channel. Your best bet is to travel with competent partners that can serve as safety boats to assist you until an exit is identified. Review the roles of safety boats, discussed below.

Swimming Toward Strainers

If you ever catch yourself swimming toward a strainer with no way to avoid it, your only option is to swim offensively, hard, and directly at it. You must build enough speed to move faster than the current. You need this extra momentum to push up and over the strainer. Reach high for branches, get your chest up out of the water, do whatever it takes to get on top of the strainer instead of being pulled under it. This is a life or death scenario.

SCOTT'S THANK YOU NOTE

I received my Swiftwater Safety Institute teaching certification under the mentorship of the highly-regarded Scott Solle. Scott makes rescue equipment and is the go-to guy for calls to recover large boats from big rivers. He doesn't discuss the cost with clients; he just sends a bill.

Scott told me about a thank-you note from a former swiftwater rescue student. The student thanked Scott for the training because, "I did just what you told me, I swam right at the log pile and then pulled myself up onto the logs. Your class saved my life!"

To my surprise, Scott didn't take this as a compliment. He explained, "I feel like I let that guy down. He did just what I told him? He shouldn't have been anywhere near those logs."

If you have no option except to charge headfirst into a strainer, you've made some significant mistakes.

Reaching Shore

After a hard swim to shore, it is tempting to stand as soon as possible; this is still a foot entrapment hazard. The current is generally slower at the shore, and the sense of urgency to stand is typically emotional, not rational. Foot entrapment is most likely in this "first-contact" setting. The best policy is to swim toward shore until your body is dragging over the rocks before you stand up.

WHY PACKRAFTERS DON'T DRINK BOOTIE BEERS

Kayakers traditionally drink a "bootie beer" if they capsize and lose their boat. The swimmer pours a beer into their bootie (neoprene footwear) and drinks from it at the end of the day. In addition to motivating the kayaker to stay in their boat (kayak roll), the swim is considered disrespectful to the river gods.

The packrafting community did not adopt the bootie beer tradition. Alaskan kayaker Jeff Shelton explains why:

> *The river gods are already so pissed off at packrafters that they don't care if you drink a bootie beer. The damage has already been done.*

Jeff's response is largely based on watching inexperienced packrafters run difficult whitewater. We swim a lot, partly because of the poor secondary stability of our boats, partly because rolling a packraft is so challenging, but mostly because many packrafters seek the thrill of whitewater before learning proper boat control. Swimming is part of our game, and this terrifies kayakers because they are often the ones who keep helping us out of the water.

Kefir, a packrafting classic. Mackenzie Slater, New Zealand.

SWIMMING WITH A BOAT AND/OR PADDLE

There are several equipment-management options after capsizing:

- **Plan A:** Hold on to your equipment and attempt a wet re-entry.
- **Plan B:** Hold on to your equipment and try to kick and swim to shore.
- **Plan C:** Abandon your equipment and go to shore using the swimming techniques discussed earlier.
- **Plan D:** Hope that your partners can rescue you.

Plan A is always to hold on to your boat and paddle. But you must be willing to release your equipment if doing so increases your chances of survival. This is especially true in cold water, continuous gradients, and above river hazards. If you don't know what is coming, let go of the boat so that you can swim to shore. Hopefully, your competent partners will help recover your equipment after they've made sure that you are out of the water and secure.

Hold the boat by reaching over the side tube: The best way to hold a packraft is by reaching over the side tubes into the cockpit. In this geometry, the boat serves as a flotation aid and can help keep you out of holes. If you can't hold on by the tube, use the perimeter line, thigh straps, or tail. Refer to the discussion of outfitting and entrapment hazards for all of these options in *Chapter 1: Packrafting Equipment*.

Move the packraft into a downstream position: When the packraft is downstream of your body, it provides a cushion between rocks or wood. Note that in this position, your downstream view is obstructed. This is another reason why it is critical to let go of your boat and swim to shore when there are unknowns downstream.

Hold the paddle: Hold the paddle, preferably braced across the top of your packraft, but alternatively in the water with you. You might be able to kick your way to shore or use one arm to hold both the boat and the paddle, side-crawling with the free arm.

If you are only holding the paddle, you can use it as a propellant or signal. If you can swim, lie on your stomach and make forward strokes with the paddle. Practicing these techniques in calm water will help provide muscle memory for a real swim. If you are unable to swim to shore (e.g., you have an injured shoulder), hold the paddle upright in the air so that your partners can track your position.

Throw the paddle to shore: Holding on to the paddle limits your swimming ability. If there is any doubt about your safety, throw the paddle to shore. Paddles will commonly snag on rocks and trees, or get stuck in eddies. It can even work to throw your paddle downriver to where you are going to swim. Intentionally throwing your paddle is almost always a good decision.

Let go of the packraft: Let go or actively push the packraft away. In general, boats are easier to recover than paddles because they get caught in holes, snag on trees or gravel bars, etc. Due to their bulk and color, packrafts can be spotted from far away.

MY FINEST SWIM

One of the reasons I love teaching swiftwater safety courses is that they force me to practice swimming. I took my finest swim right after a course, and was grateful for the timing.

On the drive to Canyon Creek, I was surprised to discover that my partner, Shasta Hood, had never paddled the section. Shasta is an ideal partner—cheerful, competent, and alert, but he'd need me to recognize the trail that portages a Class VI waterfall. Under my lead, we floated right by the trail and had to climb an exhaustingly steep hillside around the waterfall.

Back in the water, Shasta let me pick the line. Partway through a narrow and continuous section of Class IV rapids, I dropped into a hole with insufficient momentum, capsized, and prepared for a tough swim.

I saw a small eddy to my left and pushed the boat toward it, hoping it would stick. Getting rid of the boat freed me up to focus on my swim. I started in a defensive position and kept my paddle, with no space to move laterally. After swimming over three stacked drops, I threw the paddle to shore and swam into an eddy. From the eddy, I was able to walk upstream and easily recover the boat and paddle.

I'm sure I wouldn't have been as confident or capable if I hadn't just practiced swimming in the swiftwater course.

RESCUE SWIMMING

Rescue swimming involves intentionally swimming to make contact with a potentially unconscious swimmer. Rescue swimming is the highest-risk scenario for the rescuer that we will discuss. This is the last resort.

Key factors in rescue swimming include:

- Use the swiftwater entry technique to aggressively enter the water.
- Anticipate a panicked swimmer and prioritize your security.
- Make contact with the swimmer, rotate them so that they are face up, and either swim or swing them to shore on a throw rope.

Swiftwater entry: When intentionally entering moving water, an aggressive swiftwater entry provides momentum to more quickly reach your target. This technique can be useful when committing to a river crossing or acting as a rescue swimmer.

How to perform a swiftwater entry:

1. Wade into the water to your knees, or perch on a rock.
2. Launch your body horizontally *onto* the water, like Superman or a belly flop. Do not dive into the water; you want to stay at the surface of the water so that you don't hit rocks.
3. Protect your head by crossing your arms in front of your face as you land.
4. Once you hit the water, use an aggressive forward stroke to enter the faster current.

Unconscious or injured swimmer: If an unconscious or injured swimmer is in the river, a rescue swimmer might be able to make contact and bring them to shore.

1. Enter the water with the swiftwater entry technique.
2. Swim to the rescuee, make contact, and pull them to you, face up.
3. Get in a defensive swimming position. Slide an arm under the lapels on the back of the swimmer's life vest, and prepare to swim with a side crawl or catch a throw rope with your free hand.
4. If a throw rope is available, hold it against the shoulder away from the belayer.
5. Interlock your legs around one of the swimmer's legs to keep them from sliding through your grasp. This body wrap is critical if their life vest has been ripped off.

It is also possible to swim to the swimmer while on belay if wearing a rescue vest. Belayed swimming typically requires more than one rope length (tie ropes together) and people on shore to feed rope—rope drag in the water can prevent the swimmer from making progress. This is an advanced technique and should be practiced in a rescue course.

Panicked swimmer: A conscious-but-panicked swimmer might cling to you in a way that jeopardizes your safety. This is a frustrating complication, so be sure to assess the state of the swimmer before making contact.

If the swimmer is in a state of panic, try to calm them by providing information, reassurance, and clear and simple instruction. If the swimmer remains a threat to your security, you might need to stun them by slapping their helmet, body, or even splashing water in their face. Try to approach a panicked swimmer from behind so that you can hold on by their life vest lapels and place your knees or legs against their back to provide a buffer from flailing limbs. Be prepared to push the swimmer away.

EQUIPMENT FAILURE

Even if you have made all the right safety decisions, your equipment might break or get lost. We are most concerned with sudden deflation of the boat or a broken or lost paddle. Anticipate failure and have a mitigation plan.

Responding to Sudden Deflation

Packrafts are impressively puncture-resistant and, even when they do leak, it is typically a slow leak, not a catastrophic one. However, a large slice can cause fast and scary deflation. I know of several sudden deflations due to slices on rocks.

During deflation, water pressure causes the hull tubes to compress around your legs. If you are wearing thigh straps, the boat can become a "death shroud" (as described by Timmy Johnson). It is critical to kick your legs free of the packraft as soon as possible. Once free from the boat, your priority is to swim to shore. You can try to swim the boat to shore in calm water, but this is challenging. Hopefully, your competent partners will take care of the equipment for you.

Some packrafts feature independent chambers to prevent complete deflation. If your packraft uses a single chamber, you can build in some redundancy with other equipment.

Additional buoyancy for single-chamber packrafts:

- Storing cargo in sealed dry bags in the hull (packrafts with cargo zippers)
- Using a high-volume seat that extends to the knees

These quasi-chambers don't prevent the hull from rapidly deflating, but the additional buoyancy can provide more time and space to kick free from the boat.

Broken or Lost Paddle

Many packrafters have devised temporary paddle blades or repairs that have allowed them to finish their trip. Refer to *Chapter 10: Equipment Repair and Modification* for paddle repairs. For short crossings, you can hand paddle, similar to what surfers do.

SAFETY BOAT

A safety boat can assist a swimmer in the water. Safety boats are one of the most effective ways to reduce the consequences of a swim. Sometimes the safety boat is a designated role; the rest of the time, it should be the default behavior. To function as a safety boat, you must have a proper understanding of the river, boat control, and river-running skills, and be capable of self-rescue. You must also be willing to abandon the swimmer to ensure your own well-being.

A safety boat has many roles, including coaching, assisting, providing a resting platform, towing, and managing equipment.

Coaching a Swimmer

Coaching a swimmer is a mix of moral support ("You've got this!") and helping the swimmer maintain situational awareness ("Here comes the next rapid"). Be intentional with your tone. You can be forceful without inspiring panic. As a coach, you should advise the swimmer whether to abandon their equipment so they can swim to shore, or keep their equipment and try a wet re-entry. Communicate how urgently they should attempt a re-entry. Keep directions simple and don't overwhelm the swimmer with information.

Partner-assisted Wet Re-entry

If it is appropriate for a swimmer to attempt a wet re-entry, help flip their packraft upright, connect them to it, and move into a side-by-side position to stabilize the packraft while they climb in. You might be able to reach across the deck and help pull them in by their life vest lapel. A tired swimmer will need more help than a fresh swimmer.

If the water is too rowdy to float alongside the empty boat, you might have enough time to extend your paddle and hold down their far tube while they try a re-entry. Keep your eyes downriver and provide directions to the swimmer. Be prepared to peel off and take care of yourself while getting through the remaining rapids.

Resting Platform

The safety boat can serve as a resting platform for a tired swimmer. In addition to the physical benefits of resting and catching your breath, moral support has real value.

The safety boat needs to first manage their own well-being, which might necessitate convincing the swimmer to let go. Evaluate the swimmer's mindset before allowing them to latch on—a panicked swimmer can be a significant threat to the safety boat.

Towing a Swimmer

If a wet re-entry is not possible, and there are no concerns for the rescuer, the safety boat can tow the swimmer. You might tow the swimmer to shore or pull them to a better place to swim (pathlines that go where the swimmer wants to go).

Given how difficult it is to tow a swimmer, any continuous rapids or big water will likely require alternating efforts of towing and swimming. Your strategy is to paddle unhindered (not towing) so that you can navigate the rapids and then rejoin the swimmer to tow them through the calmer sections. In this application, the safety boat serves as both a resting platform and a towboat. Communication is key. Let the swimmer know when they need to let go. Maintain this approach until you identify an appropriate exit, and then either tow them to safety or instruct them to swim to shore.

Towing by the bow: A swimmer can grab onto the rescue boat's bow in a koala bear position. This position is fairly stable for both parties but makes maneuvering the boat a challenge. The koala position also exposes the swimmer's back to rocks.

Towing by the stern: Make contact and direct the swimmer to hold on to the stern by the perimeter line or tail. Towing a swimmer at the stern allows you a clear view to read downstream. The swimmer might drag over rocks, but should otherwise be comfortable. It helps for the swimmer to keep their elbows bent, because bent arms function as shock absorbers. The swimmer can help propel the boat by kicking, but they will likely need to be reminded to do so. Towing is very slow; be sure to practice this before needing to use it on the river.

Managing Equipment

When the swimmer is securely on shore or sufficiently cared for by other safety boats, you can switch your focus to loose equipment. The first priority should be the paddle since paddles are harder to spot and recover. Communicate with other people to determine if the paddle is accounted for, or when it was last seen. At the same time, monitor the loose packraft and make a plan to get it to shore.

PRO TIP!

Packrafts often get stuck recirculating in sticky holes. My first approach to retrieve the boat is to snag it with a throw bag. Pour the rope out of the throw bag, fill the bag with rocks, and try to catch the boat with the bag. If the packraft is upright, aim to land the bag in the cockpit. If the packraft is upside down, throw the bag over the boat. In both cases, use gentle tension to ease the boat free. This process might take dozens of attempts, but it only has to work once.

Managing a loose paddle:

- Toss the paddle to another boater or to shore, where it can get caught in shallow water or an eddy.
- Grab both paddles, nest them like spoons, and paddle with both. This can be challenging, especially for paddlers with small or cold hands.

PADDLING WITH TWO PADDLES

There are several ways to manage a loose packraft:

- **Bow bumping**: The easiest way to manage a loose packraft is to bump it with your bow. If the packraft is full of water, you will want to dump the water and then bump it.
- **Sandwich**: If there are two safety boats available, place the loose boat between you and drive it to shore.
- **Tether**: Type V rescue vests have a releasable "cow-tail" tow strap that can clip onto a perimeter line to tow a boat. Attaching a rescue vest to a loose boat puts the rescuer at greater risk because an empty packraft might be too light for the quick-release to function as intended.

BOW-BUMPING AN EMPTY BOAT TO SHORE

SELF-RESCUE: ROLLING A PACKRAFT

Rolling allows you to recover from capsizing without going for a swim. Rolling a packraft is difficult and should be a very low priority compared to practicing wet re-entries and boat control. Perfect your wet re-entry technique first. Note that rolling is not possible in all packraft models.

Some packrafts are easier to roll than others. The key factors are boat width and tube-diameter. A good way to judge the roll-ability of a packraft is to determine how easily it capsizes. A boat that is easy to capsize will be easier to roll back up. Performance whitewater packrafts are generally easier to roll because they are long, skinny, and feature lower-diameter side tubes.

Ensure that the seat and backband place you in the proper paddling position and pull your thigh straps as tight as possible. Thigh straps are a critical piece of equipment for a packraft roll—you need a very strong coupling between your legs and the hull. Remember that thigh straps can be an entrapment hazard. Practice capsizing and getting out of the thigh straps; you will need to do a lot of swimming to learn to roll.

Storing cargo in the hull (via a cargo zipper) does not significantly influence the rollability of a packraft. This is counter-intuitive, but since the weight is stored close to the rotation axis, it does not require significant additional torque to rotate. I've experimented with storing weight all on one side, the other side, toward the bow or stern, and can't feel any significant difference in rollability—it is always difficult!

ROMAN'S CHIEF SWIM

On the world-famous Green River in North Carolina, Timmy Johnson and I watched as Roman Dial capsized in Zwick's Backender. Zwick's is a challenging two-stage drop with a boof, strong recirculating hole, slide, and final must-make-move off an 8-foot (2.4-m) vertical drop. No big deal, right? Roman and I were pushing our limits and had been trading swims all week. We had also been successfully rolling. But Timmy and I were anxiously watching the underside of Roman's boat because the next rapid, Chief (Class IV+), is only 30 feet (9 m) below Zwick's.

Roman tried his roll once, pulled his head out of the water too early, and tipped back upside down. His second attempt was similar. Timmy and I were whispering similar mantras, along the line of, "Come on Roman, get out of the boat and swim!" Roman's head was underwater; we couldn't tell him to swim.

Roman pushed free from his boat just in time to get sucked into Chief. Chief is a pour-over, with a notorious pin rock hiding in the backwash right in the center of the drop. There is a hole to the right and an undercut cave to the left. Chief is one of the most dangerous rapids on the Green because of the pin rock that has caused at least one fatality and many close calls.

Roman knew the pin rock was there; we had run the rapid the previous day. He intentionally swam into the drop headfirst, aggressively, wanting to be in a position to push off the rock with his arms and chest. This was very well done. Roman would have likely gotten pinned if he had gone over the drop in a defensive swim position. Timmy and I sighed a huge breath of relief when Roman pushed clear of the rock. We used our next breaths to request that he abandon his roll attempts sooner the next time.

The Packraft Roll

Rolling as a capsize recovery maneuver originated with the Aleut and Inuit, who hunted by sea kayak. The packraft roll is a C-to-C kayak roll with an additional back deck maneuver. (Note that the term *Eskimo* is ill-favored to some Indigenous peoples and countries, and that "packraft roll" or "capsize maneuver" are preferred to "Eskimo roll.") Some packrafters can perform other rolls, but in my experience, this is the easiest technique to learn.

Start in a pool with partners, and take your practice to slow-moving water before attempting to roll in swiftwater. If you have access to a river kayak, begin there. If you can roll a kayak, the biggest differences in a packraft are that you need more torque from the paddle stroke and have to firmly press your torso and head to the back deck when finishing the roll.

Anticipate spending time underwater: wear warm clothing, earplugs, a nose clip, and goggles. I appreciate being able to open my eyes and watch the paddle in the water. Start with a sea kayak paddle if you can; rolling with a long paddle is easier.

The strategy of the packraft roll is the same as bracing: use the paddle as a lever arm, reach as far as possible perpendicular to the boat and catch the surface of the water with the power face. The lever arm provides the torque that allows you to snap your hips. The hip snap restores your boat upright and then pulls your torso, then your head, out of the water.

The packraft roll involves four steps:

1. Set-up
2. Swing the lever arm into position (the first C in C-to-C)
3. Snap your hips to initiate the roll (the second C in C-to-C)
4. Shift your mass to the back deck

DIG DEEPER

The physics of a packraft roll involves using a lever arm to rotate the boat to an upright position. As with bracing, the lever arm provides torque. In a roll, that torque is used to support a hip snap to flip the boat. The amount of torque that can be generated depends on the length of the lever arm (paddle), the lever arm's angle relative to the rotation axis, and the force at the end of the arm (the size of the blade).

To maximize torque, you will want to extend the paddle as far as possible and even choke back on the shaft to give you more reach. Rolling with a long paddle is easier than rolling with a short paddle.

The optimal angle for the lever arm is 90 degrees from the axis of rotation. For our application, that means extending the paddle perpendicular to the boat, in line with the hips.

It is easier to spin an object when the mass is near the rotation axis. The classic example of this angular momentum relationship is a figure skater who spins faster after bringing their arms close to their body, closer to their rotation axis. The same principle applies to the packraft roll: leaning back on the stern keeps your mass closer to the rotation axis as you come up out of the water, allowing you to rotate more easily. This concept is often translated as "keep your head in the water" during roll practice.

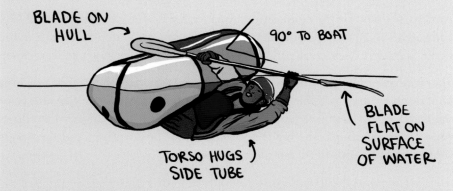

BLADE ON HULL

90° TO BOAT

BLADE FLAT ON SURFACE OF WATER

TORSO HUGS SIDE TUBE

Preparation: The Hip Snap

Before trying to roll, build muscle memory for the hip snap. Start by holding on to the edge of the pool or a dock at a lake.

1. While holding the pool edge, use your hips and knees to flip the boat upside down and right-side up. Hip control is critical but not intuitive; spend time building muscle memory for this rotation.
2. You will quickly notice that overturning the boat is easiest when you lay back on the stern, which is the position that places your mass as close to the rotation axis as possible. Use this to your advantage and find the geometry that makes rotation the easiest.
3. Once you can flip your boat back-and-forth with both hands, try it one-handed. Can you do it with only four fingers? Two?

The Set-up

While you are underwater you will want to press your torso against the front deck to protect your head and torso from impact. The roll set-up describes transitioning out of this defensive position.

1. Hug your torso over the front deck while underwater. Keep your body as close to the hull and waterline as possible.
2. Keeping your upper body against the deck, try to shift as much mass to the side tube as possible. Reach up and push the paddle into the air with both hands.
3. Hold the paddle horizontally at the surface of the water, parallel to the boat. Both hands should nearly be in contact with the hull.
4. (Optional) Moving your grip away from the front blade ("choking back") will give you a longer lever arm to generate more torque.
5. Use paddle dexterity (bend your wrists) so that the front blade's power face is in position to keep the blade from diving when the paddle sweeps across the water. An incorrect position would cause the blade to dive into the water. Goggles help to evaluate this positioning.

SET UP

PUSH BLADE OUT
OF WATER

SWING
PADDLE 90°

HIP SNAP!

SHIFT MASS
TO BACK DECK

PREPARE FOR
MORE RAPIDS!

Swing the Lever Arm Into Position

Kayakers can *sweep* the blade into the lever arm position along the water's surface because the bottom of the kayak sits low in the water. Packrafts stand tall out of the water, and since the rear blade has to stay above the boat, the forward blade is forced underwater. I have better luck *swinging* the paddle into position in the air before slapping it down to the water.

1. Push the blade up out of the water with both hands while you rotate your torso.
2. Extend the leading blade into the lever arm position, as close to 90 degrees from the boat as possible. Your back fist should stay in contact with the hull during the paddle swing. This hand position keeps your back elbow close to your ribs, which protects your shoulder from injury. Try to keep the elbow of your reaching arm slightly bent to protect the extended shoulder. There is no way around it; the shoulder of the extended arm is at risk.
3. Let the forward blade slap down onto the water. Ensure that the blade's power face is flat on the surface of the water. Any angle to the blade will cause it to dive into the water when you initiate the hip snap.

Snap Your Hips to Initiate the Roll

This is the most awkward stage of the roll. You want to leave the paddle at the surface of the water as you snap against it, using your hips to rotate the boat back to an upright position.

1. Snap your hips to *catch* the paddle, rather than *pulling* the paddle down through the water. The motion should come from your lower body while your upper body remains stationary. The paddle will dive regardless, and when it does, you will lose the ability to generate torque.
2. Drive the hip and knee near the reaching blade toward the surface while simultaneously pulling the far hip and knee down into the water.
3. Watch the forward blade as it pulls into the water. This focus helps decouple your hips from your torso, allowing the hip snap to overturn the boat.

Shift Your Mass to the Back Deck

The final stage of the packraft roll involves leaning onto the back deck. This is the biggest difference between a C-to-C kayak roll and the packraft roll.

258 THE PACKRAFT HANDBOOK

1. As your hips overturn the boat, keep hugging the hull, moving from the side tube to the stern. Unintuitively, you need to keep your head and torso in the water as long as possible. This technique keeps your mass near the rotation axis.
2. Lie on the back deck and keep your head in the water until the boat pulls it out for you.
3. Lean forward and set up for a low brace in anticipation of more rapids.

It takes practice to convince your body to lead with the hips and keep your head underwater as long as possible. Leading with the head is the number one problem with failed rolls. Watching the front blade helps keep your head underwater throughout the roll.

The packraft roll only differs from the standard C-to-C kayak roll at the very end, when you have to lie back on the stern. Otherwise, online tutorials for the C-to-C roll are relevant and helpful.

Assistance

A partner can help during roll practice in several ways. You can practice hip snaps while holding on to someone standing in the water, or even a partner in their boat. Then, have the partner stand in the water and guide your paddle to the lever arm position: power face flat on the surface, paddle oriented 90 degrees from the boat, and paddle extended as far as possible. You can build muscle memory for your torso hugging the hull, wrist position, back elbow pinned to the ribs, etc. Your partner can hold the blade in place and help push the packraft upright while you snap your hips.

Once you can get the lever arm in position on your own, have your partner move to the bow. Attempt your roll and have your partner grab the hull or perimeter lines to help turn the boat upright. Not having to do a wet re-entry for each failed attempt saves time and energy.

PRO TIP!

Surprise! In addition to being challenging, attempting to roll a packraft can cause serious injury. In shallow water, this rolling technique exposes your head and face to rocks. In all water, the paddle motion can cause shoulder dislocation or worse.

If you can touch the bottom with your paddle, you are probably better off swimming (but not putting your feet down!).

Combat Rolls: Patience and Hesitation

You might need to be patient and wait for the right conditions to attempt a roll. Frothy and aerated water in the middle of a rapid might not provide enough purchase for the blade, and therefore not enough torque for a hip snap. This is at odds with the warning against trying multiple rolls at the start of this section, but the point is that if you are going to try to roll, make it count.

Hesitation also allows your boat to get caught in the current. When the boat moves at the same speed as the current, you can more easily roll on either the upstream or downstream side (setting up on the boat's left or right side). When the boat is first caught in the current, rolling with the paddle on the downstream side is easier because the current helps push up against the lever arm. Rolling on the upstream side is more difficult because the current will catch the paddle and push it into the water.

There are also frothy settings when you don't need to hesitate. If you capsize while surfing a hole, the hole can help roll you upright. Tuck and set up quickly, getting the lever arm into position on the boat's downriver side. The upwelling water can lift the power face of the blade. However, trying to roll in a hole is asking for a shoulder injury (unexpected force on the blade). Swimming might be the right decision.

JEREMY'S HAND ROLL

The international packraft community was shocked in 2012 when footage leaked of Australian Jeremy Platt doing hand rolls (rolling without a paddle). Accolades were mixed with outrage since the rest of us had enough trouble rolling *with* a paddle.

Jeremy spent his first packrafting years on the beach, playing in the surf, where he had plenty of opportunities to get pounded by waves and practice his rolls. Surfers who develop calmness while at the mercy of factors they can't control generally make good packrafters and trip partners.

Amy Christeson and Oscar Manguy. Willow Creek, Alaska.

CHAPTER 9

RIVER RESCUE FROM SHORE

This chapter presents the second half of what you might cover in a swiftwater rescue course. These techniques are performed out of the boat, either from shore, islands, or gravel bars. In these settings, a combination of wading and ropework can bring a swimmer to shore; contact, stabilize, and extract an entrapped swimmer; and transport equipment across the river.

WHAT YOU NEED TO KNOW

This chapter should be used to accompany a swiftwater rescue course. Content and techniques will vary, but the rescue principles should be similar.

River rescue and recovery techniques from shore include:

- **Throw ropes:** Throw ropes are wonderfully effective at swinging a swimmer to shore. Throw ropes also introduce a severe entanglement hazard and require training for proper use.
- **Shallow water crossings:** Shallow water crossing techniques allow you to wade into deeper water. Note that shallow water crossing techniques are presented in the rescue context here, but these techniques will be useful to anyone who finds themselves wading in a river.
- **Entrapment:** Entrapment incidents are likely for packrafters, given how often we swim.
- **Rope systems:** You are most likely to use a rope system to transport a patient or equipment across a river. These techniques can help you assist other boating parties retrieve pinned boats, etc. It is worth noting that the mechanical advantage system is the same as used for crevasse rescue and could come in handy if you need to pull your car out of the ditch.

262 THE PACKRAFT HANDBOOK

THROW ROPES

Throw ropes are commonly used to provide safety in or below an individual rapid. The thrower sets up to throw the rope to the potential swimmer so they can swing to shore and get out of the river. Knowing where to set up safety takes time and practice.

The steps involved in deploying a throw rope include:

- **Premeditated planning:** Anticipate the swim and make a safety plan. Ensure that you can reach the swimmer and that they won't get swept into other hazards while holding the rope.

- **Throw:** Throw the rope to the swimmer when they indicate that they are ready.

- **Catch:** The swimmer needs to catch the rope and hold it against the shoulder farthest away from the thrower—hold the rope so that your body is between the thrower and your grip.

- **Belay:** The thrower will belay the swimmer, letting the current swing the swimmer to shore rather than trying to pull them upstream.

- **Secure:** Ensure that the swimmer is secure on shore.

Choosing a Throw Bag

The most popular throw ropes for packrafting are 55 to 70 feet long (16-21 m) and made of ¼-inch (6.5 mm) polypropylene river rope. A ¼-inch (6.5 mm) rope is at the lower limit for graspability. This rope is adequately strong for almost everything packrafters will encounter (950 lbs, 430 kg). For heavier loads, such as helping pull a swamped kayak out of the river, you would want a stronger rope, either wider diameter, polyester, nylon, or Dyneema-cored. Larger-diameter ropes are easier to hold onto.

The key considerations for throw bags are:

- **Rope length:** 55 to 70 ft (16-21 m)
- **Strength:** Diameter and material (polypro or Dyneema-cored)
- **Bag and stuffing:** Throw ropes are stuffed, not coiled, into throw bags. Stuffing allows the rope to unravel mid-flight.

- **Entanglement:** Throw ropes introduce entanglement hazards and require training for proper use. Store the bag securely so that rope can't unravel.

- **End knot:** If you use an end knot, make sure it is small enough to prevent someone from inserting a hand.

- **Maintenance:** Rinse the rope and allow it to dry, out of direct sunlight.

- **River knife:** If your group is using throw ropes, you should also carry river knives so that you can cut free from entanglement.

DIG DEEPER

Polypropylene and Dyneema materials are used in wet applications because they float and are hydrophobic (do not absorb water). Dyneema is stronger than polypro, but more expensive and slipperier. Most Dyneema ropes feature a kernmantle construction with a Dyneema core and polypropylene sheath for better grip. Both materials are sensitive to UV damage and should be stored out of direct sunlight.

Diameter (inch)	Diameter (mm)	Core material	Strength (lbs)	Strength (kg; kN)
¼	6.5	polypro	950	430; 4
¼	6.5	Dyneema	2,600	1,200; 11
⅜	9.5	Dyneema	5,200	2,350; 23
½	12.7	polypro	2,600	1,200; 11
½	12.7	polyester	9,000	4,000; 40

Stuffing throw bags: Throw ropes are stored in throw bags. The bag protects the rope from dirt and UV damage and allows the rope to unravel when thrown.

There are different techniques to stuff throw bags. Most people hold the bag's lip with one hand while the other hand pinches and pushes rope into the bag. A faster technique that requires more coordination is to pinch the bag on opposite sides with both pinkies, then alternate each hand, grabbing and stuffing the rope with your thumb and forefinger.

STUFFING A THROW BAG

HOLD BAG OPEN WITH PINKY AND RING FINGERS OF BOTH HANDS

X-RAY VIEW OF NICE, FLAKED ROPE

PULL ROPE INTO BAG WITH THUMB AND INDEX FINGER

Both stuffing techniques benefit from having another person untangle the rope and hold it up above the bag. If a second person isn't available, you can drape the rope over a shoulder or branch to achieve the same effect. Be wary of dragging silty ropes over your shoulder as they can wear a hole in your drysuit and introduce grit to the zipper.

Maintenance: Regularly inspect the rope for damage and try not to stand on it in practice or rescue scenarios. Remove the rope from the bag to rinse it free of sand and silt, and then allow it to dry, out of direct sunlight.

THE PERFECT COIL

This might be a legend, but I heard that someone opened his throw bag preparing to rescue a swimmer, only to discover that the rope was in a beautiful mountaineer's coil—symmetrical, tight, and tied off. He had lent the throw bag to a mountaineer friend who kindly wanted to show this river rat how to store rope properly! Let's hope a second rope was available for the swimmer.

Clean lines: Some people prefer to have a knot at the end of the throw rope that is not tied to the bag; others prefer a "clean line," no knot. There isn't a right or wrong way.

Advantages of knotting the end of a throw rope:

- The knot creates a stopper—you are less likely to let the end of the rope slip through your hand.
- The knot makes the end of the rope easy to find in the bag.
- The rope is ready to be clipped into a second rope, boat, or anchor.

Advantages of a clean line:

- People can't inadvertently feed a hand through a loop in the knot, which can become an entanglement hazard.
- You don't risk the knot catching between rocks in the river.
- If you need a different knot in the rope, you don't have to untie what was already there.

Both sides of the debate agree that the most significant concern is that someone might put a hand through the knot and get pulled into the system. If you decide to keep an end knot, tie it with a loop too small for a wrist. I use a small figure-eight.

Where to Carry a Throw Bag
Throw bags can become severe entanglement hazards if they are not stored securely. Ensure that your rope can't inadvertently feed out of the bag.

Waist belt: The best place to carry a throw bag is on a releasable waist belt. Carrying the bag on your body ensures that you have it on hand if you need to react quickly. A quick-release belt allows you to release yourself if the belt gets caught on something.

Boat: If you store the bag in your boat (e.g., in a deck bag), you are less likely to have it when needed, but otherwise, this might be your best option. Be sure to secure the rope; it should not be allowed to flop around and unravel.

Life vest: Some life vests have a pocket designed to hold a throw bag, and some people stuff a throw bag under their vest even without the pocket. These systems can work, but the added bulk at your chest can make it harder to perform a wet re-entry. Clipping a throw bag to a life vest with a carabiner is not a good option. The bag flops around, distracts you from paddling, can unravel, and snags on the boat during a wet re-entry.

Carabiners: If you use a carabiner, make sure it is a locking one, and remove it before throwing the bag. Never throw a bag with an attached carabiner. If a swimmer gets hit in the face with a piece of metal, it will distract them from catching the rope.

Target Practice

Start throw-rope practice by tossing the (sealed) bags between partners. Experiment with different throwing techniques (underhand, overhand, and sidearm) so that you are prepared for a situation where your go-to technique isn't an option, perhaps due to overhanging branches or tall bushes. Practice throwing to a stationary partner, then have your partner walk in a straight line while you calibrate throwing to a moving target.

A 30-degree trajectory is a good rule-of-thumb, and most people find an underhand toss to be more reliable than an overhand. A high throw is more likely to get blown off target in high winds than a direct throw. A sidearm can also be useful and requires less wind-up. A direct football or baseball toss is the best option for short and urgent throws.

Throwing to a Swimmer

In-water practice: Find a section of slow water with no downstream hazards to practice throwing to a swimmer. Ensure the swimmer is confident in their ability to swim to shore, and post someone downstream as safety.

1. Choose an appropriate position to throw from. If there is a strong current and you anticipate a lot of force, look for ways to brace your feet as you belay the swimmer to shore. Be wary of slick rocks that

might cause you to lose footing, and overhead branches that might snag the throw.

2. Open the throw bag and take out a few arm-lengths of rope. I like having this extra rope in case I need to adjust my position.

3. Keep the end of the rope in your off-hand while holding the bag in your throwing hand.

4. Wait until the swimmer acknowledges that they want the rope. A swimmer who doesn't expect a rope can get caught in a loose bight, putting them at greater risk. Yell, "Do you want a rope?" Wait for confirmation, vocal or physical, before throwing.

5. Aim for the head. The perfect throw will place the bag just over the swimmer's head, with the splayed rope in reach. Most new throwers release the bag too early. Remember that the shortest distance between you and the swimmer is when they are directly in front of you.

6. If the throw has missed the swimmer and they can't chase it, quickly pull it out of the water. Rope in water is an entanglement hazard.

Location: Choosing where to stage a thrower for a real rescue can be tricky. You need to be close enough to the swimmer for the rope to reach them, and then have secure footing to belay them to shore. Provide enough room to pendulum the swimmer to shore without sweeping them into another hazard.

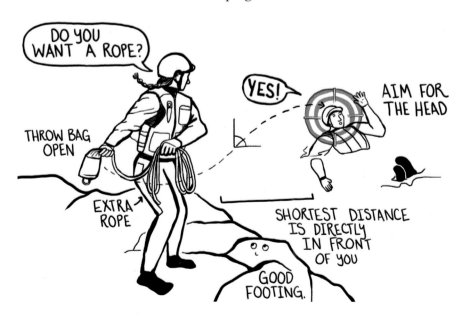

Belaying

Belaying refers to the process of supporting the tension on the rope while the river swings the swimmer to shore, like a pendulum. Your brake hand, the one actually supporting the load, holds the rope on the upstream hip. Ideally, the downstream hand feels no force.

With few exceptions, you don't want to actively pull the swimmer out of the water—let the river do the work. The exceptions to the pendulum swing are when a swimmer gets stuck in an eddy or recirculating hole. In these cases, you might need to pull the swimmer or let them climb the rope. There are also scenarios where it is beneficial to walk along the shoreline with the swimmer, reducing tension on the rope in a dynamic belay.

Standing hip belay: Place the rope around your back, at the waist, in a standing hip belay. The rope's tail should be in your upstream hand and the swimmer's end should feed around your downstream hip. This geometry allows the rope to *open* around your hips as the swimmer pendulums to shore. If you hold the swimmer's end on your upstream hip, you get *closed* in the system—the rope crosses over your waist and can spin you around, placing your back to the river. If you lose your footing in this position, you can get swept into the water.

Belay backup: A good rule-of-thumb is to have two people on shore for one person in the water. In any belay configuration, it is ideal to have someone backup the belayer by holding on to the back of their life vest by the lapels. Allow the thrower space so that you don't interfere with the throw, then help secure them.

Sitting belay: If you don't have a backup person and you need more stability than what you get in a standing hip belay, squat on the ground for a sitting belay. Bracing your feet on rocks can help stabilize you. The orientation of the rope around your waist remains the same as in a standing belay.

MY PROUDEST THROW

In 2013, Zorba Laloo invited Brad Meiklejohn, creator of the American Packrafting Association, and me on an outreach trip to Meghalaya, India. After working with local guides and teaching school kids about water safety, we went packrafting.

I barely made it through a spicy rock garden on the Umngi River and sensed that I should get a throw rope ready for the rest of our group. As soon as I got out of my boat, I saw the next paddler, Banjop Iawphniaw, capsize in the rapid. Banjop was about 100 ft (30 m) upstream from me and approaching a split in the channel. Most of the flow went left into a sustained rapid—a hard swim. The shallow channel on the right would bring him to safety.

I scanned the shoreline to find the right position to make my throw. I waded into the water to three boulders that I could brace against and threw my 55-foot rope (16 m). Our practice together paid off. The bag hit Banjop in the chest with no rope to spare, and he maintained a hold long enough to swing into the right-hand channel and out of danger.

Banjop Iawphniaw. Meghalaya, India.

PRO TIP!

Remember to guide the swimmer all the way to shore. Make contact; don't assume that they are okay just because they are in shallow water at the river's edge.

Dynamic belay: Be aware that the swimmer feels the same force as you. If you pull (create more force), the swimmer will have to hold on tighter. If you ever catch yourself celebrating and thinking, "I've caught a whopper!" the swimmer is certainly struggling to hold the rope.

Likewise, any load at the end of a rope under tension will sink; the water pressure pushes the object down. You and the swimmer will both feel a greater force if the swimmer gets dunked.

This is one reason I prefer to belay from my waist rather than use a "friction belay" around a tree or rock. With a friction belay, I can't monitor how much force the swimmer feels. A dynamic, or moving, belay allows you to move downstream with the swimmer and adjust the rope's tension. This is only an option when there is no risk of leading the swimmer into a hazard.

Vector pull: It can be helpful to have another rescuer walk the shore toward the swimmer while holding onto the rope (letting the rope feed through their hand). This leverage trick, a vector pull, adjusts the pull angle and helps bring the swimmer to shore. Other applications for a vector pull are presented later.

Receiving a Throw

The swimmer should be in the defensive swimming position, feet first and at the water's surface, scanning downriver. Signal the thrower that you want the bag, with voice or body language—one arm held upright is the correct "ready" signal.

If the rope lands upstream, you might be able to catch it by back paddling or turning onto your stomach to swim. If the rope lands downstream, switch to an offensive position and aggressively swim to it. Remember to grab the rope; try not to let the rope slide through your hands, waiting for the empty bag at the end. Neoprene gloves can make it easier to grip a rope in cold water.

Once you have caught the rope, get back in a defensive swimming position. Hold the rope against the shoulder that is farthest from the thrower. This "opposite shoulder" technique keeps you on your back, face out of the water, with bent arms as shock absorbers. The current will rotate your body into line with the rope as you pendulum to shore. If you hold the rope at the shoulder nearest to the thrower, the force on the rope will pull your arms straight, cause you to spin facedown into the water, and then get dunked by the force of the current.

Entanglement: The swimmer needs to prepare for the possibility of entanglement. If it looks like a loop of rope might fall on you (instead of a straight segment), you need to swat the loop away and then swim to retrieve the rope. A loop or bight around your arm or neck is an entanglement hazard. You should have a river knife on your life vest to cut yourself out of accidental entanglement. The likelihood of entanglement is increased when more than one rope has been thrown, which happens due to poor communication.

PRO TIP!

Never wrap a rope around your arm or wrist, either when receiving a throw or belaying. Spiral wrapping your arm can lead to entanglement and submersion.

Multiple Throws

When possible, stage other throwers downriver for redundancy. If the first throw misses, pull the rope out of the water while the second rope is thrown. Having multiple ropes in the water significantly increases the risk of entanglement for the swimmer. Communication is critical when multiple ropes are part of a rescue.

Rapid coil: If there is only one throw rope and your first throw doesn't reach the swimmer, you have limited time for a second attempt. With a rapid coil, you might be able to make a second throw before the swimmer is out of range.

There are several rapid coil techniques. The common theme is that each coil is orderly and carefully placed in your hand, minimizing crossing strands. You can try a butterfly coil, an alpine coil, or an alpine coil with progressively smaller diameter loops.

Rapid coiling technique:

1. Pull the rope out of the water and start coiling from the free end (not the bag).

2. Keep track of the swimmer while you coil the rope. You might be able to move down the bank during or after coiling, bringing yourself closer to the swimmer.

3. It can help to drag each coil over the ground, or use your leg as a backstop, to keep the coils from tangling.

4. When you have coiled enough rope to make the throw, transfer the coils to your throwing hand, holding the bag in your off-hand.

5. Keep hold of the bag with your off-hand and throw the coiled rope. I find the sidearm technique to be the most effective—it seems to splay the coils out in the air, limiting tangling.

The swimmer needs to be especially alert to the possibility of a coil landing over their head or arm. If you're the swimmer and the rope is about to land on you, swing your arm to swat the rope away, then swim to it.

RAPID COIL

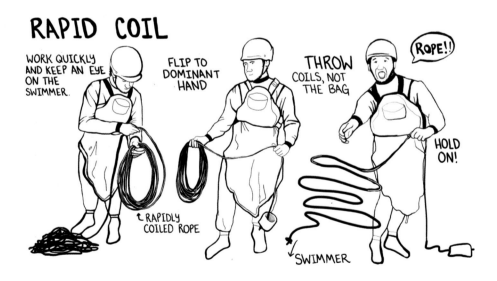

WORK QUICKLY AND KEEP AN EYE ON THE SWIMMER.

FLIP TO DOMINANT HAND

THROW COILS, NOT THE BAG

ROPE!!

HOLD ON!

↳ RAPIDLY COILED ROPE

↙ SWIMMER

PRO TIP!

Loose rope in turbulent water is almost guaranteed to get wrapped around a limb. Practice tying a clove hitch to see how easily two loops can turn into a locking hitch. Any time ropes are part of the rescue system, be prepared to cut yourself free.

SHALLOW WATER CROSSINGS (WADING)

Each individual has a different point at which they can no longer control their motion while wading into the water. The strategy with shallow water crossings is to use the combined mass of your team members to wade into deeper water. These techniques are useful for rescues, but also anytime you want to cross rivers. If hiking, search for the widest crossing. Wide crossings should feature shallower and slower water. Trekking poles are a great asset for stability and probing water depth.

The shallow water crossing techniques can give you a little extra reach when throwing a rope, or allow access to an entrapped swimmer. For an entrapment rescue, the wading group of rescuers can create an eddy around the rescuee and attempt to extract them. For such a simple technique, shallow water crossings can make a big difference in a rescue.

You can practice shallow water crossings in places without downstream river hazards. Start on the bank and walk into the river until you reach the point where you lose control. You should be able to wade farther across the channel as you add partners.

Everyone attempting a shallow water crossing needs to wear full safety equipment, especially life vest and helmet. Be prepared to get swept off your feet, and be certain that you can swim to shore without encountering any hazards. There are a variety of effective wading techniques; I'll outline those taught by the Swiftwater Safety Institute.

Shallow water crossing practice, Willow Creek, Alaska.

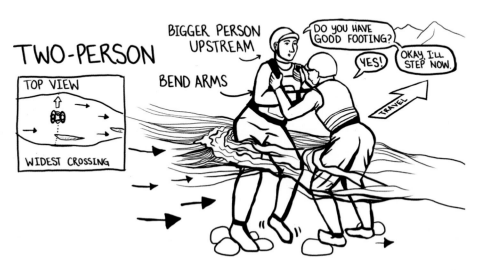

Solo (with Optional Pole or Paddle)

If alone, find a stout pole to use as a brace. Some people use their paddle for this, but I find it difficult to control the blade angle, causing me to fight the paddle when I want to focus on my footing.

Solo crossing:

1. Face upstream so that the water passes between your legs; keep your legs wide.
2. Move laterally with side steps, keeping at least two points of contact (legs or pole) on the river bottom at all times.
3. Take the time to search for secure footing before committing to the next step.

Two-person (A-frame)

When two people are available, form an A-frame by facing each other and grabbing each other's life vest lapels with both hands. The bigger person should be on the upstream side, and both partners will communicate as they search for sound footing and coordinate side-stepping into deeper water.

Three-person (Tripod or Pivot)

A third person can be added to the A-frame so that all three are holding on to each other's life vest lapels, keeping their heads together, and facing inward to allow for eye contact and verbal communication.

Three-person shallow water crossing:

1. When the person in the upstream position is stable, they remain stationary while the others pivot across the current.
2. When the next person rotates into position with their back to the current, they become the new anchor, and the others pivot into the current.

The three-person group might be able to wade across without pivoting, pivoting just provides a designated anchor. Communication is key. The anchor needs to let the others know when they are stable; the pivoting members need to communicate when they have set a new anchor and are ready for the next rotation.

Wedge

Large groups can attempt crossing as a wedge. This technique allows rescuers to reach significantly farther into the channel and provide a stable eddy for a rescuer to work on a patient or extract equipment.

Group shallow water crossing:

1. Place the largest person at the front of the wedge, facing upstream, and preferably with a stout pole to brace against.
2. Stack two people behind the anchor, also facing upstream, holding onto the leader's life vest lapels.
3. Stack three people behind the row of two, crossing each other's arm to hold on to the lapels of the row in front, and keeping the wedge compact. Additional people can stack onto the back of the wedge.

The entire wedge moves laterally by side-stepping into the channel. The leader will feel a very strong current but is supported by the rest of the wedge. The people in the back of the wedge are unlikely to feel any significant current, which allows them to help with an extrication (see below).

ENTRAPMENT

Entrapment occurs when a limb or body gets caught in the riverbed or obstacle. A frustrating aspect of entrapment is that the rescuee is often in shallow water—just out of reach. The rescuee has to fight against the constant force of the current and will eventually collapse into the water and possibly drown. There might only be minutes to provide rescue, depending on the temperature and force of the water. *To avoid entrapment, do not stand in the river unless you can control your movement.*

Entrapment, and especially foot entrapment, is a significant perceived hazard for packrafters because we are often on low-volume rivers and out of our boats. However, thankfully, there have not been any reported incidents. The hazard feels likely because packrafters often try to stand or push off the river bottom when attempting wet re-entries. It seems probable that pushing off the river bottom will eventually lead to a foot getting stuck between rocks or sunken debris.

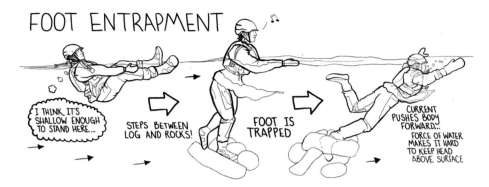

Possible entrapment scenarios include:

- Walking on an uneven riverbed and slipping a foot into a keyhole gap between rocks or wood and then twisting or otherwise catching in place.
- Swimming into a strainer and getting caught in or under the branches.
- Getting pulled into a sieve rockpile.
- Getting snagged by a non-locking carabiner on your life vest that prevents you from freeing yourself.

The rescuer's first objective is to stabilize the rescuee with a rope or by creating an eddy. Once the rescuee is stabilized, the rescue team can try to extract the limb or body. Extraction usually requires pulling the limb or body out the same way it went in, which almost always means forcing it against the current. Pulling against the current can be difficult or impossible, depending on its strength. However, as with our river-running principles, it can be advantageous to use the river's force to help with the extraction. Several extractions were made possible when rescuers changed the fluid dynamics directly upstream of the rescuee.

Single-shore Rescues

Because entrapment victims are typically in shallow water and near shore, it is likely that the rescue party will be on a single shore, not spread on both sides of the channel. There are several techniques to stabilize and extract an entrapped swimmer from a single shore. Keep the rescue system simple and honor the rescue priorities. These techniques should be practiced in a swiftwater rescue course.

Shallow water crossings: The simplest way to approach a rescuee might be to wade to them, using shallow water crossing techniques.

After evaluating downstream hazards, use a wading technique to get people directly above the entrapped rescuee. By creating an eddy for the rescuee, they might be able to extract their foot. If not, someone from the back of the rescue group can work with the rescuee to determine which foot is stuck, then attempt to reach down the rescuee's leg to pull on their foot, remove the shoe, or anything else that might free the foot. Working in the water is surprisingly challenging due to the buoyancy of the rescuer's life vest. Do not remove your life vest.

When the rescuee is free, position them on their back, grab them by their life vest lapels, and float them back to shore behind the wading group.

Single-shore stabilization: If a shallow water crossing rescue isn't an option, prepare for a single-shore stabilization. Your objective is to get a bight of rope around the rescuee to hold them upright until you can get them out of the water.

One way to get a rope around an entrapped swimmer is by holding both ends of the rope and throwing the middle section over their torso. This technique is possible to a distance of about 10 feet (3 m) from shore.

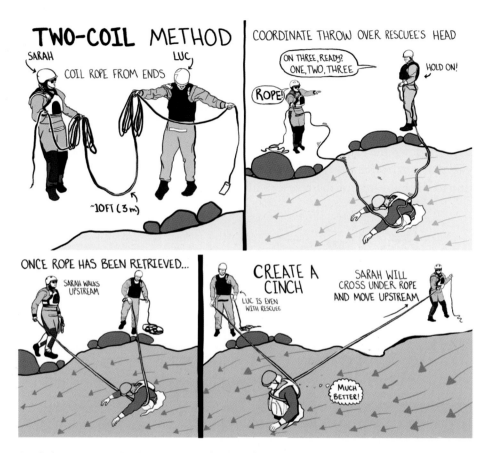

Stabilization with the two-coil ("Kiwi") method:

1. Have two people coil a single rope, starting at the ends and coiling toward the middle. Let's call these people Sarah and Luc to match the illustration.

2. Leave approximately 10 feet (3 m) of rope uncoiled at the middle and coordinate throwing efforts to toss this section of rope over the rescuee's torso (the motion will be like swinging a jump rope). This might take several attempts. Re-coil the rope each time.

3. Once the rope is over the rescuee's torso, instruct them to grab the rope and ideally move it to their armpits.

4. Sarah, who was originally downstream, quickly walks upstream and passes *under* Luc's rope to form a cinch around the rescuee. Sarah continues moving upstream as far as possible, maybe even attaching a

second rope. The rescuee will feel the most support when the rope is in-line with the current.

5. Luc, who was initially upstream, moves down the bank to a position even with the rescuee. Luc holds just enough tension to maintain the cinch. Don't pull sideways unless the rescuee is freed. If the rescuee can free themselves with the support of the upstream rope, the cinch should allow the lower rescuer (Luc) to pull them to shore.

Stabilization by rope retrieval: Another possible technique to get a cinch around an entrapped swimmer is to throw a rope behind the rescuee and then retrieve it downstream.

1. Hold the end of a throw rope and throw the bag to the upstream side of the rescuee. The current will pull the rope against the rescuee and carry the bag directly downriver.

2. Depending on the shore geometry, a group might access the empty bag with a shallow water crossing.

3. You can also try snagging the rope with a second rope. Fill an empty throw bag with rocks and toss the bag over the rope in the river. Carefully pull the bag of rocks to shore, hoping to snag the first rope. It might take several attempts to snag the first rope.

4. Direct the rescuee to grab the rope, ideally positioning it under their armpits.

5. Walk the downstream end of the rope up the bank, crossing under the belayer's line to form a cinch around the rescuee.

Belayed lower: If a shallow water crossing or stabilization rope are not options, another technique is to belay a rescuer down to the entrapped swimmer. Putting a rescuer in the river on a rope significantly increases the rescuer's risk exposure—especially when you know the swimmer is stuck on something. A rescue vest is designed for this kind of rescue. There is a workaround for rescuers without rescue vests, but it puts them at significant risk. *This is a high-risk system that should be practiced in a swiftwater rescue course.*

The belayer should position themselves as directly upstream from the rescuee as possible. Belaying from the side is ineffective at bracing the rescuer as they wade downstream. The belayer might be able to wade into the water for a more upstream position, especially if a group can create an eddy for them.

If the rescuer has a rescue vest, attach the rope to the releasable belt. Given the significant force you might experience while making contact with the patient, consider feeding the belt through the friction plate, not just the buckle (see *Chapter 1: Packrafting Equipment*).

If you don't have a rescue vest, tie a large loop at the end of the rope; the opening should be about eight feet (2.5 m) long; the longer the better. Place the loop around your torso and under your arms. To be clear: do not tie or fix yourself to the rope. A small loop is an entrapment concern, and this rescue technique puts the rescuer at serious risk.

Practice escaping from the loop of rope before getting in the water:
1. Pull your arms to your body in a defensive boxing or "chicken wing" position.
2. Twist your torso so that you can place an elbow in the loop.
3. With your forearm against the rope, twist your torso in the opposite direction and then push the loop up and over your body.
4. Lift your feet off the riverbed and get in the defensive swimming position.

The rescuer will communicate with the belayer using hand signals to indicate "stop" and "lower me." Make a plan for communication before you go into the water. It works well to hold the signaling hand high, using a fist for stop and a small (or large) forward wave for gradual (or fast) lowering.

If the rescuer is using the releasable belt on a rescue vest, they can either walk or sit in the defensive swimming position while being lowered. If the rescuer is in a loop of rope, sitting is not an option. *Don't try this technique if the water is too swift to descend by foot.*

If you can contact the rescuee, work to free their leg. If you are using the releasable belt on a rescue vest, slide your arm under the lapels of their life vest, wrap your legs koala-style over them, and pendulum to shore on the rope. Otherwise, stay upstream of the rescuee, and try to walk with them to shore. Assume that the rescuee is exhausted and unable to manage their own motion.

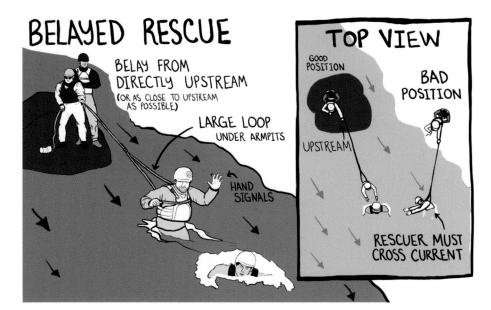

Double-shore Rescues

If the channel is narrow enough to throw a rope across, you can set up a double-shore stabilization line. The additional challenges of a double-shore rescue are crossing the river and communication between riverbanks.

As with the single-shore stabilization, the objective is to support the rescuee in freeing themselves. If they are unable to free themselves, and depending on the strength of the current, a rescuer might lower themselves down the rope hand-over-hand to the rescuee. In this position, the rescuer might free the trapped foot or limb.

Another technique practiced in some swiftwater rescue courses is to use a second rope to pull the rescuee's ankles upstream. The rope needs to be weighted, which can be done by filling throw bags with rocks. This is a desperate measure.

Stabilization by getting a rope across the river:

1. Throw a rope to the downstream side of the entrapped rescuee and walk both ends upstream.
2. The rescuee can hold the rope with straight arms to push themselves away from the object they are stuck on. Another option is for the rescuee to feed the rope under their armpits so that they are supported

by the rope and catch their breath. You might need to yell, "Place the rope under your arms!"

3. With the rope in place, walk both ends upstream as far as possible.

4. Extending the rope with a second rope (figure-eight knots and a locking carabiner) will allow you to get farther upstream, providing a better pull to support the rescuee. The farther upstream the better; a 120-degree angle between belayers is a minimum.

5. A second throw rope can also be used as a cinch line around the rescuee. Clip one end of the rope to the stabilization line with a locking carabiner and pull the rope tight around the rescuee, toward the opposite bank. If the rescuee is freed, the cinch line can be used to pull them to shore.

Head-down Rescuee

If an entrapped swimmer is head-down in the water, you can justify risking injury to save them from drowning. In this scenario, you might consider paddling or swimming to the rescuee to try to knock or pull them free of the obstruction.

"NOBODY DIES ON MY BIRTHDAY"

Hours before the official start of the annual Sixmile Kayak Fest in Hope, Alaska, kayakers were taking warm-up laps through the first canyon—a Class IV stretch of water. A spectator noticed an overturned kayak coming down the river and then saw the swimmer get stuck mid-river. The spectator alerted nearby kayakers, and several highly experienced rescuers were quickly on-hand.

Within minutes, the rescuers got a rope to the trapped swimmer, who was able to keep his head out of the water while holding on to the rope. After holding the rope for four minutes, exhaustion forced him to let go, and his head dropped into the water. Concluding that there wasn't time for anything else, Obadiah Jenkins, a local kayaker recognized for his considerable experience and cool head—who just happened to be celebrating his 33rd birthday—jumped into the river and swam directly toward the pinned swimmer and the unknown entrapment hazard, putting himself at severe risk. Building momentum with aggressive strokes, Obadiah plowed into the rescuee headfirst, which successfully broke him free, as well as the wood he had caught on. The patient was revived with CPR.

ROPE SYSTEMS AND MECHANICAL ADVANTAGE

You can use rope systems to extract a pinned boat or transport people and equipment across the river. Even a simple rope system will take some time to set up, so they are rarely feasible for urgent efforts.

This section starts by reviewing useful knots and anchors and progresses to using mechanical advantage (pulleys) to install a tensioned line over the river. These techniques are standard in swiftwater safety courses.

Note that for rope systems under tension, the basic 55-foot (17-m) polypropylene ¼-inch (6.5 mm) rope is inadequate; you will want a longer and stronger rope (e.g., Dyneema-cored).

> ## *PRO TIP!*
>
> Rope systems in rivers are often built with less attention to backup and redundancy than vertical climbing and rescue systems. The major difference is that river rope systems are generally used to transport equipment rather than people, so the consequence of system failure is less severe.
>
> Another difference is that river systems are less likely to experience a shock load, unlike a climbing rope used to catch a fall.
>
> A complexity in river rope systems that climbing rescuers don't often have to account for is that we might want to anticipate a changing pull direction. Once a pinned boat is pulled free, the direction of pull on the anchor will change as the boat swings to shore. Self-equalizing anchors are often the better choice in river systems.

Knots and Anchors

Different knots are suited for different applications, depending on direction of pull, ease of untying, etc. Online tutorials, such as www.animatedknots.com are a great way to learn knots.

As a general rule of thumb, a knot reduces the strength of a rope by one third. Multiple knots in a rope do not additively weaken the rope, the strength will still be reduced by one third. Don't forget to dress (organize) the knot and leave a tail about the width of your hand.

Useful knots in river rope systems:

- **Figure-eight (follow-through, on a bight, and bend)**: Excellent in-line strength, good for making prusiks
- **Bowline**: Easy to untie, a good option when you don't have webbing to wrap around the anchor
- **Butterfly**: Strong mid-rope knot
- **Double Fisherman's**: To join ropes or make prusiks
- **Water knot**: To tie webbing around anchors
- **Clove hitch**: A self-locking hitch that can be used on an anchor
- **Munter hitch**: Belay or **progress capture** without a belay device
- **Girth hitch**: For quick anchors

- **Basket hitch**: For quick anchors
- **Prusik**: Used for progress capture in rope systems. A prusik is a loop tied from accessory cord attached to a rope with a friction hitch. The prusik allows you to haul on the rope and also capture slack when pulling a rope tight.

Anchors: Anything solidly on shore can serve as an anchor—trees ("5 and alive" [inches, 2.5 cm]) and rocks are typical. Attaching a rope to an anchor can be as simple as tying the rope around the object. The bowline knot is a popular choice because it is easy to untie. If you have cord or webbing to use as anchor material, tie it around the anchor and clip in with a locking carabiner.

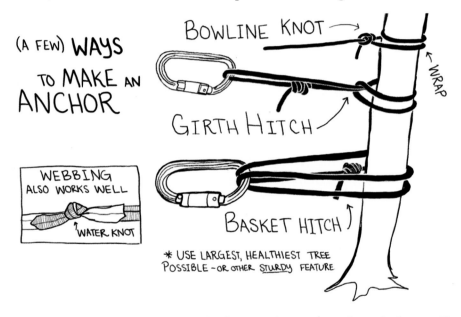

Load-sharing anchors: For light loads, a single tree or rock might be a sufficient anchor. For larger loads, or weaker anchors, load-sharing distributes the force to multiple anchors and provides redundancy if one anchor slips or breaks.

Multiple anchors can be connected by webbing, rope, or cord. The preferred angle between the strands of anchor material is between 45 and 90 degrees. The angle between anchors matters because the anchors feel greater force than the load as soon as the angle exceeds 120 degrees. Large anchor angles can lead to anchor failure.

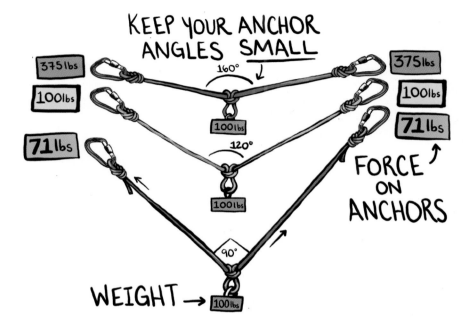

Vector pull: You can use force magnification on an anchor to your advantage. Consider a rope under tension between a tree (anchor) and a pinned boat. The rope effectively connects two anchors (the tree and the boat) at an angle of 180-degrees. Clipping a second line to the rope and pulling, ideally at a 90-degree angle, will magnify the forces felt by the pinned boat and potentially pop it free. Whipping or sliding the clipped rope close to the pinned boat will result in a more effective direction of pull.

I briefly mentioned this same trick in the throw rope section: you can hook the rope and walk down the shore toward the swimmer, creating a vector pull between the belayer and the swimmer. Force magnification helps pull the swimmer to shore.

Vector pulls can be a simple and elegant solution worth trying before setting up a complicated mechanical advantage system. The hardest part will likely be attaching a rope to the pinned boat. Approach a pinned boat from the downstream side if possible, because whatever has pinned the boat can likely trap you as well.

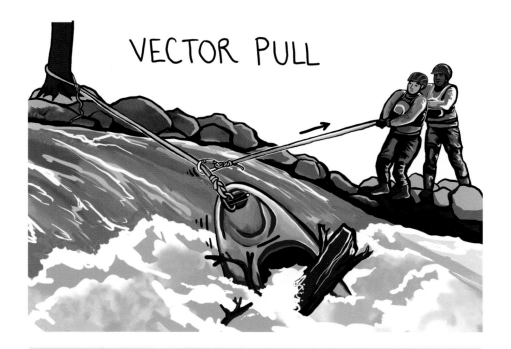

DIG DEEPER

To get a feel for force magnification on anchors, grab an approximately 10-foot (3 m) section of rope or webbing and two partners to act as anchors. Have the two anchors hold the ends of the rope and stand side-by-side. Grab the middle of the rope and pull it away from the two anchors. We'll simplify this geometry and say the two sections of rope have a 0-degree angle between them. In this arrangement, each anchor feels half the force of your pull. Give the rope a hard pull; it will be difficult to pull the anchors off their feet because they each feel half of your pulling force.

Reset and move the two anchors away from each other, holding the rope taut between them at a 180-degree angle. Grab the midpoint of the rope and pull it away from the anchors. In this orientation, it should be quite easy to pull the anchors off their feet. Theoretically, the anchors would feel an infinite load at a true 180-degree angle. In this exercise, each anchor likely feels four or five times your force. This is why the vector pull technique works.

Have the two anchors reset and create a 120-degree angle between your pull and each anchor. This arrangement results in balanced forces: the force on each anchor is equal to your pulling force.

Fixed and focused anchors: Load-sharing anchors can be set up as self-equalizing or fixed and focused. Paddlers with a climbing background will be familiar with the fixed and focused technique; tie an overhand ("frost") knot in the webbing at the attachment point. This anchor system is redundant—one anchor or webbing section can break without losing the entire system. Fixed and focused anchors are common in the climbing world because the force is straight down and doesn't change (gravity). Many river applications will have a dynamic direction of pull, e.g., a pinned boat pulled free from a rock that then drifts down the river. For these applications, a self-equalizing anchor is a better option.

Self-equalizing anchors, the Magic X: A convenient trick to make a self-equalizing anchor is the Magic X. Hold both strands of the webbing loop where you will attach a carabiner. Take one strand and twist it to create a loop. Clip the loop and the second strand with the carabiner. Notice how the webbing adjusts (self-equalizes) as you pull the carabiner from side to side. This anchor system is redundant—one anchor could fail—but you would lose everything if the webbing breaks. Also, note that if one anchor fails, the webbing length will double before catching the load, shocking the system. A sufficient shock could cause the second anchor to fail.

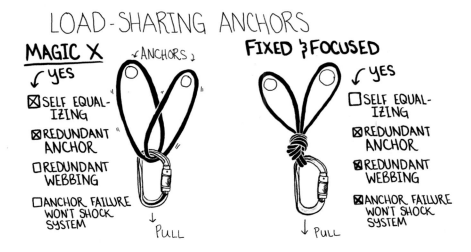

Mechanical Advantage

To pull on an object with more force, the simplest technique is to enlist more pullers. The next simplest option is to try a vector pull (see the previous section). If neither of those approaches works, consider a mechanical advantage system.

Mechanical advantage systems use pulleys to magnify the force on a load or pull a rope tight between two anchors. Basic mechanical advantage systems, such as the Z-pull, require minimal hardware and can be deployed in minutes by experienced teams. While setting up a Z-pull, your concerns should be the entrapment hazard caused by loose rope in the river and that the rope or anchors might fail under tension. Practice these systems on dry land and preferably as part of an in-person course.

Z-pull: This 3:1 mechanical advantage system is a convenient one to remember. In theory, one person can pull with the force of three people. Let's imagine a scenario where you assist a party to extract their pinned canoe from the river.

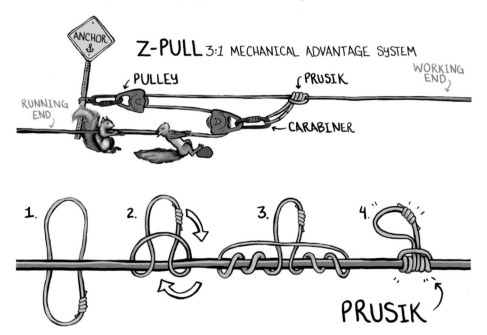

Z-pull supplies:

- **Pulleys (2)**: Pulleys are optional, but a system without pulleys has significant friction and reduces the mechanical advantage to approximately 2:1. Basic and inexpensive pulleys intended for climbing and crevasse rescue are appropriate for our purposes.

- **Prusiks (2)**: Prusiks are slings of cord used to grab onto a line under tension. Use a figure-eight bend or double fisherman's knot to tie a sling from approximately four feet (120 cm) of accessory cord. The diameter of the prusik cord should be approximately two-thirds the rope diameter, with a lower limit of 5 mm. By this guideline, our popular ¼-inch (6.5 mm) throw ropes would be best matched with a 4 mm prusik, but a 4 mm prusik can cut into the rope. We are better off with a 5 mm cord and additional loops to the prusik hitch to generate more friction. A 6 mm prusik would be a good choice for ⅜-inch (9.5 mm) rope.

- **Locking carabiners (2)**: Some people prefer auto-locking carabiners because you can't forget to lock them. All locking carabiners can be hard to operate with cold hands.

Setting up a Z-pull:

1. Attach the "working" end of the rope to the load (the canoe, in this example).
2. Lay the "standing" end of the rope on the ground in a "Z" shape. The free end of the rope ("running") is what you will pull.
3. Use a pulley and carabiner to attach the corner of the Z that is most inland to the anchor.
4. Use a pulley, carabiner, and prusik to attach the remaining Z corner to the standing part of the rope (the section that leads to the canoe). The prusik might need three or four wraps due to the suboptimal prusik-to-throw-rope diameter ratio.
5. To hold tension and capture your progress after pulling on the canoe, attach a second prusik to the standing part of the rope at the anchor. Wrap the prusik around the rope that leads to the canoe, and clip it into the anchor. Someone will need to manage this prusik, sliding it away from the pulley as other people pull on the free end. Prusik management is discussed below.

ANCHOR

HOW TO KEEP ROPE UNDER TENSION

MOVE PRUSIK AWAY TO CAPTURE PROGRESS

Theoretically, in this 3:1 system, a pull with one unit of force will exert three units of force on the canoe. With pulleys, the ratio is more likely at 2.5:1 (due to friction). With bare carabiners, the ratio is closer to 2:1 (even more friction).

How hard to pull: The appropriate number of haulers depends on the application. The safest approach is to start with one or two haulers and monitor the anchor and the load as you pull. Gauge the strength of the system to determine if you can add more hauling power.

The weakest link in our system is the throw rope. If you are using the basic ¼-inch (6.5 mm) polypropylene throw rope, three people pulling with 100 lbs of force each (45 kg) will be at or beyond the strength rating of the rope.

DIG DEEPER

Let's assume you are using the basic ¼-inch (6.5 mm) polypropylene throw rope rated at 950 lbs (430 kg) and have a true 3:1 mechanical advantage system. Adding a knot reduces the rope's strength by approximately one third, to 630 lbs (285 kg). If the rope can handle 630 lbs and the mechanical advantage is 3:1, the pulling force is limited to 210 lbs (95 kg). If each person can pull with 100 lbs of force (45 kg), three haulers would exceed the rope's strength, and the system would fail.

A Dyneema-cored rope of the same diameter bumps the rope strength to 2,600 lbs (1,200 kg). By the same analysis, the system should be able to support six haulers.

Management: Everyone should be working on the upstream side of the rope in case the rope breaks or the anchor fails. If you are downstream of the rope during a failure, the rope or anchor can pull you into the water.

The progress capture prusik at the anchor requires tending. Self-capturing pulleys are available, but they don't work well on our narrow-diameter throw ropes. The attendant should work with their back to the system in case something breaks. Slide the prusik knot up the line to capture progress and keep it from getting sucked into the pulley.

As hauling progresses, the prusik nearest to the load will get pulled toward the anchor. You might need to lock the capture progress prusik and move the other prusik toward the load for a second round of pulling.

DIG DEEPER

I struggled to visualize the mechanical advantage of rope systems until I was taught the T-count method. We can use the T-count method to confirm that the Z-pull is a 3:1 system.

THE T-COUNT METHOD

① PULL WITH ONE UNIT OF TENSION (T)
ANCHOR

② 1T INTO THE PULLEY
1T OUT OF THE PULLEY

LOAD

← 1T

PRUSIK FEELS 2T

2T

← 1T

← 1T

③ 1T INTO PULLEY
1T OUT

→ 1T

→ 1T

④ 1T FROM ROPE +
2T FROM PRUSIK = 3T!

Start at the free end of the rope and assign a pull worth one unit of tension (1 T). Trace this 1 T up the rope to the first pulley. One T of force goes into the pulley, and 1 T of force comes out. Since each strand of rope holds 1 T, the pulley (and attached prusik) must balance forces by holding 2 Ts. If this feels like a leap of faith, revisit the inset exercise from earlier, where two partners stood as side-by-side anchors and opposed your force as you pulled on the rope between them. The geometry is the same. In this case, the pulley/prusik pulls with 2 Ts, and half of that force, 1 T, is felt by each strand coming out of the pulley. We'll leave these 2 Ts banked at the pulley/prusik and keep working along the rope through the rest of the system.

Continue following the rope that comes out of the pulley toward the load. The 1 T that came out of the pulley goes into the pulley at the anchor: 1 T in, 1 T out. As with the first pulley, this pulley banks 2 Ts of force (at the anchor), and the strand of rope that comes out of the pulley still only has only 1 T of force.

Follow the 1 T of force that came out of the pulley at the anchor. Continue down the rope until you reach the prusik. The prusik banked 2 Ts and, when combined with the 1 T of the rope, we get a total of 3 Ts—a 3:1 system.

Tension Diagonal

A tension diagonal is a zip-line that uses the river's force to transport equipment or people across the channel. The rope needs to be under tension because slack can lead to the load getting stuck mid-river. The river can most effectively transport the load when the diagonal is at a steep angle relative to the current.

We want to use the river's force to move the load across the river, so the anchor on the "from" side of transport will be upstream of the "to" side. An angle of 45 to 60 degrees is preferred. Anything less than 45 degrees will likely result in the load getting stuck mid-channel due to the rope's stretch.

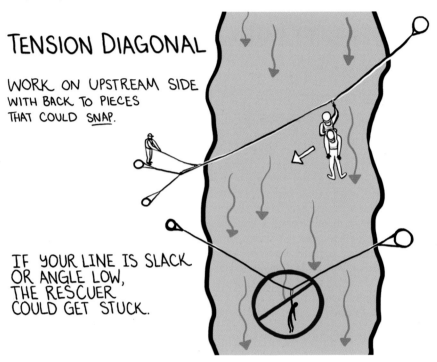

TENSION DIAGONAL

WORK ON UPSTREAM SIDE WITH BACK TO PIECES THAT COULD SNAP.

IF YOUR LINE IS SLACK OR ANGLE LOW, THE RESCUER COULD GET STUCK.

Setting up a tension diagonal:

1. Choose an anchor on each shore. Set anchors to position the rope at knee to waist height above the water.
2. Tie the rope to one anchor, and set up a 3:1 Z-pull at the second anchor. It doesn't matter which anchor has the 3:1 system, but consider which bank has the most workable space.
3. Any time you have a rope across a channel, keep a lookout for other boaters coming downstream. Be prepared to cut your line (ideally from the downstream side) if it might endanger another boating party.
4. Clip your load to the tension diagonal and let the current sweep it downstream. You can help haul the load by attaching a throw rope and pulling to shore.

A rescue vest is ideal for transporting an injured patient on a tension diagonal because you can clip into the releasable belt and free your hands to support the patient. It is possible to ferry across the river without a rescue vest, but it can be difficult to hold on to the rope.

To transport an injured patient without a rescue vest:

1. Clip a loop of cord (e.g., an extra prusik) into a pulley or carabiner on the rope.
2. Position the prusik's knot at the bottom of the loop, and close your hand over both sides of the loop so that the heel of your hand rests on the knot. *Do not put a wrist through the prusik loop (an entrapment hazard!) and make sure the patient and rescuer can easily release themselves.* You, the rescuer, can lie on your back, similar to the defensive swimmer position, and feed an arm through the back of the patient's life vest lapels.
3. Wrap your legs around the patient's legs in a koala hug.
4. Drift down the rope, letting the current pull you across the river.

This scenario puts the rescuer and patient at significant risk. Practice these techniques in a swiftwater safety course.

RIVER RESCUE AND RECOVERY: REVIEW

These chapters covered an overwhelming amount of material, so let's step back and revisit the philosophy and key considerations.

- **Keep it simple**: The best rescue is the one that can be performed efficiently and with the least exposure to the rescue team.
- **Preparedness**: Your brain—what you know and *have practiced*—is your most valuable asset.
- **Motivation and attitude**: We are out there for fun . . . and maybe to develop skills and gain a sense of accomplishment. But the overarching goal must be to start and end at home, safely. Your attitude sets the stage for your experience on the water.
- **Hazards**: Hazards are part of the paddling landscape. Water safety is anticipating what can go wrong, discussing your risk tolerance, and making a plan. The water doesn't care, so you have to.
- **River force**: Use or influence the river's force whenever possible.

Meg McKinney repairing a floor in the middle of the Alaska Range, Alaska.

CHAPTER 10

EQUIPMENT REPAIR AND MODIFICATION

Packrafting equipment is durable, but if you use it long enough, eventually you will have to fix or replace something. Field repairs are part of the game and can make the difference between a minor inconvenience and a major disaster. Field repairs are ideally quick and easy.

The most common damage you are likely to experience is:

- Slow-leaks in the packraft hull or inflatable components
- Torn drysuit gaskets
- Ripped deck or skirt material

The process for glue repairs and modifications (installing tie-downs and other attachment points for thigh straps, cargo, etc.) is the same. Jump to the *Permanent Glue Repairs and Modifications* section for tie-down installation.

WHAT YOU NEED TO KNOW

Equipment breaks down, both from neglect and intended use, especially in the water environment. Carry repair supplies that match your paddling objectives; the most common damage can be repaired with various tapes or Aquaseal.

Field repairs often merit more permanent solutions once back home. Severe damage can be fixed by rafting shops, gear repair specialists, or manufacturers. But you can do much of this work on your own.

REPAIR SUPPLIES

Repair supplies can make the difference between staying on the water or having to hike out. Your repair kit's contents will depend on your objective and how much weight you are willing to carry. At a minimum, carry vinyl underwater tape since it can patch slow leaks and torn gaskets, even when wet.

I carry approximately two feet (60 cm) each of multiple tapes—including vinyl underwater and/or sheathing tape for the exterior of the hull and Gorilla tape for the interior—as well as any adhesive patches that came with the boat.

	Aquaseal	Sheathing tape	Vinyl underwater tape	Patch-N-Go	Tenacious tape	Gorilla tape	Light-duty glue	Heavy-duty glue	Heat weld	Lubrication	Cleaning
Packraft hull (interior)	X		X		X	X					
Packraft hull (exterior)	X	X	X	X			X	X			
Packraft floor	X	X	X	X	X	X	X	X			
Tie-down install							X	X			
Thigh strap install								X			
Leaking valve	X										
Inflatable seat, etc.	X								X		
Skirt or deck	X	X				X					
Drysuit fabric	X				X						
Drysuit gasket	X		X		X						
Broken paddle						X					
Stiff zipper										X	
Non-sealing zipper	X									X	X

Minimal field repair kit:

- Vinyl underwater tape
- Patch-N-Go tape
- Gorilla tape
- Aquaseal UV
- A cotton drying cloth or alcohol swabs

Expedition field repair kit:

- Vinyl underwater tape
- Aquaseal UV or FD
- Gorilla tape
- Sheathing tape
- Patch-N-Go tape
- Multi-tool with pliers
- Needle and dental floss
- Zipper repair kit (see below)
- Spare tube material, ideally long enough to cover a cargo zipper. Store material flat or folded, not rolled.
- Valve gasket, spare cap, and nozzle, if relevant
- Alcohol swabs
- Ski-strap (for paddle repair)
- Accessory straps (webbing with a ladderlock buckle)

Paddle repair kit:

- Ski or accessory straps
- Gorilla tape
- FiberFix

Zipper repair kit:

- Zipper lubricant (TiZip lubricating grease or another non-paraffin zipper lubricant)
- Cleaning cloth
- A small brush (toothbrush)
- Irrigation syringe (10 ml. Optional, but good to have in a first aid kit anyway.)
- A pick (e.g., dental pick, needle)

REPAIR TAPES

Tape is incredibly versatile and can be used to repair pinholes, gashes up to several inches long, torn drysuit gaskets, and broken paddle shafts. Different tapes are appropriate for different surfaces. Review the list below and carry multiple tapes to accommodate different repairs.

If possible, apply tape to both the inside and outside of the puncture or tear. Some tapes will not adhere to the hull's exterior side, as specified in the descriptions below. Tape should extend at least one inch (2 cm) beyond the puncture or tear edges. Round the corners on a tape patch to make the repair less prone to peeling.

Sheathing tape: Tyvek (United States), Tuck (Canada). Sheathing tape is designed for house wrap vapor barriers. Sheathing tape has no stretch and features aggressive acrylic adhesive. Firmly apply the tape using a lighter, rock, or another hard surface. The adhesive is so sticky that you will likely not be able to cleanly remove the tape after it has cured. Sheathing tape is available at hardware stores.

Vinyl underwater tapes: Gorilla Waterproof Patch & Seal, Nashua Aqua-Seal, Flex Tape. These tapes work on wet boats! Vinyl underwater tapes come with a thick layer of adhesive that allows you to press water out to the tape's edges. Once applied, the tape is difficult to remove. Vinyl underwater tape also works to temporarily seal a torn drysuit gasket. I carry about eight inches (20 cm) of vinyl underwater tape in a small ziplock bag in my life vest and have used it on wet boats for an instant repair. Vinyl underwater tapes are available in the plumbing section of hardware stores and online.

Patch-N-Go, Kirch's Kwik Patch. Patch-N-Go is designed to be a permanent patch. Patch-N-Go is the right tape for a careful repair job; the only more durable option is to glue patch material to the boat. Patch-N-Go can be purchased from packraft brands or online.

Tenacious tape. Tenacious tape has more stretch than sheathing tape. Tenacious tape is best on uncoated nylon (the interior of some hulls) and not as good for TPU-coated nylon (the exterior of most hulls). Some outdoor retail stores carry Tenacious tape.

Gorilla and duct tape. Like Tenacious tape, Gorilla and duct tape stick better to uncoated nylon (interior) than to TPU-coated nylon (exterior). These tapes are good candidates for torn drysuit gaskets. While wearing the suit, wrap the gasket several times to create a temporary seal. Gorilla and duct tapes are available in hardware and grocery stores.

It feels like blasphemy to say it, but duct tape is not very useful for packrafting. Gorilla tape is much more effective in cold and wet conditions compared to duct tape.

PRO TIP!

Vinyl underwater tape is the most useful tape I carry. I was suspicious of the "works underwater!" marketing, but I'm a total convert. I've used this tape to seal a hole between rapids on the Grand Canyon section of the Colorado River, on a friend's boat while we both drifted down the river, and to seal a leaking gasket.

AQUASEAL

Use Aquaseal to seal pinholes, small leaks, or repair gaskets. If possible, tape the inside of the tube before applying Aquaseal to the outside. A dab works on pinholes; a bead with ¼-inch (6 mm) overlap works on everything else. Apply Aquaseal in a thin layer; thick layers are more inclined to peel. Aquaseal repairs generally don't need to be redone at home. If the repair starts to peel at the edges, replace it with slow-cure Aquaseal or a tape or glue repair.

There are currently three Aquaseal varieties with different cure times. Longer cure times typically result in more durable repairs. Aquaseal can be purchased in outdoor gear shops or online.

Aquaseal varieties:

- **Aquaseal FD**: Cures in 10 to 14 hours, longer in wet/cold conditions.
- **Aquaseal FD with Cure Accelerator**: Cures in two hours.
- **Aquaseal UV**: Cures instantly when exposed to sunlight. You can also purchase a UV keychain light for around 10 USD.

DAMAGED PACKRAFT

Severely damaged packrafts have been successfully repaired in the field. Carry various tapes, Aquaseal, and a needle and thread in your repair kit. Carry zipper lubrication and repair supplies if your boat features a waterproof zipper.

Repair instructions for these components are discussed in this section:

- Hull
- Floor
- Inflatable components (seat, backband, etc.)
- Valves
- Zippers
- Decks and coaming
- Tie-downs and attachment-plates

Finding Leaks

Some leaks are easy to locate because you know what caused them.

To find slow leaks:

1. Inflate the boat to maximum pressure.
2. Listen for leaking air; place an ear on the hull to hone-in on the zone that is leaking.
3. Bring your face close to the boat while scanning for leaks. Your face (especially your eyes) is more sensitive to airflow than your hands.
4. Spray a 1:1 ratio of soap and water on the boat and watch for bubble formation.
5. Submerge sections of the boat in a pool or calm water and watch for a stream of bubbles.
6. For extremely mysterious leaks in boats with cargo zippers, fill the hull with water. Wet material or beads of water on the outside of the hull indicate leaks. Open the zipper and allow the boat to dry thoroughly.

Leaking Floor

The packraft's floor can tear when it drags over boulders and gravel. Significant abrasion on the floor will lead to small holes. I start looking for holes when I feel like the cockpit is collecting more water than I expect. Floor leaks are most common where your heels press into the floor or under the seat, especially if the seat pushes a hard valve into the floor. More serious floor damage can occur if a sharp spine of rock slices through.

Fortunately, floor material is generally thicker than tube material, and leaks are usually slow and not an immediate safety concern. Even a significant tear (and water-filled cockpit) can be manageable until you get to camp.

Finding leaks: Search for pinholes by shining a light at the floor. Hold the boat upright so that the floor is vertical and have a partner illuminate the side of the floor opposite you. This technique is most effective in the dark.

Field repair: Repair pinholes with tape or a thin coat of Aquaseal. Apply tape or Aquaseal to the floor's inside surface, since the outside will continue to scrape over rocks. I consider an Aquaseal repair permanent unless the hole is large.

To repair the floor with tape instead of Aquaseal:
1. Dry the inside surface of the floor.
2. Preheat the tape in cold temperatures by placing it against your body or another heat source.
3. Cut a length of tape that extends at least an inch (2 cm) beyond the hole. Round the corners of the tape.
4. Affix the tape over the hole. Apply pressure to the tape by using a lighter, rock, or similar firm object.
5. Applying heat to the tape once it is in place also helps improve adhesion. I've used a water bottle filled with boiling water for this effect.

Home repair: Significant tears, especially if they are not linear, might require gluing a patch of floor material over the damaged section. Follow the *Permanent Glue Repairs and Modifications* directions at the end of the chapter.

Leaking Hull
Hulls are most commonly damaged when the packraft comes into contact with sharp rocks. Holes often form at and below the waterline, where the boat has more contact with rocks. Holes can also form when the material pinches between a hard object and a rock, e.g., if something loaded through a cargo zipper is pressed firmly against the floor and then drags against a rock.

ERIN AND HIG'S BEAR CLAW REPAIR

Near the end of a 4,000-mile (6,400 km) trek from Seattle to the Aleutian Islands, Erin McKittrick and Brentwood "Hig" Higman set up camp along a salmon stream. While eating dinner on the other side of a sand dune, a brown bear destroyed their camp, shredding their tent, sleeping pads, and slicing a two-foot (60 cm) tear in a packraft.

After twelve months of travel, Erin and Hig were no strangers to field repairs. It didn't hurt that Eric Parsons, sewer and creator of Revelate Designs bike bags, had joined for this leg of the journey.

Hig repaired the boat using a baseball stitch, carefully aligning the two sides of the complex tear by matching up pre-existing scratches. Matching the sides ensured that there were no puckers in the repaired tube. When the slice was sealed within a few inches (10 cm), Hig glued as much of the tear from the boat's inside as possible (without cargo zipper access). He then applied two thin coats of Aquaseal over the stitching. Hig's repair held for the rest of their trip and a subsequent 800-mile (1,300 km) marine packraft tour around Cook Inlet, Alaska.

Field repair: Minor leaks can be repaired with tape or Aquaseal. All repairs should be done on clean and dry boats (except for vinyl underwater tape, which can be applied wet). Alcohol swabs help the drying process, but dry cloth works too. When conditions are very wet, boil water, fill a bottle and place it against the area that needs to dry before applying the tape. If you can access the inside of the hull (through a cargo zipper), repair both sides of the hull material.

The likelihood of a successful field repair diminishes in proportion to the size of the tear. If a significant field repair is your best option, try sewing the tear closed before applying Aquaseal or tape. Stitching can serve as a ripstop so that if the repair fails, it will hopefully be a slow enough leak that you can get to shore. I keep a needle taped to my multitool's handle and I carry a spool of dental floss to use as thread. Pliers (on a multitool) can help push or pull the needle through thick fabric.

Sew the large tear with a baseball stitch, which pulls the material's edges together. Then apply Aquaseal to the seam and needle holes. An application of tape over the Aquaseal doesn't hurt.

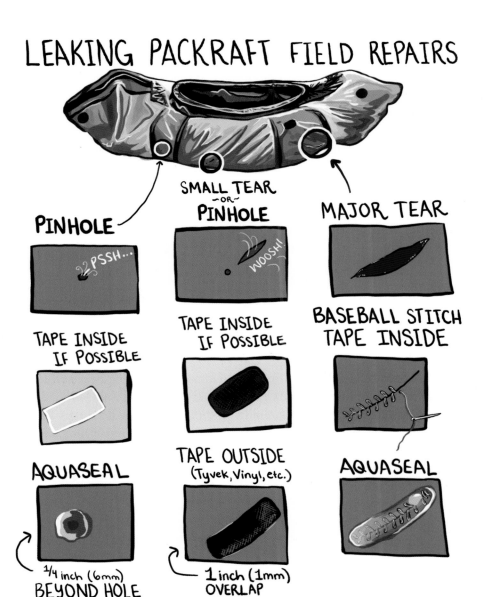

LEAKING PACKRAFT FIELD REPAIRS

How to sew a baseball stitch:

1. Start at one end of the tear and insert the needle from the inside of the opening.
2. Feed the needle to the inside of the tear's other side, using a spacing of approximately ⅛-inch (3 mm).
3. Continue sewing the gash closed, always feeding the needle from the inside.
4. Adjust the stitch tension so that the fabric is brought together.

Home repair: Permanent hull repairs can be made at home; follow the *Permanent Glue Repairs and Modifications* directions at the end of this chapter.

Leaking Seat, Backband, or Other Inflatable Accessories

Inflatable components are most likely to fail as a result of holes, tears, or leaking valves.

Field repair: Repair small holes and tears with a thin coat of Aquaseal. Tape typically doesn't work well on areas that have curvature, are exposed to water, or experience wear when getting in and out of the boat. Refer to the *Leaking Valve* section below for valve repair.

Home repair: Inflatables are often manufactured by welding heat-seal fabric. You can re-weld seams with a household iron. If the original weld fails or develops a leak at an edge, try to re-weld it. In theory, you only need half an inch (1 cm) of welded material, but a wider weld will make the repair more secure.

Re-welding heat-seal fabric:

1. Deflate the inflatable component and allow it to dry.
2. Calibrate your iron by starting at a low heat setting and applying light pressure to a superficial corner of the fabric—there is often a narrow strip of unwelded material external to the original weld. Keep the iron moving constantly. Frequently check the corner to see if it has started to weld. Increase the heat setting until you see the corner weld. If the material develops a sheen or wrinkles, the iron is too hot.
3. Align the edges of the seam or tear so that the glossy (inner) material is face-to-face.
4. Apply the calibrated iron for about ten seconds, continually moving the iron.

5. Allow the material to cool and test the weld. If the weld peels, try a higher heat setting or longer weld time.

'TWAS THE NIGHT BEFORE TWENTY BELOW

The night before venturing into the Arctic National Wildlife Refuge for a ski trip, I inflated my sleeping pad and discovered a two-inch (5 cm) leak along the edge. We were sleeping at a lodge and I borrowed an iron to weld the edge of the pad.

If I hadn't used my pad that night, I wouldn't have discovered the leak and would have had to abandon the ski trip after one cold and sleepless night. I appreciated having the confidence to weld my pad, which I gained from repairing blown packraft seats.

Leaking Valves

Packraft hulls typically have one or two inflation valves, designed for inflation by bag or mouth. Inflatable seats or backbands also use mouth valves. Valves are glued into the boat or accessory fabric, so valve failure can either be at the hull attachment or the nozzle.

Field repair: Examine a leaking valve to determine if the leak is coming from the nozzle, cap, or fabric around the valve. Valves will either have one attachment point that is flush to the hull, or two, one at the hull and the other at the end of a valve arm (a short length of tubing). The attachment point at the hull is a common source for leaks. Refer to the *Finding Leaks* section earlier if you have trouble finding the leak.

Gasket: Large valves typically include a gasket in the valve cap. Check to see if the gasket is missing. Fortunately, gasket leaks are slow, and you should be able to frequently re-inflate your boat until you are off the water. Lost gaskets are common; I carry a spare gasket in my repair kit. The valve on some inflation bags also includes a spare gasket.

Debris: Look for debris in the nozzle and cap threads that might prevent the valve from sealing. Use pressurized irrigation to clean the cap and threads. Pressurized irrigation is easiest with an irrigation syringe (from your first aid kit), but a hydration bladder mouth valve or a hole cut in the corner of a plastic bag can also work.

Hull attachment leak: If the leak originates in the hull material, clean and dry the surface and then apply Aquaseal. Aquaseal is a better option than tape around the valve or valve-arm edges.

Nozzle leak: If the leak originates where the nozzle is glued into the arm, remove and replace the nozzle.

To remove and replace a nozzle:

1. Work the nozzle free of the arm. A small screwdriver on a multitool is effective.
2. Scrape the old glue from the nozzle and arm.
3. If the arm is damaged (cracked tubing or with glue residue), cut the damaged section off, leaving enough clean tubing to accommodate the nozzle's reinstallation.
4. Apply a bead of Aquaseal around the nozzle and insert it back into the arm.
5. Place tape over the nozzle assembly to prevent it from working out of the tubing before the Aquaseal cures.
6. Allow the Aquaseal to dry, then test for leaks.

Lost valve cap: If you cannot repair a leaky nozzle, you will want to seal the valve as best you can. Find an object to use as a plug, such as a tape-padded section of a branch. Secure the plug in place with more tape. Anticipate needing to re-inflate your boat frequently for the duration of your trip.

> ## *PRO TIP!*
> You might be able to convert the inflation bag's nozzle into a cap. Plug the nozzle with a ball of tape or other material and use tape to secure the plug in place.

Home repair: Repairing major valve failure, such as delamination, is best done by the manufacturer. Valves are such critical components that I am disinclined to attempt any non-trivial repairs.

Leaking Cargo Zipper

A stiff zipper needs lubricant, a non-sealing zipper needs repair and cleaning.

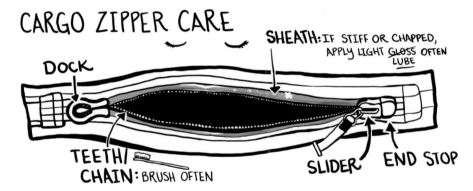

CARGO ZIPPER CARE

SHEATH: IF STIFF OR CHAPPED, APPLY LIGHT GLOSS OFTEN LUBE

DOCK

TEETH/CHAIN: BRUSH OFTEN

SLIDER   END STOP

Lubrication: Only lubricate a clean zipper. Frequent light lubrication is better than infrequent heavy lubrication. Directions from the zipper manufacturer are clear about not lubricating the zipper teeth. If you feel that you must lubricate the teeth, apply a very light coat, and remove any excess lubricant.

Cargo zipper lubrication:

1. Pull the slider into the dock to close the zipper.
2. Lubricate the sheath, not the teeth! A smooth polyurethane sheath protects the zipper's teeth. Spread TiZip lubricating grease on a scrap of cloth and work the lubricant into the chain's sheath, both the sides and the top surface.
3. Apply a dab of lubricant to the zipper's docking end and the transition from dock to chain.

4. Use a clean rag to wipe off any excess lubricant; you don't want the zipper to be wet enough to attract dirt.
5. Open and close the zipper several times to spread the lube and test for smooth operation.

Field repair: A non-sealing zipper needs repair and cleaning.

Cleaning a waterproof zipper:

1. With the zipper open, examine the zipper teeth for particulates.
2. Try to free debris by gently bending the zipper, using air pressure (your breath or an empty hydration syringe), a brush, or a small pick. Air compressors are a great help when available.
3. Clean the zipper teeth with a small brush and warm soapy water. Don't use solvents or aggressive cleaning solutions.

If debris is caught at the end stop (opposite from the docking end), you will need to split the chain to access the teeth.

Splitting a zipper chain to clean the end stop:

1. Pull the slider about six inches (15 cm) from the end stop.
2. Place thin slippery material, like a thick plastic bag, in front of the slider. Pull the zipper-pull and catch the plastic between the teeth. The exposed plastic behind the slider provides a breaking point for you to separate the chain by hand.
3. Gently work the separation back to the end stop. Clean the debris from the end stop.

To seal a split zipper:

1. Manually close one inch (3 cm) of zipper, starting at the end stop. Hold one side of the zipper in each hand and work the halves together, watching to make sure the teeth interlock.
2. With one inch (3 cm) of a sealed zipper, the slider should now successfully re-seal the entire chain.

Repeat the cleaning process until the zipper closes, then lubricate the zipper. Note that manually closing the zipper is an option at any position along the chain, just be careful not to force the zipper closed when there might be debris between the teeth.

CLEANING THE END STOP

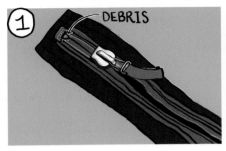

IF DEBRIS ARE CAUGHT IN ZIPPER...

PULL PLASTIC IN TO OPEN TEETH AND GIVE ACCESS TO END STOP.

WORK SEPARATION BACK TO END STOP. CLEAN DEBRIS.

MANUALLY CLOSE ZIPPER ONE INCH (2.5 cm) BEFORE USING ZIPPER.

Home repair: In theory, the entire zipper can be removed and replaced at home. This is an intimidating repair. Follow the gluing directions at the end of the chapter if you are so inclined.

Ripped Deck or Sprayskirt

Packraft decks and skirts are generally made with thin ripstop nylon. This fabric keeps weight down but is prone to tearing.

Field repair: You can repair small holes and tears with tape or Aquaseal. You might need to sew more extensive damage before applying tape. Gorilla and Tyvek tape are good candidates.

Home repair: If the deck has ripped from the hull, your best hope is a heavy-duty tape like Gorilla tape. Tyvek is a good second choice. Given the water exposure and tension on decks and skirts, you might need to send these repairs to the manufacturer. Severe deck damage might motivate you to convert your boat into a self-bailer.

Broken Coaming

Currently, deck coaming consists of aluminum poles, PEX tubing segments, or a combination of both.

Field repair: Broken or lost coaming sections can be replaced with flexible willow or alder branches.

Home repair: Check with the brand for aluminum replacement parts. You can purchase PEX tubing at a local hardware store. The printed size refers to the inside diameter ("nominal"). For example, ⅜-inch PEX has an inside diameter of ⅜-inch (9.5 mm) and an outside diameter of ½ inch (12.7 mm).

Broken Tie-downs and Torn Attachment Points

Tie-downs and attachment points can fail by delaminating, tearing, or the metal D-ring can bend or break.

Field repair: D-rings can be replaced with a loop of cord tied with a square knot.

Home repair: If you need to remove a patch (for example, removing a torn tie-down), reheat it with a heat gun and gradually peel it from the edges. This is hard on the fingers (hot), but it is better to use your fingers than pry the patch with a tool that might damage the hull. Be careful not to overheat the hull.

DAMAGED DRYSUIT

Drysuits are most likely to fail at the gasket, or develop slow leaks in the suit material. Torn gaskets and slow leaks can be sealed with tape in the field and can be permanently repaired at home.

Torn Gaskets

Field repair: A torn gasket can be temporarily sealed by taping the gasket closed over the wrist or neck. Vinyl underwater, Gorilla, or duct tape are the best candidates.

Home repair: Permanently replacing gaskets is easy. Save your money and do this one yourself.

How to replace latex gaskets:

1. Trim the gasket to ½-inch (1 cm) from the original glue.
2. Find a rigid cylinder that fits snuggly through the gasket. Mason jars, water bottles, or food cans work for the wrists; cooking pots work for the neck.
3. Apply a continuous bead of Aquaseal to the remaining original gasket material. Use a scrap of cardboard or plastic to spread the bead and make sure that it is continuous.
4. Stretch the new gasket over the bead, overlapping the original gasket.
5. Use masking tape to hold the gasket in place and prevent it from slipping out of position while the Aquaseal cures.

GASKET REPLACEMENT

1. TRIM OLD GASKET
(EITHER BEFORE OR AFTER STRETCHING IT OVER JAR)

½ inch
1 cm

2. APPLY AQUASEAL
TO OLD GASKET

3. STRETCH NEW GASKET
OVER CYLINDER AND TAPE IN PLACE

MASKING TAPE

316 THE PACKRAFT HANDBOOK

Leaking Drysuit

With any significant use, your drysuit will begin to accumulate slow leaks.

Field repair: You can patch small holes with Aquaseal or Tenacious tape. Repair larger leaks with GORE-TEX or other waterproof fabric repair kits.

Home pressure test: The best way to identify drysuit leaks is with a pressure test. Most manufacturers offer this test and will patch your drysuit at an affordable price.

To perform a pressure test at home:
1. Turn the drysuit inside-out.
2. Reach through the neck to close the zippers.
3. Use rigid cylinders (water bottles, jars, etc.) to seal the gaskets.
4. Sneak a compressed air valve or bike pump nozzle into one of the gaskets to inflate the suit. An electric air pump works as well, but you will have to keep it powered to maintain pressure.
5. Spray a 1:1 water and soap mixture on the suit, look for bubbles, and mark with a pen.
6. Once the suit is dry, seal leaks with a thin coat of Aquaseal or Tenacious tape.

PADDLE

Paddle damage includes stuck, broken, or lost segments.

Stuck Paddle

Four-piece paddles are likely to stick at each joint if they are left assembled and stored wet. If the connection is so tight that it requires two people to separate, *lightly* sand the joint's male end to reduce its diameter. Err on the side of removing too little material since you can always sand more.

Lost Blade

A lost blade can be substituted with a bight of flexible wood (willow, alder, or coaming PEX). Attach the bight to the shaft with several ski straps, hose clamps, or cord, spanning at least six inches (15 cm) of the shaft. Once the bight is secure, wrap it with fabric, tape, or a stuff sack.

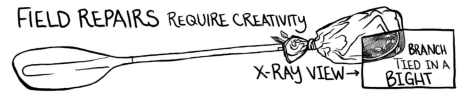

FIELD REPAIRS REQUIRE CREATIVITY

X-RAY VIEW→

BRANCH TIED IN A BIGHT

Broken Shaft

The most common place for a paddle to snap is at the ferrule, the length of slightly smaller-diameter pipe that fits inside the shaft where the pieces connect.

Field repair (splinting): A broken or cracked shaft can be splinted with branches, tent stakes or poles. Secure both ends of the splint with ski straps, tape, or cord. The longer the splint, the more secure the repair.

Field repair (FiberFix): A more robust field repair for a broken shaft is FiberFix, a resin-infused fiberglass wrap.

To splint a shaft with FiberFix:

1. Sand the shaft with sandpaper.
2. Soak the fiberglass for 10 seconds in warm water, and then wrap it around the broken shaft.
3. Use the included vinyl strip to wrap the repair tightly, which compresses the wrap layers and forms a stronger bond.
4. Wait 10 minutes for the epoxy to cure.

TOM'S FIBERFIX REPAIR

I broke my paddle (took a swim in a spicy rapid, and somehow snapped it over my right quad when the blade got lodged against a rock—or I think that's what happened). I had read about FiberFix and had some in my repair kit. The repair was quite strong. Since this was the last day of our trip, a friend and I tried to break the paddle back at camp. We tried torsion and then bridged the paddle across two picnic benches. We gave up trying to break it since I decided the repair was strong enough to keep the paddle as a spare.

-Tom Wetherell

Home repair: A permanent shaft repair involves gluing in a new ferrule that acts as an internal splint. This might not be possible, depending on the position of the break.

You will need to find piping to use as a ferrule. Ideally, you can find piping that happens to fit snugly inside the broken shaft. If not, another option is to grind a ¼-inch gap (6 mm) along piping that is nearly the same diameter as your paddle. The gap allows the ferrule to squeeze, decreasing its diameter to fit inside the main shaft. An eight-inch (20 cm) section of the shaft from a friend's broken paddle might be your best hope.

To glue a new ferrule in a broken paddle:
1. Sand all surfaces that will be glued.
2. Use marine epoxy to glue one half of the ferrule inside the outer shaft and allow it to cure.
3. Glue the remaining outer shaft in place over the exposed half of the ferrule.

Shortening a paddle: Shortening a paddle is intimidating, and I'm more inclined to sell rather than risk messing up this process. Shortening a paddle involves the same process as above, except that instead of gluing both shafts to the ferrule, one shaft will be held in place with a spring clip. If there is an existing ferrule already in place, skip step (3) below and either re-use the existing buttonhole or drill one that doesn't interfere with it.

To shorten a paddle:
1. Use a hacksaw (24 TPI) to remove the broken or excess shaft material.
2. Use a sanding block (180 grit, wet) to smooth and square any cut ends.
3. Glue half of the ferrule in place.
4. Use a drill bit that matches the existing spring clip buttonhole, assemble the shafts, tape them together, and drill through both sections.
5. Seal all cut surfaces (paddle shaft and drilled holes) with epoxy.

PERMANENT GLUE REPAIRS AND MODIFICATIONS

Permanent glue work can be done to repair packrafts or add tie-downs or attachment points for thigh straps or other outfitting. These glues and solvents are toxic and can be hard to find; you might prefer to have the manufacturer or local raft outfitters do this work.

Review the entire process before starting your glue work. Online videos and tutorials will be helpful as well.

Notes on the gluing process:

- **Adhesive strength**: Light-load repairs (or tie-downs) can be made with a one-part flexible adhesive. Large and heavy-load repairs (and tie-downs) merit a stronger adhesive and longer glue process.

- **Material**: Most packraft exteriors are one-sided TPU-coated nylon, so these directions will only cover TPU-coated nylon modifications. The adhesives I discuss should work on rubber and PVC materials, but do your homework first. Order repair material from your boat manufacturer. Any TPU-coated nylon should work, but the manufacturer will know what is best for your boat.

- **Inflation**: Whenever possible, glue repairs should be done on an inflated boat.

- **Heat reactivation**: Glue repairs are significantly stronger when the glue has been reactivated with a heat gun or hair dryer. However, be careful not to overheat the packraft, especially near its welds and seams.

- **Seams**: Repairs that extend over seam tape might still leak along the edges of the tape. Use Aquaseal to seal the seam after gluing the patch in place.

Tie-downs and Attachment Points

Tie-downs and attachment points can be used to outfit your packraft for cargo, perimeter lines, towing points, or thigh straps. There are several tie-down and attachment point options intended for different uses.

Tie-down options:

- Packraft brands sell lightweight plates made of thin TPU-coated material with either a grab loop (webbing), D-ring (metal), or slot (strap plate). These packraft-specific plates are unofficially rated to approximately 300 lbs (135 kg) of force, more than adequate for perimeter lines, securing cargo to the bow, and thigh straps for people that do not intend to roll the packraft.

- Packraft brands sell attachment points designed for use with thigh straps.
- For greater loads, use PVC or urethane-coated D-rings by big raft brands (e.g., Aire, NRS). These D-ring patches are heavier and bulkier than tie-downs manufactured for packrafts.

A PVC D-ring being installed for thigh straps.

Thigh Strap Installation

Thigh straps can be added to any packraft. Your options include:

- **Minimalist:** Accessory straps (flat webbing with a buckle) work as ultralight thigh straps. Minimalist straps are generally inadequate to roll, but do help with boat control. Tie one end of the strap to the hip or ankle attachment point and use the buckle to tighten the other end. *Do not install anything with a loop or excessive tail*; these would be entrapment hazards.
- **Packraft-specific thigh straps:** Packraft-specific straps are the best option for high-performance and low weight and bulk. Four-point straps provide more control and make the thigh straps less risky because the shorter span between strap segments is less likely to trap a foot or leg.

- **Inflatable kayak thigh straps:** You can purchase two-point thigh straps intended for inflatable kayaks (NRS or AIRE). These straps often come with heavy metal buckles.

To determine the installation positions for attachment points, refer to the illustrations in *Chapter 1: Packrafting Equipment*, partners' boats, and photos of packrafts online. The distance between the hip and ankle attachment points should be approximately 30 inches (75 cm). Try to leave at least an inch (2 cm) between attachments and seams, the floor, and the skirt so that you don't risk weakening existing glue or seams. You can experiment with attachment positions by taping straps to the hull; Gorilla tape works well.

Choose attachment points based on availability, weight considerations, and whether you intend to roll your packraft (capsize recovery). If you do not plan to roll your packraft, lightweight attachment points are the most affordable and least bulky option. Rolling your packraft can exceed the tear strength of lightweight attachment points, especially at the hip position. I've torn several of these, always at the hip position.

If you intend to roll, your best option is to use attachment points intended for thigh straps. If packraft attachment points are unavailable in your area, marine and raft shops sell D-rings.

When installing the attachment point, orient the D-ring or webbing loop in line with the strap's pull direction to minimize the peeling force on the attachment plate.

Date night. Anchorage, Alaska.

322 THE PACKRAFT HANDBOOK

Loctite Vinyl, Fabric & Plastic Flexible Adhesive, and Equivalents

You can glue light-load tie-downs or minor patches with a polyurethane adhesive like Loctite Vinyl, Fabric & Plastic Flexible Adhesive. This one-part glue is available in hardware stores and is significantly easier to work with than Clifton or Stabond.

Gluing with the Loctite one-part adhesive:

1. Prepare the surface by cleaning, drying, and lightly sanding with 150 to 220 grit sandpaper.
2. A "wet bond" involves applying an even coat of glue to both surfaces and pressing them together. Masking tape can help prevent the patch from peeling while the glue cures. Allow the glue to cure for 24 hours (check the directions if you are using other one-part glues).
3. A "contact bond" takes longer to cure but can be stronger. Apply an even coat of glue to both surfaces and allow it to dry for 10 to 30 minutes. Apply a second coat to both surfaces and allow it to dry. Reactivate the glue by heating both surfaces with a heat gun or hair dryer (low heat). When the glued surface starts to shine, assemble the pieces, apply pressure, and tape with masking tape. Wait 24 hours before exposing the repair to water.

Stabond, Clifton, and Equivalents

The preferred adhesives for significant repairs are urethane compatible glues such as Stabond, Clifton, Helaplast, or Wiggins Bostik.

Permanent adhesives:

- **Stabond Adhesive (UK-148):** In my opinion, Stabond is the best glue for TPU-coated fabric common in packrafts. This adhesive consists of two parts: glue and accelerator. Stabond has a shelf life of one year. The shelf life is real; expired components will not work as well. If possible, check the expiration date before purchasing to ensure that you aren't getting old stock.
- **Clifton Urethane Adhesive (LA 4123):** Clifton adhesive is a one-part cement for PVC and urethane materials, but it requires the same gluing process as Stabond. An accelerator is available for the adhesive, but it isn't needed. Clifton adhesive has a shelf life of one year.

- **International options:** Packrafters outside of the United States might need to find other polyurethane-based (PU) adhesives. Helaplast is an option in Europe, Wiggins Bostik 999 is available in New Zealand.

Materials:

- Stabond (UK-148, two parts) or other adhesive
- PVC solvent (MEK, or MEK-substitute)
- Patch material or attachment-plate
- Pencil, pen, or marker
- (2) Disposable 1-inch (2.5 cm) paintbrushes (not foam)
- Stirring stick
- (2) Disposable containers
- Measuring cup or graduated cylinder with 1 oz/ml graduations
- Disposable gloves
- Heat gun (or hair dryer)
- Roller hand tool (or round edge of a tool, large spoon, etc.)
- Face mask and ventilation

Preparation: Cut the repair material to extend at least 1 inch (2.5 cm) beyond small holes and at least 1.5 inches (3 cm) beyond large tears. Round the corners of the patch material. Tape the inside surface of the hole or tear if the boat has a cargo zipper. Even without a zipper, try to work tape into the inside of the boat to seal part of the gap and allow for low-pressure inflation.

Gluing directions:

1. Clean and dry the area to be glued. If possible, inflate the boat.
2. Outline the patch/attachment point position with a pen or marker.
3. (Optional) Lightly sand the area you're about to glue with 150 to 220 grit sandpaper.
4. Pour a small amount of MEK into a disposable container. Apply a very thin coat of MEK with a disposable brush to the patch *and* the location marked on the boat. Repeat this process five times, letting the MEK dry between applications. You should see the luster of the hull dull slightly.
5. (Stabond only) In a disposable container, mix the Stabond adhesive at a 10:1 ratio of glue to accelerator. A small measuring cup or graduated cylinder is a big help here. Mix thoroughly (60 seconds). The glue will

324   THE PACKRAFT HANDBOOK

become tacky in 10 minutes, so you will need to work quickly on the next steps. The amount of glue to mix will depend on your application. Since it is only workable for 10 minutes, mixing multiple small batches is a good idea.

6. Apply a thin application of glue to both surfaces that will be glued (hull and patch) using a disposable brush. Don't overwork the glue; use as few strokes as possible, no globs. If an area is thin, return to it with the next application. Allow the glue to dry (3 to 5 minutes) and then repeat this process. Clifton recommends two coats; I use five for Stabond. When gluing multiple patches or attachment-plates, it is most efficient to cycle through the positions, applying a coat to each surface. The first patch is usually dry and ready for a new coat when you return to it. Dry glue has a dull luster; wet glue is glossy.

7. Reactivate both glue surfaces with a heat-gun or hair dryer on a low-heat setting. Place your hand next to the boat surface, or holding the patch, while you heat it with the heat gun. If your hand gets too hot, move the heat source away. Your hand is the thermal gauge. Work the heat gun over the surface and monitor the glue's luster for a change from dull to glossy. If your hand gets too hot or you see any bubbling, the heat source is too close. The patch material will likely curl at the edges; this is okay.

8. While the glue is reactivated, apply the patch to the hull. Start contact at the patch's edge and roll the patch into position. Be careful not to trap air bubbles.

9. Use a roller hand tool or another blunt surface (e.g., a screwdriver handle) to apply significant pressure to the patch. Work from the center to the edges to drive air bubbles out. If the patch looks like it might curl, masking tape will help hold it in place while curing.

10. Let the glue cure for 24 hours. Keep the boat inflated during this time, if possible.

GLUE REPAIR

1. CUT PATCH 1½-2 inches (4-5 cm) BIGGER THAN TEAR

hole

2. OUTLINE POSITION ON HULL

3. SAND (ONCE). ETCH WITH MEK FIVE TIMES.

← SANDPAPER

4. APPLY GLUE TO BOTH SURFACES

←BOAT

FIVE TIMES

PATCH
↓

5. RE-ACTIVATE GLUE WITH HEAT GUN

NOT TOO HOT!

6. APPLY PATCH WORKING FROM ONE SIDE

7. REMOVE AIR BUBBLES WITH ROLLER

Clinton Hodges's dislocated shoulder in a makeshift sling. © Óscar Lage

CHAPTER 11

MEDICAL EMERGENCIES

While we all hope to extend the period between injuries by mitigating risks, at some point playing outside will result in an injury for you or your partners. This chapter presents a few topics and scenarios that take place in recreational boating.

The best tool in your emergency kit is a smoothly operating mind. Once something bad happens to you or your partner, it *is* possible to make things worse. The right action is sometimes the quickest, but no patient benefits from panicked assistance. Time spent preparing for unexpected injuries or other setbacks provides your brain clarity when what you do next matters most.

This chapter begins with a discussion of coordinating a rescue and then covers the most common boating injuries as listed in the American Whitewater accident database as of 2020.

WHAT YOU NEED TO KNOW

The injuries you are most likely to see packrafting are the same as other outdoor activities: sprains, broken bones, infections, and so on. The best preparation to manage these injuries is Wilderness First Responder training, or equivalent. Everyone should have basic first aid and CPR instruction.

There have been relatively few packrafting fatalities by drowning, fourteen as of publication. But death by drowning is our greatest concern, and as the sport grows more popular, we can expect more close calls. Risk management and the other concepts throughout *The Packraft Handbook* are intended to prevent you from drowning, but if you are part of a team that experiences drowning, medical training in rescue breathing and CPR might mean the difference between life and death.

This chapter is not an adequate substitution for medical training.

CALLING FOR HELP

Before considering an evacuation, determine whether your situation is urgent (threatens life, limb, or eyesight) or non-urgent (everything else). An urgent evacuation will likely involve rescue professionals. A non-urgent evacuation might involve private assets, such as airplanes or motorboats, or be possible without external assistance.

The following protocols are based on United States resources but the principles are the same elsewhere.

Who to call: Call the emergency phone number in your region: 911 in the United States and Canada, 112 or 999 in Europe, 111 in New Zealand, etc. The dispatchers work with rescue coordination centers and will determine what kind of rescue asset might be able to reach you. If not 911, call the State Troopers (United States). Review the different satellite communication options in *Chapter 1: Packrafting Equipment* for communication where cell phones aren't an option.

The critical pieces of information to communicate are:

- **Location:** Use a GPS or phone to report your latitude and longitude, preferably in decimal degrees.
- **Nature of injury:** Describe the severity of the injury.
- **Condition of the patient:** Urgent versus non-urgent.
- **Accessibility:** Near a road? Airstrip? Can a helicopter land?
- **Special equipment:** Is any special equipment required? Hoist? River vessel?
- **Supplies on hand:** Food, water, equipment, etc.

PRO TIP!

Anticipate a long wait. Ensure that the patient is protected from additional injury and is as comfortable as possible. Insulation (warmth), food, and water are critical.

As a very general guideline: an urgent evacuation with two-way communication might take 4 to 6 hours; a one-way SOS response can take 24 hours (United States).

Kate Fitzgerald packaged for an evacuation. Ski and packraft traverse, Alaska.

What happens when you push the SOS button?: When you push the SOS button on a messenger or personal locator beacon (PLB), your location and distress signal is sent to an international rescue coordination center (IRCC). The IRCC is staffed 24/7 and maintains a database of rescue assets. The database is queried with your location, and nearby assets are alerted. At the same time, the IRCC staff look up your device's emergency contacts and try to reach them to verify that you are out on a trip—keep your account contacts updated! If you have a two-way device, the rescue staff will try to contact you to collect more information.

The IRCC then transfers your case to a regional RCC. These smaller coordination centers are alliances of state (Troopers) and federal (Coast Guard, Air National Guard, etc.) rescue centers. The RCC then pushes your rescue through a governed hierarchy:

1. **Private (e.g., LifeMed):** These are the rescue professionals with the most medical training, but they can't necessarily access remote locations and adverse conditions.
2. **Municipal:** Fire department, Search and Rescue organizations, etc.
3. **State (Troopers)**

4. **Federal (Coast Guard, Air National Guard, National Park Service, etc.):** Federal assets are the best at accessing difficult terrain and conditions. Incidents in National Parks are passed to NPS assets first.

The RCC and involved agencies determine who will respond to your evacuation. A private asset like LifeMed might conclude that they can't reach you, so your case will get passed to the next asset. Or, a flight might be mid-air and receive notification about a more urgent evacuation and reroute. It is critical to accurately communicate your situation.

PRE-EXISTING MEDICAL CONDITIONS

Despite what our inner superstars claim, we aren't invincible. Some of us have life-threatening reactions to insect stings and peanuts, and you will see your share of hornets and Snickers bars while portaging.

Take the time to identify potential health issues within the group. Ensure you know who in your party might need quick sugar (diabetics on insulin), an Epi-Pen (know how to administer it), have other allergies (carry Benadryl [Diphenhydramine]), or cardiac conditions that predispose them to life-threatening arrhythmias. These conversations help strengthen the bonds of friendship that largely motivate our outdoor time in the first place.

DROWNING

Death by drowning is our greatest concern while working or playing in water environments; all of our risk assessment and safety precautions are intended to reduce the likelihood of drowning.

The American Whitewater accident database reveals a number of causes that led to death by drowning: not wearing a life vest, entrapment in rocks or strainers, and so on. As with our approach throughout *The Packraft Handbook*, understanding what can go wrong allows us to train for an appropriate response. What goes wrong during drowning is that the patient's brain doesn't get enough oxygen. The priority is to get oxygen into the patient's lungs so that it can enter the bloodstream and be transported to the brain. Seek medical training so that you are prepared to get oxygen to the patient's brain with rescue breathing and/or CPR. Your training can absolutely save a life.

Whitewater
Accident & Fatality
SANKEY VISUALIZATION — 4/1/1924 to 7/22/2020

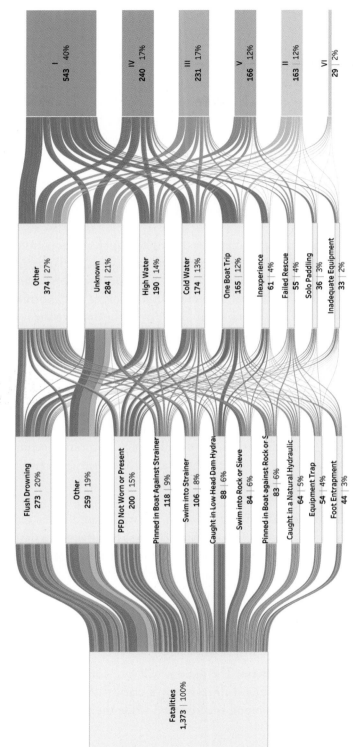

Fatality	Causes	Factors	River Difficulty
Fatalities 1,373 | 100%	Flush Drowning 273 | 20%	Other 374 | 27%	I 543 | 40%
	Other 259 | 19%	Unknown 284 | 21%	IV 240 | 17%
	PFD Not Worn or Present 200 | 15%	High Water 190 | 14%	III 231 | 17%
	Pinned in Boat Against Strainer 118 | 9%	Cold Water 174 | 13%	V 166 | 12%
	Swim into Strainer 106 | 8%	One Boat Trip 165 | 12%	II 163 | 12%
	Caught in Low Head Dam Hydrau... 88 | 6%	Inexperience 61 | 4%	VI 29 | 2%
	Swim into Rock or Sieve 84 | 6%	Failed Rescue 55 | 4%	
	Pinned in Boat against Rock or S... 83 | 6%	Solo Paddling 36 | 3%	
	Caught in a Natural Hydraulic 64 | 5%	Inadequate Equipment 33 | 2%	
	Equipment Trap 54 | 4%		
	Foot Entrapment 44 | 3%		

SOURCE AW Accident Database | DATA AS OF 7/28/20 | DESIGN Gabe DeWitt

The Definition of Drowning

The concept of drowning is complicated by somewhat arbitrary categorization: near drowning, flush drowning, secondary drowning, and so on. What really matters is that drowning is a *process* that can be interrupted and reversed.

According to the World Health Organization,

> **Drowning is the process of experiencing respiratory impairment from submersion/immersion in liquid. Drowning outcomes are classified as death, morbidity, and no morbidity.**

By this definition, if you have ever coughed to clear water from your airway in the pool or river, you have experienced drowning. The "morbidity" term refers to a change in functionality due to the drowning process: whether or not the patient returns to normal. A patient that recovers with normal breathing and alertness is said to have no morbidity. A patient that experiences brain damage due to oxygen starvation has severe morbidity.

Note that "Flush Drowning" in the American Whitewater database is another arbitrary categorization that refers to drowning without a clear cause.

The Drowning Process

Drowning proceeds in stages and typically takes three to ten minutes before culminating in cardiac arrest. The duration of this process depends on the patient's exertion level (heart rate) and the amount of oxygen in their bloodstream.

The stages of drowning:

- **Surprise**: Surprise at being in the water can induce fear, voluntary breath-control (choosing to hold one's breath), and a natural reaction that limits kicking of the legs. These reactions reduce your ability to catch your breath and swim in turbulent water.

- **Involuntary breath-holding**: When a trace of water (a thimbleful) enters the airway (trachea), the body reflexively blocks the airway to prevent water from reaching the lungs. The patient is likely to be seen struggling, silently, in this stage.

- **Unconsciousness**: The patient will lose consciousness when oxygen levels in the blood drop below a critical threshold. The remaining oxygen in the blood is consumed while the patient is unconscious. If the drowning process is interrupted, rescue breathing can resuscitate the patient. The degree of morbidity will depend on how long the brain went without oxygen.

- **Cardiac arrest**: Sustained unconsciousness can lead to convulsions, a blue skin tone, and ultimately, cardiac arrest. You might be able to resuscitate a patient with CPR, as discussed below.

DIG DEEPER

Many of the drownings in the American Whitewater database occurred in cold water. Drownings are more likely in cold water due to "cold water immersion syndrome."

The first stage of cold water immersion syndrome is an automatic gasp that closes the lungs. This reaction, referred to as the mammalian dive reflex, serves to store and preserve oxygen in our lungs.

After the initial reflexive gasp, the body tries to recover with rapid but shallow breathing. Limited lung capacity, combined with shallow breaths, panic, and turbulent water contributes to the aspiration of splashed water droplets. Coughing is the body's natural defense against aspiration.

The second stage of cold water immersion syndrome is swimming failure. Our bodies seek to preserve core temperature and vital functionality by transporting blood from our extremities to our core. Blood loss in arms and legs reduces motor control, tactile functionality, and feeling. Our body effectively prevents our limbs from being able to swim.

There are third and fourth stages to cold water immersion syndrome, including hypothermia, but whitewater patients aren't likely to get there; we are more likely to lose consciousness—another natural reflex designed to prevent additional water from getting into our lungs.

Both the normal and cold-water drowning processes can be delayed with training and proper equipment:

- Intentional swimming practice can train your body to be less surprised in the water.
- Dressing for the swim, and wearing a drysuit, can slow the cooling process that leads to loss of motor control and hypothermia.
- A properly fitting life vest designed for turbulent water can help to keep your head above water.

Treating a Drowned Patient

The priority in all drownings is to get oxygen to the patient! The air we breathe contains approximately 21% oxygen. Rescue breathing provides the patient with your exhaled air, which contains approximately 17% oxygen.

The immediate treatment for an unconscious patient is rescue breathing (also known as positive pressure ventilation and mouth-to-mouth resuscitation), and if there is no pulse, CPR. Breathing through a CPR mask with a one-way valve is ideal, especially if there is foam (see the inset below), but mouth-to-mouth is also an option. Pocket-size CPR masks can be carried in your life vest for emergency access.

Rescue breathing and CPR:

1. Completely remove the patient's life vest. Effective CPR needs a hard surface underneath the torso.
2. Unless there was significant trauma (waterfalls), tilt the patient's head back slightly to open the airway and initiate rescue breathing. If you suspect an injury to the cervical spine, one rescuer would need to stabilize the cervical spine during rescue breathing.
3. Rescue breathing consists of a *gentle breath* over a 1 to 2 second period, followed by a 4-6 second rest between breaths.
4. If there is no pulse, perform standard 30-2 CPR on the patient (thirty compressions followed by two breaths).
5. Anticipate needing to roll the patient from their back to a recovery position on their side so that they don't aspirate their vomit.

If the patient remains unconscious for more than 30 minutes, or was unconscious underwater for more than 60 minutes, CPR is no longer justified. Permanent brain damage is expected within 10 to 15 minutes of being unconscious due to a lack of oxygen to the brain. However, see the caveat in the hypothermia section; cold water can depress vital signs and justify sustained treatment.

PRO TIP!

Drowning patients might exude significant amounts of foam from their mouth or nose. This foam is produced in the lungs by the interaction of water with a naturally-occurring surfactant. Your priority is to provide oxygen (rescue breathing), which can be done through the foam—*ventilate through the foam.*

CASE STUDY: MARTY RINKE

Marty Rinke drowned on the Lion's Head section of the Matanuska River, Alaska, in 2017. Marty was an accomplished paddler, leading a group of four on his backyard run. He was trained in swiftwater rescue and was wearing full safety equipment.

Marty paddled into a hole and capsized. He held onto his packraft and attempted a wet re-entry three times. After the third attempt, he was separated from his packraft and unable to recover. Exhaustion and water-inhalation soon led to a loss of consciousness. Marty was pulled to shore but did not regain consciousness despite CPR.

Marty's partners and widow shared these details, hoping to make a difference for someone else.

Marty Rinke at the terminus of the Matanuska Glacier, Alaska. © Abby Quimby

Pulmonary edema: Any patient who was unconscious in the water is a candidate for pulmonary edema. Pulmonary edema is a dangerous condition caused by cellular fluid transfer into the lungs from the blood. Symptoms can take 24 hours to develop, starting with a dry cough, progressing to a crackle, respiratory distress, gurgling sounds, and respiratory failure.

This is the tricky part: if the patient never went unconscious, or went unconscious because they fainted (not due to water in the lungs), there is no risk of pulmonary edema. But if the patient went unconscious because a thimbleful of water got into their lungs, that water can trigger the continuous transfer of cellular fluid. Because you are unlikely to know what led to loss of consciousness, you should consider an urgent evacuation of anyone that was unconscious in the water. If the patient has foam at the nose or mouth, or they have remaining respiratory distress or crackling sounds in the lungs, get them to a hospital for monitoring.

HYPOTHERMIA

Hypothermia refers to a low body temperature. Mild hypothermia is indicated by shivering (which produces heat), pale skin (blood is drawn into the core for warming), and an altered mental state. Severe hypothermia is indicated by discontinued shivering and further deterioration of the mental state.

Hypothermia is a severe concern for paddlers in cold water. Half (52%) of the American Whitewater hypothermia injuries resulted in death. The best way to prevent hypothermia is to make good paddle-or-portage decisions and wear a drysuit.

Treatment: To treat mild hypothermia, immediately rewarm the patient. The best heat source is internal, so provide them with easy sugars such as a GU shot, candy, or soda. These fuels burn hot and fast, so anticipate moving onto medium-burn fuels (carbohydrates) and slow-burn fuels (fats) as the patient recovers. Provide warm fluids to drink. Remove wet clothing and dry the body. Place the patient in a sleeping bag, but remember that the bag only traps heat; it doesn't generate heat. Hot water bottles and chemical hand warmers are excellent heat sources, but be careful not to place external heat sources directly on the skin, which can be unknowingly burned due to a lack of sensitivity (numbness from cold).

If field treatment is not effective or the patient shows severe hypothermia symptoms, initiate an urgent evacuation.

PRO TIP!

Cold water can extend survival time for unconscious swimmers, which leads to the saying, "Nobody is dead until warm and dead." Hypothermia will depress vital signs and can make a recovery seem impossible. Monitor vital signs, and don't give up.

A COLD SWIM

My most ambitious adventure was a self-supported, 30-day, 370-mile (600 km) traverse of Mt. Logan in Yukon Territory, Canada. After weeks of using our pack-rafts as sleds, we finished the traverse with a float down the glacial Chitina River. The trip featured several hardships, mostly for me, including getting caught in an avalanche at the base of Mt. Logan, and snow-blindness at 19,000 feet (5,800 m). We were eager to get to the river for some "free" miles of travel.

In a classic demonstration of safety drift, we kept pushing the day's objective, hoping to get low enough on the Chitina to reach tree line so we could harvest wood for a fire. Because I had the most paddling experience, I led the group through Class II features, but was surprised by turbulent water and capsized. I managed to keep a hold on my boat and kick my way to shore, despite the additional weight of my water-filled ski boots.

I was in the water for less than a minute, but I was too cold to take care of myself by the time I reached the shore. My partners helped me out of my wet clothing and provided hot drinks. We were very fortunate to have reached a beach with driftwood—the fire provided an important heat source.

Besides not wearing a drysuit, my rapid cold response was likely a result of having lost 10+ pounds (4.5 kg) during the previous four weeks. Being underweight made me more vulnerable to cold-water hazards.

Luc Mehl at the headwaters of the Chitina River, Alaska. © Graham Kraft

WATERBORNE ILLNESSES

River-runners across the world are prone to waterborne illnesses due to drinking water contaminated with microorganisms. Water treatment that kills microorganisms is discussed in the next chapter. Most stomach bugs will clear through your intestinal tract within a day or two.

Giardia is the intestinal infection that receives the most attention from the boating community, followed by cryptosporidium. Symptoms of giardia and cryptosporidium typically take seven days to set in and include watery diarrhea, stool that floats ("greasy" for giardia), an upset stomach, cramps, and nausea. Any parasitic infection can cause severe dehydration. Loperamide (Imodium) can help as an anti-diarrheal, but you should seek medical help if symptoms persist. Clinics will take a stool sample and prescribe medication.

DISLOCATED SHOULDER

Shoulder injuries are common in water sports, with dislocated shoulders being the most prevalent. A shoulder is said to dislocate when indirect torque on the arm causes the humeral head to pop out of the socket. Unexpected torque transmitted through the arm occurs when the paddle blade gets caught by powerful water or rock. Dislocations occur most frequently when performing a high brace with improper technique: hands above neck level, elbows elevated. Recall the "reading a watch" guideline that reminds you not to raise your wrists above eye level.

The major concern with a dislocated shoulder is that the arm's neurovascular bundle may be impinged, leading to reduced circulation or ischemia (inadequate blood supply) of the distal hand and fingers. It is worth attempting to reduce (re-set) the dislocation in a remote setting (more than two hours from help), especially if the involved hand is numb, cold, or pale in appearance. If you aren't able to reduce the shoulder, and the hand is not getting blood flow, the patient might lose it.

The Cunningham technique: The humeral head wants to be back in the socket; the problem is that the strained deltoids and other arm and shoulder muscles prevent reduction. A non-invasive method for shoulder reduction is the Cunningham technique. The Cunningham technique involves relaxing tight muscles to allow a natural reduction.

CUNNINGHAM TECHNIQUE for SHOULDER REDUCTION

The Cunningham technique for shoulder reduction:

1. Help the patient relax as much as possible.
2. Have the patient sit upright with good posture.
3. Sit across from the patient and help them place their hand on top of your shoulder. Rest your wrist in the crook of their elbow, where you can apply slight downward traction.
4. Encourage the patient to continue to sit upright with good posture and roll their shoulders back (proud chest).
5. Gently massage the muscles of the arm and shoulder, especially the biceps and deltoids.
6. Reassure the patient to help them relax. The light massaging should feel good, and if the patient's muscles relax sufficiently, the humeral head will slip back into the joint.
7. Monitor the circulation, sensitivity, and motion of the hand of the injured side in case the neurovascular bundle was damaged.

There are many reduction techniques that are beyond the scope of this guide, including solo techniques that you might be able to perform in the water.

If you are unable to reduce the dislocation, begin an evacuation. If the reduction is successful and there is normal circulation in the fingers, there is no need for an urgent evacuation.

DMITRY'S DISLOCATED SHOULDER

I was pushed up sideways against a rock in shallow water. I used a high brace on the rocks upstream to keep my head out of the water. But then the current caught my boat and rolled it beneath me. I knew I messed up: my hands were above my head, and sure enough, my shoulder popped out.

I pulled my skirt and swam. I was full of adrenaline, and swimming wasn't painful. My friend was able to get my shoulder back in the socket with the baseball technique. He put my arm in a sling and then swung me to the other shore with a throw rope. I was able to hike out.

-Dmitry Surnin

Dislocated versus separated: A dislocated shoulder can be difficult to distinguish from a separated shoulder (torn AC joint). Perhaps the most helpful clue is to determine the mechanism of injury. A dislocated shoulder is the result of indirect torque, whereas a separated shoulder is typically due to impact, e.g., trying to catch a fall while on skis or bike. Both injuries will show a divot between the humerus and AC joint. A dislocated shoulder will have lost all mobility, whereas a separated shoulder will have some mobility in lower positions, albeit painful.

HEAD INJURY

Serious head injuries are not as unusual as you might expect, and when they occur, they often result in death (74% of the head injuries in the American Whitewater database). The easiest way to prevent head injury is to wear a helmet. Don't forget to continue wearing your helmet out of the water—slipping and falling on rocks can directly impact the head.

Traumatic Brain Injury: Blunt force to the head can cause a Traumatic Brain Injury (TBI). Mild to moderate TBIs are often called concussions.

Criteria for TBI may include:

- Loss of consciousness
- Amnesia
- Any altered mental state, regardless of how long it lasted

The anticipated problem with a TBI is that blood or swelling in the skull will cause increased intracranial pressure (ICP). Signs of increased ICP include severe headache, persistent vomiting, and deteriorating mental state. Any of these indicators merits an urgent evacuation.

TRAUMA

Bleeding is bad. If there is excessive bleeding from an extremity (hemorrhage), compress the wound with significant pressure to restrict the flow of blood. If that doesn't work, then use a tourniquet, a two-inch wide (5 cm) soft band applied two to four inches (5-10 cm) above the wound. Note that tourniquets are dangerous when left on too long (over an hour). If bleeding is from a junctional wound (neck, groin, armpit), be prepared to maintain pressure until your patient is delivered to a higher level of care.

If the bleeding is inside and you can't see it, you won't be able to do much. Fortunately, we are generally well protected by our life vests and the water's fluid pressure. Only 11% of the American Whitewater trauma injuries resulted in death.

Signs of internal bleeding include:

- Increased pulse
- Increased rate of respiration
- Decreased skin tone or quality
- Declining mental state

One critical indicator of internal bleeding is a declining mental state. The body can compensate for volume loss (blood) with increased pulse and respiration, and if the body successfully clots the source of bleeding, symptoms will return to normal (homeostasis).

The best we can do in the field is to get the patient comfortable and as relaxed as possible, aiding the body to clot the wound naturally. If the rupture does not clot, hypoxia of the brain will cause brain damage and a rapidly declining mental state. This is most likely to occur within the first hour after the injury and, if it is going to stabilize, should do so within about six hours. Decompensated volume loss (declining mental state) requires an urgent evacuation.

SPINAL INJURY

Spinal injuries are very infrequent (6% of the American Whitewater database) and rarely lead to death.

Indications of spinal injuries include:

- Point tenderness along the vertebrae
- Tingling, numbness, or electric sensations within the extremities
- Faulty sensation in hands and feet (e.g., the inability to correctly identify a sharp versus soft point of contact while eyes are closed)
- Inability to flex/extend hands and feet

Most spinal injuries involve breaking the vertebrae processes (the bones that stick out) and do not include the spinal cord. If a patient has any of the symptoms above, begin an urgent evacuation.

FIRST AID KIT

Water sports don't require any unusual additions to your backcountry first aid kit. The contents of your first aid kit depend on your group, experience, and objectives. In-person training is the best way to learn what to carry and how to use it. Items to consider bringing are listed below.

The most used equipment in my first aid kit is LeukoTape P, for blister prevention. Apply this tape at the first hint of a hotspot. This breathable tape's adhesive is very aggressive and some friends develop minor rashes.

Pain killer, both over-the-counter and prescription strength, are the next most used components of my kit.

Supplies:

- Non-allergenic gloves
- EpiPen (for insect allergies)
- Blister care tape (LeukoTape P)
- Gauze (four-by-four-inch pads and rolls)

- Povidone-iodine or Tincture of Benzoin (antiseptic)
- Irrigation syringe
- Bandages
- Splint materials (you can use the cord, throw ropes, tape from your repair kit, etc.)
- Pocket CPR Face Shield (should be carried in life vest or pocket)
- Chemical heat packs

Medications:
- Diphenhydramine (Benadryl)
- Nonsteroidal anti-inflammatory drugs (aspirin, ibuprofen, naproxen, etc.)
- Tylenol
- Imodium
- Prescription antibiotics: e.g., ciprofloxacin
- Prescription pain medication: e.g., oxycodone
- Prescription muscle relaxants: these might help reduce a dislocated shoulder

PART IV

PUTTING THE "PACK" IN PACKRAFTING

No vessel is better suited for creative routes and off-the-beaten-path destinations than a packraft. Whether you bought a packraft to fill a specific need or having a packraft has revealed a new world of possibility, it is likely just one component in a bigger system.

Part IV presents recommendations for backpacking and camping equipment, carrying cargo on the packraft, and planning and executing your next great adventure—be it across the neighborhood or across the globe. The possibilities are endless; hopefully these resources will help you discover new beginnings.

Danny Powers. Mt. Fairweather Traverse, Alaska.

Packrafters in the Arctic National Wildlife Refuge, Alaska.

CHAPTER 12

BACKPACKING, CAMPING, AND CARGO

Including your packraft on backpacking or multisport adventures opens a world of possibilities. This chapter presents equipment considerations and how to strap cargo to your boat (backpacks, bikes, skis, meat). Cargo changes the maneuverability of the boat and can introduce entrapment hazards. You will likely want to choose easier paddling objectives to compensate for the loaded packraft's limited handling and recoverability.

WHAT YOU NEED TO KNOW

If the packraft is part of a larger system, consider these concerns:

- **Going too heavy:** Carrying too much equipment can prevent you from reaching your goals. Identify unnecessary gear and share common needs between the group. Cut weight in "the big three" categories: shelter, sleeping system, and pack.
- **Going too light:** Being too weight-conscious can result in unpreparedness when something goes wrong. Safety equipment, repair kits, and first aid are important to include in your outings.
- **Carrying cargo:** Carrying cargo will make the packraft slower to maneuver and harder to recover if you capsize. Practice in a controlled environment first.

My experience is heavily influenced by off-trail trips in Alaska and might be less relevant in your part of the world, especially if you are closer to resupply points or support.

PACKING YOUR PACKRAFT AND PADDLE

Folding and rolling your packraft: There isn't a right way to roll a packraft before loading it in a backpack. I get the most compact roll by folding the boat into lengthwise thirds, with each side tube folded toward the center, then rolling the folded boat from the bow. I kneel on the roll to keep it as tight as possible and keep an accessory strap within reach so that I can capture the roll at its tightest. I'm careful not to force too tight of a roll at the cargo zipper.

PRO TIP!

Suck the air out of your seat and boat to make the most compact package. If I'm packing the packraft at home, I'll even place a vacuum on the inflation valve to remove as much air as possible.

Packing your paddle: A very common mishap is losing or damaging a four-piece paddle segment during transport (backpack, bike, car, etc.).

Best-practices for packing paddles:

- Store paddle segments inside your pack, if possible. Some pack material (Dyneema) has a low tear strength when rigid objects are forced into the fabric under tension. Load the shafts first, then fill the rest of the volume.
- If the shafts don't fit inside your pack, tie them securely to the outside. Consider taping a small loop of cord to the shaft that allows you to tie it in place.
- Note that the segment attachments (ferrules) are at risk of damage when exposed. Be intentional about where you carry the shafts and find a way to protect the ends.

- Some people place a rubber cap on the paddle shaft and use it as a walking stick. This application makes me nervous about damaging the shaft.
- Refer to *Chapter 10: Equipment Repair and Modification* for methods of replacing missing or broken paddle segments.

Chris Erickson carrying a one-piece paddle in the Alaska Range, Alaska.

CARRYING CARGO ON A PACKRAFT

Popular packraft cargo includes other passengers, pets, wild game, overnight camping gear, bikes, and skis. Loading cargo in and on your packraft dramatically affects maneuverability and recoverability; get familiar with how your boat handles and performs in a controlled setting before heading out to moving or remote water. I match the increased vulnerability of carrying cargo by reducing my exposure—choosing to float easier rivers.

Cargo best-practices:
- Attach cargo in a way that minimizes entrapment hazards.
- Practice maneuvering the loaded boat in a controlled setting.
- Determine if a wet re-entry is possible and, if not, make a plan for recovery.

DOUBLING UP WITH JOHN

In 2011, John Sykes and I decided to save weight by sharing my packraft during a 110-mile (180-km) traverse of the Alaska Range. Fresh out of college, John was a new adventure partner for me. Even though he was younger, John consistently did a better job of recognizing hazards and initiating risk assessment—great characteristics for a mountain partner! But in this case, due to having more packrafting experience, John deferred to me. Oops.

We went to a neighborhood lake to experiment with two-in-one boating configurations. We decided on the "beast with two backs" arrangement: sitting on the bow and stern, facing each other.

Our route started with a crossing of the broad Delta River. The beast with two backs approach turned out to be very unstable in moving water, and we nearly capsized. We had convinced our partners Todd Kasteler and Tyler Johnson to abandon their second boat, and they did capsize. Soaking wet, Tyler ran back to the car to grab his packraft so that he and Todd wouldn't have to double up again.

If John and I had practiced doubling up in moving water, we would have either found a better arrangement or concluded that doubling up was a bad idea. We finished the route in the more intimate "honeymoon" position: 6'4" John sitting in my lap (193 cm).

John Sykes and Luc Mehl. Delta River, Alaska. © Todd Kasteler

PRO TIP!

Don't attach deck bags to a packraft with non-locking carabiners or clips. Non-locking hardware poses a snagging and entanglement hazard.

Attaching Cargo to the Bow

Deck bag: Deck bags are low-volume waterproof bags that strap onto the packraft's bow or stern. Deck bags are excellent for storing items that you need access to during the day: food, water, clothing, maps, etc. Deck bags can also be used as an accessory pouch to boost the volume of your backpack while hiking.

Larger loads: If you can't store cargo inside the hull (cargo zipper), your best option is to strap it to the bow. Resist the temptation to load bags in the cockpit with you. In addition to possibly losing the bags during a swim, anything stored in the cockpit is an entrapment hazard.

If your packraft doesn't come with tie-down attachments, install your own. Four tie-downs are ideal, positioned along the bow's perimeter, to also be used for a perimeter line. Refer to the *Permanent Glue Repairs and Modifications* section in *Chapter 10: Equipment Repair and Modification*.

How to attach a backpack to the bow:

- Store relevant gear in dry bags; the pack will get wet.
- Reduce entrapment hazards by tightening all straps on the pack and tucking loose ends away. Pay special attention to loops; leave the hip belt unclipped.

■ Feed accessory straps or tie cord between tie-downs and through pack straps to secure the pack in place. Secure any loose tails to reduce entanglement hazards.

Having a load on the bow moves the center of gravity forward and upward. The packraft will be less stable and harder to maneuver; adjust your objectives accordingly. I feel comfortable in Class IV with weight in my tubes, but move that weight to the bow and I'm only comfortable in Class II water.

Practice swimming and wet re-entries in a controlled setting (refer to *Chapter 8: River Rescue from the Water*). In brief, it works best to use the pack to turn the boat right-side up. Grab the pack in both hands and twist it to turn the boat over.

PRO TIP!

When you have to make frequent transitions between hiking and paddling, attach your backpack to the bow with shoulder straps and hip belt facing outward and wearable. This system allows you to put on the pack with the packraft still attached. The packraft sticks out to the side or stands tall, but it works for frequent short portages.

Note that leaving the shoulder straps exposed is an entanglement hazard.

Sarah Histand. West Fork Yentna River, Alaska.

Cargo Zippers

Some packrafts come with a waterproof zipper on the hull (stern or side tube) that allows you to store equipment inside the boat. Other packrafts utilize a roll-top closure, which follows the same loading guidelines.

Advantages of storing cargo inside the boat:

- Cargo stays dry.
- Loading weight in the tubes lowers the boat's center of gravity, which makes it more stable.
- It is easier to see over an unloaded bow.
- Overturning a capsized packraft is easier than if the backpack is on the bow.
- Edging is easier with cargo in the tubes.

The disadvantage of zippers is the added cost and the possibility of slow leaks or total failures. Total failure is improbable, but dirt in the teeth can cause slow leaks and zipper damage. Cargo zippers require regular maintenance, especially if you are visiting silty rivers and camping on sand. Before working on your zipper, identify whether the problem is that the slider is hard to pull or if the zipper doesn't seal. A stiff zipper needs lubricant, a non-sealing zipper needs repair and cleaning. Carry a zipper cleaning and lubrication kit (refer to *Chapter 10: Equipment Repair and Modification*).

Cargo zipper best-practices:

- Be careful not to load dirty gear through the zipper.
- Rinse the zipper before you open and close it.
- Pull the zipper slide gently and in line with the zipper.
- Be careful not to overstretch the docking end of the zipper when loading cargo.
- Don't fold the zipper tightly when rolling your boat for packing or storage.
- Open the zipper and allow it to dry after every use.
- Store the packraft with the zipper closed.
- New packrafts have dry zippers. Lubricate the zipper before your first outing.

Load distribution: Distribute cargo by putting equal weight in each side, between your knee and hip positions. The packraft should sit flat in the water.

Have a friend look at the boat's profile to determine if the bow or stern sits deeper in the water. When the boat is not balanced in the water, tracking and speed both worsen.

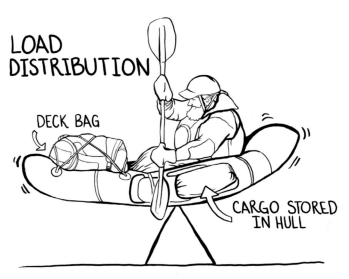

The cargo will shift, especially during portages, unless it is attached in place. Some boats include an attachment point that allows you to clip a dry-bag into position.

Attaching a Bike to a Packraft (Bikerafting)

The combination of biking and packrafting is alluring and has made some fantastic trips possible, but attaching a bike to a packraft increases your vulnerability and should be offset by adjusting exposure or paddling easier water. Practice paddling and capsizing on a lake and then mellow water before considering a long crossing or rapids.

Attach a bike to the packraft's bow with cord or straps. Ski straps ("Voile straps") work well due to their strength, slight stretch, and easy-to-secure buckles. Ski straps come in multiple lengths; you will want straps 16 to 20 inches long (40-50 cm). Straps that are too long can be double-wrapped; straps that are too short can be chained together. The mounting technique described below requires eight straps.

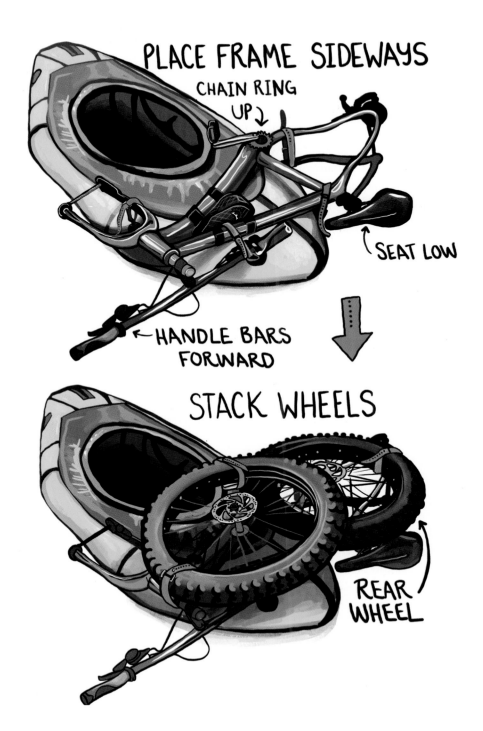

If your boat doesn't have four tie-downs on the bow, add them yourself (refer to *Chapter 10: Equipment Repair and Modification*).

Attaching a bike to a packraft:
1. Feed ski straps through each of the four attachment points.
2. If your bike has a dropper post, set the seat in the lowest position. Do anything else that will allow your bike to be a more compact package.
3. Remove the pedal from the non-drive side of the bike and store it somewhere secure.
4. Remove the front wheel and re-install the axle through the fork.
5. Optionally, remove the rear wheel.
6. Place the frame sideways on the bow with the chainring facing up and the seat and handlebars facing forward. This geometry places less fragile and pointed things at the bow, where the risk of damage or snagging is higher.
7. Start strapping the frame at the chainstays (back left tie-down from the boater's perspective) and work your way around to the fork (back right). Check that all four straps are tight and secure.
8. Stack the wheels on top of the frame. It works well to stack the rear wheel first, cassette face down, in a position that hides the sharp cassette teeth and doesn't involve any metal-to-metal contact on the frame.
9. Use a bungee cord, static cord, or more ski straps to secure the wheels to the frame.
10. Use any remaining straps or cord to make the attachment more secure.

Check that the bike weight balances laterally. If the boat leans left or right, adjust the wheels to re-center the load.

If you have a backpack (and no cargo zipper), flatten the pack before stacking and securing it on top of the bike—the higher and heavier the load is, the less stable. You might be able to deflate your seat and sit on the pack, but sitting tall is less stable than sitting low.

PRO TIP!
It might be impossible to re-enter a bikerafting load after capsizing. Some bike-rafters have found that they can climb on top of the overturned raft and gradually paddle to shore. Have a plan, a support crew, and remember to prioritize yourself.

Attaching Skis to a Packraft

It is a real treat to finish a ski mountaineering trip with a river float. However, our same primary concerns still apply: entrapment, limited boat control, and difficult to impossible recoveries from capsizing.

Across the bow: You can attach skis and poles across the bow with the standard four tie-downs. Use cord or ski straps to secure the skis in place. Find a way to keep the ski's sharp edges from contacting the packraft, such as wrapping them with willow, cord, and clothing.

On the side tubes: The bow attachment system is not ideal for any difficult or sustained paddling because the skis will interfere with paddle strokes. A better approach is to strap the skis and poles lengthwise along the sides. You will need a rear tie-down, which might require installing it yourself. Use ski straps to secure the tips and tails of the skis to the tie-downs. Wrap the skis to keep the sharp edges off the tubes.

A disadvantage of the lengthwise carrying system is that the bindings rest in a position that your hands strike. Try moving the skis forward or back to create a better paddling geometry, or pad the bindings with clothing.

Practice overturning your boat before needing to do it on your trip. Be especially careful not to pass an arm or leg through the tight spaces between the skis and the hull.

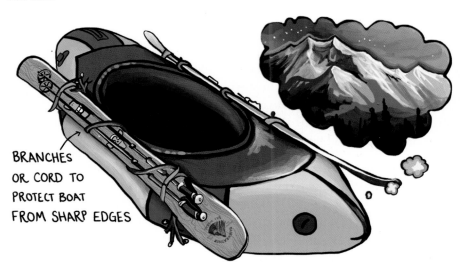

BRANCHES OR CORD TO PROTECT BOAT FROM SHARP EDGES

Carrying Meat and Other Heavy Loads

Carrying heavy loads (> 100 lbs, 45 kg) in a packraft is a risky endeavor. The additional weight works against the boat's buoyancy and brings the waterline closer to the top of the tubes, making your boat easier to swamp. The packraft will be slower and harder to maneuver. Give serious consideration to the type of water you are willing to paddle with a heavily loaded boat.

Heavy loads are generally unstable when secured to the bow and stern. Storing weight in the cockpit helps lower the boat's center of gravity, but sitting on top of the cargo raises the center of gravity. Your best bet is to pack the cargo in the cockpit in a way that allows you to sit as low as possible. You might need to dangle your feet over the sides. This geometry prevents you from proper paddle position and could be an entrapment hazard.

Walk the boat through any rough or turbulent water. If your boat's stability isn't apparent when you first get in, it will be after the first choppy water. Wade alongside the boat while holding onto the load in a way that allows you to keep the boat upright. Don't risk foot entrapment by wading with the boat in swiftwater; get out and portage.

Depending on the riverbank, you might be able to use a throw rope to line your packraft in the water while you walk the shore. But lining a packraft could easily result in flipping the boat and soaking or losing the load. Towing a packraft as a cargo trailer presents the same challenges. You can't steer the trailer and need to manage the rope around rocks, branches, and riverbends. These options are only feasible on the calmest of waters.

Yet another challenge is keeping meat dry and protected from impact. Here are some tips from a hunter friend:

- **Plastic bags:** Double-wrap the meat in heavy-duty plastic bags. Seal the bags securely. Carry spare bags to allow for multiple re-baggings.

- **Air the meat out when possible:** Unpack the meat and expose it to the air whenever possible, certainly overnight. Sealed bags promote bacterial growth and rot.

- **Flotation:** Place additional flotation on the packraft floor, such as a thick (3-inch, 8 cm) inflatable sleeping pad. The extra flotation serves multiple purposes, including keeping the meat elevated (out of water in the cockpit), adding buoyancy to counter the heavy load, and protecting the meat from hitting rocks on the river bottom.

PRINCIPLES OF ULTRALIGHT BACKPACKING

Whether you come to packrafting with backpacking experience or using a packraft motivates you to do more hiking, reducing your pack weight will help. You can shave weight by identifying what you don't need, sharing equipment between the group, and upgrading to lighter equipment. The concern with going too light is that you might be unprepared for surprises.

Advantages of carrying a light load:

- **Reduce wear and tear on your joints, especially the feet and knees:** When our bodies aren't suffering, we can enjoy hiking and tune in to our surroundings.

- **Cover ground more efficiently:** Efficiency might mean more miles per day or more time to fish and take photographs, depending on your objectives.

- **More willing to portage:** If your load is light, you will probably be more willing to portage.

In addition to these tangible advantages, I appreciate the simplicity of traveling with less stuff. It is refreshing and empowering to recognize that I only need a handful of items in the woods. Traveling light helps me to embrace the beauty of being outside.

EMBRACING THE BEAUTY OF BEING OUTSIDE

PACKRAFT
LIFE VEST
ELECTRIC BEAR FENCE
SPARE PADDLE
SPARE STOVE →
← HELMET
← BOW BAG
THROW BAG
18 DAYS OF FOOD
BEAR SPRAY
TENT
SLEEPING BAG
CLOTHES
DRY SUIT
FUEL
WATER FILTER
WATERCOLORS
BRUSHES
SKETCHBOOK

The Goldilocks Principle

Too much equipment can be a problem, but so can too little. Carrying too much equipment is inefficient and compels you to move slowly. Moving slowly requires you to carry more food and fuel, adding weight to your pack. You can escape this feedback loop by planning shorter trips, having resupply stations, or carrying less weight.

Too little equipment can be a safety concern. In the form of safety equipment, carrying more weight could have prevented several known packraft fatalities. Choosing appropriate safety equipment for remote trips is discussed below.

Finding Goldilocks' "just right" packing list takes trial and error. It is common to go too light one weekend, have a close call or uncomfortable night, and then overcompensate (too heavy) on the next trip until you hone in on "just right." The important part is that these lessons should be learned in environments with low consequences.

For reference, I aim to keep my base weight (camping gear and boating gear) to about 35 pounds (16 kg).

Safety Equipment: Should it Stay or Go?

There isn't any way around it: cutting weight by abandoning safety equipment increases your vulnerability and, therefore, your risk. We should always carry a full set of safety equipment, but some packrafters will choose to cut corners on remote trips to save weight. This is a sensitive subject for me since inadequate safety equipment was the primary factor in Rob Kehrer's drowning—the primary motivation for *The Packraft Handbook*. If you choose to cut safety equipment, it should be a calculated decision, based on river research and a discussion with your trip partners.

Hazard: The easiest way to reduce risk is to choose rivers with fewer hazards: low-hazard rivers are better options if you aren't carrying a complete safety kit. Of course, we can't control many environmental hazards, such as water level, so even an otherwise easy section of water might have surprises.

Exposure: You can reduce risk by limiting your exposure, e.g., portaging. If you are carrying a partial safety kit, you should be more willing to portage. We often commit to portaging rapids during the trip-planning phase, as part of the decision to carry less safety equipment. The hard part can be honoring the commitment to portage. If you get caught up in the moment and decide to run rapids with a poor safety net, you match high exposure with high vulnerability, a dangerous combination. If in doubt, portage! No other boat is as well-suited for portaging.

Vulnerability: Your vulnerability is determined in part by the equipment you choose to bring. Let's get specific:

- **Life vest:** Life vests are arguably the most important piece of safety equipment. Wear a life vest unless your outing is an excuse to go swimming. Type III life vests can be as light as 1 lb (0.5 kg), a minor weight penalty given the reduced vulnerability payoff. Inflatable life vests may be lighter but are not appropriate for whitewater. I easily justify a foam life vest for all of my outings and carry a heavier vest if the objective is to paddle whitewater.

- **Drysuit:** A drysuit can make the difference between life and death in cold water. If you will be in cold water or far from shore, you should wear a drysuit.

- **Throw rope, helmet, and rescue hardware:** These are the items most likely to get cut when saving weight. If you choose to venture without a full safety kit, make sure you have a clear understanding of your paddling objective and the consequences of swimming.

ROB KEHRER

Rob Kehrer drowned while participating in the Alaska Mountain Wilderness Classic. Everyone in the Classics—100 to 200 mile (160-320 km) unsupported wildland traverses—sacrifices comfort and safety to cover a lot of ground in a short amount of time. Like Rob, I decided to cut four pounds (2 kg) by not carrying a drysuit. We both portaged the Class IV rapids of the Tana River Canyon, but Rob capsized below the canyon and was separated from his boat.

I can't help imagining going back in time and making a decision that would have saved his life. He walked the rapids; he managed that exposure correctly. His mistake was choosing not to carry a drysuit, and it didn't help that sacrificing safety equipment was the norm in the Classic community. Carrying the extra four pounds of a drysuit would have made Rob less vulnerable and might have saved his life.

Rob Kehrer. Thompson Pass, Alaska.

ICELAND: TO SELF-SUPPORT OR NOT

I met British kayaker Dan Rea-Dickins when we were both visiting Zorba Laloo in Meghalaya, India. After a few days on the water, Dan proposed a 200-mile (320 km) ski and packraft crossing of Iceland. The idea was to travel unsupported, carrying all of our equipment from start to finish.

While researching the river, I realized that we would spend some time on Jökulsá á Fjöllum's big water Class IV rapids and would likely encounter hazards beyond my skill level. I recognized that I needed a full safety kit: helmet, rescue vest, and throw rope, and that I should not run the river with skis attached to my raft.

Carrying the requisite river safety gear over the glacier would be possible, but not fun. Knowing that the river would involve paddling or portaging Class IV big water, we changed our plans.

We were able to arrange a gear swap near where we skied down the Vatnajökul Glacier, thanks to the generosity of Dan's friends at Viking Rafting. They brought our packraft safety kits and took our skis and crevasse rescue equipment. We sacrificed "style points," an unsupported traverse, for "life points," making sound decisions based on risk assessment.

James Smith. Jökulsá á Fjöllum, Iceland.

The Weight, Durability, and Expense Triangle

There is a common expression regarding sporting equipment: "Weight, durability, expense. Choose two." In other words, you can buy something light and durable, but it won't be cheap. Or you can buy something light and cheap, but it won't be durable. It has worked well for me to upgrade an item or two for each big trip, paying more to have something that is both light and durable.

Needs Versus Wants

One way to help lighten your load is to separate your packing list into "need" and "want" piles. Your definition of needs and wants will probably change over time, but this approach can help you identify the gear to leave behind.

Multiple Uses and Sharing Equipment

One of the most effective ways to cut weight is to share equipment amongst your team. By sharing the stove, water filter, repair kit, etc., everyone saves weight. Identify group gear and split it between the group.

BROOKS RANGE REDUNDANCY

Roman Dial shares a story about a packrafting trip that failed in part because the party carried two of everything.

Roman flew in to help a father and son recover from a lost packraft deep in the heart of the Brooks Range. The duo was in the too-heavy category, and the son had never packrafted before committing to this remote river.

Hoisting the father's heavy [75 lb, 34 kg] pack to gauge how fast to walk the two, I asked the son, "What's in your dad's pack?"

"Tent, cooking gear, first aid kit, my dad's camping gear. Food."

"What'd you have?" I asked, surprised that the father had carried everything and wondering how the son could flip a nearly empty boat.

"Oh, the same stuff. Tent, cooking gear, first aid kit, and everything else, like the shotgun, some books, binoculars, more food. You know, camping gear."

"Why'd you duplicate everything?" I asked incredulously.

"Oh, in case we lost something. And it's a good thing we did duplicate because that's what happened!"

I went silent at that admission, having spent forty years working on just how to get my weight to be as light as possible: sharing among the group members was a key strategy. Their plan ran counter to all my experience.

THE BIG THREE: SHELTER, SLEEPING SYSTEM, PACK

The right camping gear for you is probably what you already own or can borrow. When you have the opportunity to upgrade your gear, consider prioritizing the "big three": shelter, sleeping system, and backpack.

My weight targets for summer trips in Alaska (32-75°F, 0-24°C) are:

- Shelter: 1 lb (0.5 kg) per person.
- Sleeping bag: Less than 2 lbs (1 kg) per person.
- Sleeping pad: R-value of 4 and weight of 0.75 lbs (0.35 kg).
- Backpack: 3 lbs (1.4 kg) or less.

Lighter options are available, but I've honed in on these weights to meet my weight/durability/expense target in Alaska.

Shelter

The lightest shelter option is no shelter. This works great until it starts raining, and you spend a restless night in your drysuit under the packraft.

Tarps: The next lightest option is a tarp shelter. Ultralight tarps pitched between trees, trekking poles, or paddle shafts can work well to keep you dry. Tarps can't withstand high winds and don't provide a barrier from mosquitos or other insects.

Mids: Pyramid-style shelters, "mids," are tarp shelters that form a full enclosure. Mids require a single pole in the center; a paddle or trekking poles work well. With proper setup, mids can withstand significant wind.

Drying out after the storm. Talkeetna Mountains, Alaska.

Mids are popular with the ultralight and packraft communities because the shelters are spacious and can be set up nearly anywhere. The open floor is appreciated when you are soaking wet and want to quickly get out of the rain. Mids are quite effective at trapping heat and can quickly change your cold and miserable experience to warm and comfortable. If the soil is saturated, you can use a deflated packraft as a moisture barrier.

The main disadvantage with mids, from my perspective in Alaska, is that they don't keep the mosquitos out unless you have a bug liner, which adds bulk and weight. I end up sleeping with a bug headnet.

Tents: Floored tents are heavier than tarps and mids because of the added material and poles. That said, tent design and materials continue to improve, and high-end, two-person tents are approaching the 2 lb (1 kg) mark. Tents provide better storm resistance and a warmer and drier barrier from the elements.

Sarah Histand. North River, Alaska.

As a general rule, the number of poles is proportional to the storm resistance of the tent. Two-pole tunnel tents do well when aligned directly into the wind but are not as stable as tents with three or more poles.

My shelter weight goal for summer camping is 1 lb (0.5 kg) per person. Tarps and mids fall below this mark; expedition tents are well above it.

ZIPLOCKS AND HUMAN FURNACES

I was still looking for partners with just a few days remaining before the start of the 2020 Wilderness Classic event. The Classics are hard on my body, and I wanted to find partners that were planning a comfortable pace. My previous partners said they planned to sleep six hours, which sounded great until I realized that they meant six hours total over the 160-mile (260 km, 4+ day) course. Next I checked in with Lee Helzer and Alan Rogers, who I hadn't traveled with but knew from previous Classics. Lee and Alan planned to sleep six hours a night, and welcomed me onto their team.

Several days into our crossing of the Talkeetna Mountains, we watched a storm roll across the mountains. We all recognized the bank of ominous clouds as guaranteed heavy rain. The wall of clouds was distinct and trackable, so we determined that we had time before it would start to rain. We did, but in that time, we walked out of good camping and into the brush.

When the sky ripped open, we had to grit our teeth and keep moving to find a place to camp. We waded across a creek and filled our water bottles. We each carried a single liter bottle, but needed more water to cook and rehydrate our bodies. Lee suggested that we dig out our empty plastic food bags and fill them with water to carry to camp. Most of the bags had small leaks, but we hoped to find a camp nearby. We climbed back into the alpine and hastily erected the mid at the first opportunity.

We were all cold and soaked to the skin despite our raingear. But our bodies heated the air in the mid within minutes, and we started peeling off wet layers. Alan fired up the stove and boiled the bagged water as we settled in for a cozy night.

Alan Rogers and Lee Helzer. Kosina Creek, Alaska.

Sleeping System

The lightest sleeping system is to sleep in warm clothes on top of your packraft. A set of synthetic puffy pants and jacket is sufficient in some climates.

Cowboy fire: A cowboy fire can help you get through the night where wood is available, and fires are permitted.

Sleeping with a cowboy fire:

1. Eat a high-calorie dinner.
2. Sleeping on a pile of branches or closed-cell foam pad makes a huge difference to reduce the heat that you lose to the ground. Air mattresses are not a good option because flying embers could pop the mat.
3. Collect enough wood to maintain a fire through the night.
4. Stack the wood within reach of the fire.
5. Doze until you get cold, then add wood to the fire.
6. If you get cold during the night, use a stove to quickly make a hot drink.

The more comfortable option is to carry a sleeping bag and pad. I easily justify the weight of a good sleeping system because I count on sleep to help my body recover from the day's exertion.

Sleeping bag: Sleeping bags are available with synthetic or down insulation. Synthetic bags insulate when wet and also dry more quickly. Down bags are lighter and more compressible. **My weight objective for a summer sleeping bag (in Alaska) is under two pounds (1 kg) per person.** Some packrafters will shave more weight by sleeping in insulated quilts or blankets.

You can boost your sleeping bag's insulation by wearing clothing in the bag, sharing bags, or sleeping with a hot-water bottle in an insulated koozie.

PRO TIP!

On cold nights, sleep with a one-liter bottle filled with boiling water. Wrap the bottle in clothing to extend the heat release through the night.

Sleeping pad: The other part of the sleeping system is the pad. A sleeping pad provides two services: thermal insulation from the ground, and comfort. Your pad options are closed-cell foam or inflatable. Foam pads are cheap and durable but not as comfortable, compact, or warm as inflatables. The disadvantages of inflatable pads are their expense and the need to prevent and manage punctures. Since I'm carrying a packraft repair kit, I'm confident that I can repair an inflatable sleeping pad as well. But I play defense, placing a packraft, pack, drysuit, or other equipment under my pad to protect it from rocky campsites.

The R-value, resistance to heat flow, of a 1 lb (0.5 kg) closed-cell foam pad is around 2. The R-value for an inflatable pad of similar weight can be as high as 7. **My summer sleeping pad target is an R-value of 4 and a weight of 0.75 lbs (0.35 kg).**

The extra cushion of inflatable pads is more welcome as I age, especially when I put in long days. I find that a comfortable sleeping system makes up for its weight by allowing me to hike more on recovered muscles.

Backpack

The most significant pack weight savings might come from the pack itself. I upgraded from a beloved Dana Designs Terraplane, eight pounds (3.6 kg), to a three-pound (1.4 kg) pack by Hyperlite Mountain Gear. **My target weight for a packrafting backpack is three pounds (1.4 kg).** I use a lighter pack on day trips and a heavier pack for ski expeditions.

Hiking on a rock-covered glacier. Eastern Alaska Range, Alaska.

You are probably best-off starting with the pack you've already got and checking with partners about the packs that work in your region. Useful features on a packrafting pack include:

- A hip belt for load distribution.
- Pack material that doesn't absorb water.
- A narrow or otherwise flexible backpack frame that allows the pack to be inserted through the cargo zipper, if relevant.
- External pockets or a lid for quick access to frequently needed items such as food and water.

Choosing a pack volume can be tricky. High-volume packs (greater than 70 liters, 4,400 cubic inches) allow you to store more of your bulky packraft equipment inside the pack. But with mid-volume packs, you can strap those items to the outside. The deciding factor between high or mid-volume packs is likely to be the duration of your trips—how much food and fuel you need to carry.

PRO TIP!

Carrying weight is most comfortable when it is loaded close to your spine and in the middle of your pack. I bury the clothing that I won't need on the bottom of my pack, then load heavy food and the packraft against my spine, using light and bulky gear to fill out the pack's outer portions. I place things I need to access at the top of the pack: clothing, rain gear, snacks, etc.

CONSUMABLES: FOOD, WATER, AND FUEL

Consumables are the items in your pack that get used up. Determining the right amount of food, water, and fuel to carry takes trial and error. Carrying too little can make you uncomfortable and low on energy. Carrying too much can be burdensome.

- **Food**: Food is fuel for the internal fire that keeps us warm and func-tional. Two pounds (1 kg) of food per person per day is a good target for adults.
- **Water**: A common guideline is to drink at least two liters of water per day, but this is inadequate for high exertion or hot environments.

Water weighs 2.2 lbs (1 kg) per liter, so water weight adds up quickly. Water treatment is discussed below.

- **Fuel**: No-cook meals relieve you from needing to carry a stove and fuel. Dehydrated meals are the next best option for minimal fuel consumption. I like having a stove as part of my safety net: we can quickly make a sugary hot drink after a cold swim.

Food

A useful rule of thumb for ultralight food weight is two pounds (1 kg) per person per day. Half of that weight is typically snack foods to eat throughout the day and a quarter for each of breakfast and dinner. Smaller hikers can get away with less food; larger and young hikers might need more. Not all foods are created equal regarding energy, so a useful metric is to aim for four calories per gram or more. Two pounds (1 kg) per day of 4 cal/g food makes for an approximately 4,000 calorie daily diet.

As you spend more time outside, you will understand what your body needs and when. For example, it is common to need less food at the start of a trip (when you are still burning town-food and body fat) and more food at the end (no reserves). I might only eat 1.5 lbs/day (0.7 kg) initially and save the remainder to boost my meals at the end of the trip. You might also anticipate needing less food on boating days (low exertion) and more on walking days (high exertion). Or, you might crave salty foods on hot days and sugars on cold days. Learning how our bodies work is part of what I love about long trips.

Food-as-fire: My Wilderness First Responder instructor Deb Ajango presented foods as fuels for an internal fire. Food is the fuel source for our bodies, like wood is the fuel source for a fire.

Fuels for the human fire:

- **Fast-burning fuel:** Tinder; simple sugars, such as candy and dried fruit.
- **Moderate-burning fuel:** Small logs; complex carbohydrates, like chips, crackers, cookies, ramen, and pasta.
- **Slow-burning fuel:** Large logs; fats, including butter, cheese, meat, and nuts.

I like the food-as-fire mindset because it helps me determine what I need to eat during the day. If I'm cold or notice someone else shivering, fast-burning foods will be most effective at heating our bodies. If I'm comfortable and not particularly hungry, slow-burning foods are a better option. Slow-burning foods before bed help keep me warm through the night.

Trail mix can contain all of these fuels, which explains why it is such a popular staple for backpacking. My other go-to food choices include ramen (cheap, high-calorie, and can be eaten cooked or dry), dried meats, and cookies.

Dinners: Dinners should include as many slow-burning fuels as possible, and I'll often supplement dinner with butter, coconut oil, or cheese powder. Dehydrated meals are effective for me, though I need at least two official servings per meal. We generally don't bring meals that require active cooking unless downtime and socializing are trip goals. The easiest way to reduce fuel weight is to need less fuel, and the easiest way to need less fuel is to bring meals that don't need to be cooked. Pizza, sandwiches, and burritos work well for me.

Sarah Histand, Ben Histand, and Diana Johnson. Alatna River, Alaska.

Water

If food is fuel, water is the lubricant that keeps our bodies running.

I prefer to save weight by carrying little to no water whenever possible. This is generally an appropriate habit in Alaska, where there are abundant water sources. When we do find water, we treat it to prevent waterborne illnesses (see *Chapter 11: Medical Emergencies*).

Drinking water can be treated by many methods:

- **Boiling:** Boiling is the safest option but requires time and fuel.

- **Mechanical water filters:** Mechanical pumps feel bulky by today's standards, but they are tried and true. In-line squeeze options are fast and less bulky. Mechanical filters get clogged with time, and the in-line options are particularly sensitive to silt.

- **Chemical treatment:** Iodine or chlorine treatment is effective against giardia but not the other major threat, cryptosporidium. Chlorine dioxide (AquaMira) has a low to moderate effectiveness against cryptosporidium. I carry iodine and use it when I don't want to risk clogging a mechanical filter. Most chemical treatment leaves an aftertaste.

- **UV filters:** UV filters such as Steripens provide for rapid filtering but require batteries and clear water.

All filter methods benefit from removing silt from the water. You can pre-filter muddy and glacial water through fabric (cheesecloth or a bandana). Silt can also settle out, either by leaving water to sit overnight or collecting water from stranded pools.

JOHN'S SIP 'N GO

Deep in the Alaska Range, John Sykes let us know that his knee was acting up, and he had serious concerns about continuing. The weather had been poor, and we were moving quickly to stay warm. We had not done a good job of staying hydrated, and it seemed reasonable that dehydration was part of the problem.

We took a break and drank as much water as possible. When we started moving again, John coined a "Sip 'n Go" technique of filling his cup at every available water source and sipping the water as he walked. I am convinced that rehydrating lubricated John's knee, and he didn't have any other issues, even with another 100 miles (160 km) of travel.

Cooking and Fuel

I appreciate the reliability and power of a canister or liquid gas stove and have never experimented with lighter options, such as alcohol. I enjoy campfires, but having a reliable heat source that I can use from the shelter is part of my safety net. I know that hot water bottles wrapped in a foam koozie or clothing can get me through the night, and I like having enough fuel to help me through an emergency.

Canister stoves: Canister stoves are lightweight and easy to use. Fuel is readily available in most regions, but not all, and the empty canisters can be difficult to recycle. For maximum efficiency, canister stove systems (JetBoil, MSR Reactor, etc.) include an integrated pot and lid. These integrated systems allow you to boil more water with the same amount of fuel or, equivalently, to carry less fuel. Some models allow you to invert the canister, which is more efficient at cold temperatures (subzero). **We use canister stove systems on our summer trips and carry 0.5 oz of fuel per person per day.** This is enough fuel for boiling water in the morning and evening, but not enough for more involved cooking.

Liquid fuel stoves: Liquid fuel stoves are heavier than canister stoves but better options at altitude, cold temperatures, and long trips, since you don't have to carry empty fuel canisters. Priming and igniting liquid gas stoves can take some getting used to, but these stoves are reliable and durable. The MSR Whisperlite and equivalents are justifiably popular options. **We typically have fuel left over if we carry 1 oz per person per day.**

PRO TIP!

Consider carrying both types of stoves if you will be flying or traveling internationally.

Sarah and I missed a flight to Kotzebue (Northwest Alaska) one summer because I forgot to declare a handgun (for protection from bears) in my luggage. After airport security released me and I rebooked my flight, my new status on the security watchlist resulted in a thorough screening of my luggage. In Kotzebue, I discovered that my (empty) liquid fuel bottles and fuel pump had been confiscated. We were very fortunate to have packed a canister stove "just in case," and were able to purchase fuel canisters at the grocery store.

Sidenote: The guy next to me at airport security was busted for hiding marijuana at the bottom of a jar of peanut butter. Pro tip! Drug-sniffing dogs love peanut butter!

OTHER PRIORITY EQUIPMENT

My priority equipment consists of supplies that will keep me safe when things go wrong. These items will vary depending on location, experience, and objectives.

General priority equipment:

- **Firestarter:** Lighter and/or matches
- **First aid kit:** See *Chapter 11: Medical Emergencies.*
- **Satellite communication device:** See *Chapter 1: Packrafting Equipment.*
- **Navigation:** See *Chapter 13: Research and Trip Planning* for information on digital navigation.
- **Puffy layers:** Hooded jackets and pants with synthetic insulation are light, warm, and quick to dry.
- **Ski straps and accessory straps:** I have found myriad uses for these straps to attach and repair equipment.

Camping in bear country requires additional attention and equipment:

- **Bear deterrent:** Bear spray is statistically more effective than firearms. Some life vests have a pocket large enough to hold bear spray. Otherwise, a deck bag is a good storage location. If you do carry a firearm, be sure to train with it beforehand.
- **Store food in an approved container away from camp:** We prefer carrying Kevlar Ursacks instead of hard-sided bear canisters.
- **Don't surprise bears:** Make an extra effort to announce your presence in areas with limited visibility (brush) or hearing (near running water). Travel in the open when possible and make noise with your voice, bells, or whistles. This is one of the few times I don't follow a Leave No Trace guideline. Specifically, "Let nature's sounds prevail."
- **Travel in a group:** It's rare for groups of two or more to experience a bear mauling incident.

CONSERVATION AND STEWARDSHIP

Most of us are drawn to packrafting because it enables us to visit pristine lands with clean air and water. Adopting the seven Leave No Trace principles helps everyone enjoy pristine wildlands.

Leave No Trace Principles for river corridors:

- **Plan ahead and prepare**: Learn about river-specific issues. Create a trip plan, check for permitting needs, and respect private property.

- **Travel and camp on durable surfaces**: Keeping track of equipment, and keeping it clean, is easiest on a surface of small pebbles. We prefer not to camp on sand because it gets on all of our gear and zippers. Avoid camping at tributaries because animals converge in those spaces and can be disrupted by your presence. Move camp frequently and replace any dislodged rocks.

- **Dispose of waste properly**: Leave excess packaging at home and don't burn plastic or foil. Bury human waste 150 ft (45 m) from the water in a small pit. Leave plants intact and try to displace the soil in one unit. Pack out or burn toilet paper. Liquid waste can be dumped directly into the main current of rivers over 500 cfs (14 cumecs). Scatter liquid waste 200 feet (60 m) from smaller waterways.

- **Leave what you find**: This includes invasive species you might have "found" on your previous trip . . . clean your equipment between trips.

- **Minimize campfire impacts**: Avoid using fires if possible. If you do build fires, do it on sand, gravel, or in a pan so that you can wash the ashes into the current. Don't build fire rings or dig pits.

- **Respect wildlife**: In Alaska, we like to camp in open areas to be less likely to surprise bears or other animals. People using bear bags would want to camp close to tall trees or store the food bags an appropriate distance from camp, but still in sight.

- **Be considerate of other visitors.**

Conservation: In addition to practicing the Leave No Trace principles on your trips, consider getting more active with conservation efforts. Most regions have active conservation organizations that need volunteers or donations. Donating to environmental law firms is increasingly relevant, as more and more conservation work is happening in the courts. Some of the big players in river conservation work in the United States are American Whitewater, American Rivers, Backcountry Hunters and Anglers, Trout Unlimited, and Earthjustice. If Alaska takes up as much space in your heart as it does mine, consider donating to the Trustees for Alaska to assist in their conservation efforts.

Inclusion: Everyone would benefit from seeing what we get to see, but not everyone can do so. Consider supporting local efforts that help under-represented populations access the outdoors.

Indigenous people and lands: The United States and other countries were initially populated by Indigenous peoples who often had little or no say about the taking of their homelands. Packrafters can begin to correct for past injustices by being respectful when we packraft on Indigenous lands. This book was inspired by a lifetime living and playing in the traditional homelands of the Dënéndeh and Dena'ina.

Grizzly bear family. Fairweather Range, Alaska.

Sarah Heck checking the map. Aniakchak Crater, Alaska.

CHAPTER 13

RESEARCH AND TRIP PLANNING

One of the Leave No Trace guidelines is to plan ahead and prepare so that you can visit natural places safely and respectfully. Preparedness allows me to enjoy the trip more, seek ambitious objectives, and recover from the inevitable setbacks. Many destinations are described in guide books and online forums, but secluded destinations will require additional research effort. For me, that effort takes place online, using digital mapping and imagery resources.

WHAT YOU NEED TO KNOW

Research and trip planning involves:

- **Research:** Research your destination. Try to understand the river characteristic, appropriate flow levels, seasonal variation, and storm response. Determine if an open-water crossing is likely to have strong currents, tides, or wind. Get a weather forecast before and during your trip.
- **Vulnerability and objectives:** Recognize that remote travel increases your vulnerability, and consider downgrading your technical objectives accordingly.
- **Planning:** Make a plan and leave it with an in-town contact. Include the details that will help them coordinate a search effort if you are overdue.
- **Digital mapping:** You don't need to embrace digital mapping resources (GPS, Google Earth, etc.), but going digital can improve your safety buffer and creates new opportunities.

CHOOSING WHERE TO MAKE MISTAKES

Pushing beyond your comfort level can be healthy—we learn from mistakes. Know when it is okay to make mistakes and how to reduce your vulnerability by building a metaphorical safety net. Mentors are precious in this process. If you don't have access to a mentor, consider a guide. A good instructor or guide can help determine appropriate challenges in safe settings.

Develop boat control skills in a controlled setting before applying them to a remote river. Learning from mistakes is easier when you are close to safety, with capable partners, on familiar rivers, and carrying full safety kits. Making mistakes, even minor ones, on a remote trip could be serious.

PACKRAFTING IN REMOTE PLACES

The American Packrafting Association has published these guidelines in response to a rapid increase in close calls and packraft rescues in remote settings.

Before You Go: Spend the time required to become proficient in packrafting and wilderness travel before setting out for remote regions. The margin of error in packrafting is small; remoteness and changeability of conditions reduce that margin even further. Before setting out on a packrafting adventure in a remote area, you should:

- *Seek out mentors, instructional courses, and swiftwater rescue training. Also, keep in mind a course certificate is no substitute for hard-won experience.*
- *Be properly equipped and familiar with necessary safety equipment, especially personal flotation devices, thermal protection, footwear, and repair kits.*
- *Hire a guide, or travel with people who are already experienced with the region.*
- *Complete shorter, more accessible packrafting routes before attempting longer trips.*

Another piece of advice from remote travel experts is to be self-sufficient and prepared for the worst. Can you hike out to the road system without a phone or GPS? A satellite phone is not a rescue plan; you can't count on being rescued from a remote river.

Finally, as pockets of wildlands become increasingly rare, it is important to visit respectfully. Acquire legal permitting for access and respect local cultures. I appreciate the Leave No Trace principles presented in the previous chapter. In brief, do everything in your effort to limit the impact of your passage.

Josh Mumm, John Sykes, and Luc Mehl. Yukon, Canada. © Joshua Foreman

CREATING A TRIP PLAN

Start every trip with a trip plan. The trip plan should be a document that you leave with reliable help at home. This documentation can be hugely helpful to your in-town contacts if they are called upon to help with a search. The trip plan also helps to ensure that everyone has the same expectations.

A trip plan should be a shareable document that includes:

- **Itinerary**: Put-in, take-out, anticipated days on the water, hiking, etc.
- **Contact information:** Contact information for trip members and family.
- **Rescue assets:** Contact information for rescue assets, such as flight operators and the State Troopers.
- **Equipment:** A list of your key equipment and a description of the larger items that might be spotted from the air (packrafts, tent, etc.).
- **First aid:** Information about allergies, medications, and what you are carrying in your first aid kit.
- **Due date:** A due date or date at which to start planning an overdue search.

382 THE PACKRAFT HANDBOOK

In-town contact: Find a friend capable of coordinating help who is willing to serve as an in-town contact. Experienced trip partners often make better contacts than parents or spouses. In the case of an emergency, the in-town contact manages communication until rescue professionals take over. You might also send messages to friends and family, but the in-town contact has a copy of the itinerary, knows the plan, knows when to get worried, and knows how to coordinate help.

Pace: Knowing how long you will be on your outing helps you decide what gear to bring and when your in-town contact should start to worry. Separate your trip into convenient segments and assign expected travel time for each segment, for example, miles (km) per day hiking versus boating.

I use the digital mapping tools below to trace river distances and then make my best guess at pace. My pace estimates are based on previous trips recorded in my river diary. As I collect more trip data, my predictions get more accurate. As a starting point, I might expect to travel at five mph (8 km/hr) on braided rivers, three mph (5 km/hr) through meandering sections, and ten to twelve miles per day (16-20 km) hiking off-trail in Alaska.

Adding rest days to your itinerary allows you to limit your exposure by not paddling in unsafe conditions.

> ## *PRO TIP!*
> You can collect pace data by recording your moving speed with a phone application while walking, running, or biking. Take note of how quickly the trail slides by during these activities. In the water, paddle close to the river bank and then watch how quickly the bank moves past. With practice, you can develop a sense of the water's speed compared to your familiar activities.

WATER RESEARCH

The more you know about your destination, the better you can prepare. Not having to stress about conditions during your trip allows you to more fully enjoy your surroundings. A great asset in developing a feel for different river conditions is to keep a river diary, as outlined at the end of *Chapter 4: How Rivers Work.*

The key components of water research are:

- **Open-water crossings**: In addition to knowing the length of the crossing, collect information about tides, currents, wind patterns, and other vessel traffic.

- **River characteristic:** Is the nature of the river appropriate in terms of character, gradient, and expected water level, given the group's experience?

- **Timing:** When is the right time to go? Which water levels or crossing conditions are fitting?

- **Response to rain:** How does the area respond to rain?

- **Weather:** Track the weather forecast and precipitation history before and after your trip to anticipate changing water levels and wind.

Use guidebooks, online and digital mapping resources, and local knowledge to research your paddling objective. The internet is an excellent resource for finding information about most rivers and canoe systems. Blogs, trip reports, social media, forums, and websites such as American Whitewater (United States) provide a wealth of information. Park rangers and local pilots are likely to know about your area of interest, though it can be hard to translate from their vantage to what we see on the ground.

When traveling across state or country borders, research the rules and regulations for watercraft. Many countries require boats to pass through customs and biosecurity scans. Refer to *Chapter 1: Packrafting Equipment* for instructions on cleaning contaminants off your boat.

River Character, Discharge, and Gradient
River character: Determine, broadly, the character of the river: braided, meandering, or bedrock. Does the valley ever pinch? Are there canyon sections?

When there aren't people to ask, the best way to determine the river character is to study maps, satellite imagery, and aerial imagery. Google Earth and Esri satellite imagery are free, easy to access, and enormously valuable. Both Google Earth and Esri (Esri Wayback) provide access to historical imagery that allows you to study multiple paddling seasons. These digital resources are discussed in more detail later in this chapter.

Discharge: Discharge is most meaningful when compared to familiar rivers. The actual discharge or water level on a nearby river is often not as helpful as the trend (rising or dropping). If the destination doesn't have a published river gauge, the next best option is a qualitative sense of discharge from paddlers in the area, a nearby gauge, maps, or satellite imagery. Use the map interface of gauge providers (USGS and NOAA in the United States) to search for gauged rivers near your destination. The most helpful gauges will be on rivers with similar catchment areas. If there are no gauges in the area, maps and high-resolution imagery can at least give you a sense of low, moderate, or high discharge levels based on the catchment area and width of the channel.

Recall from *Chapter 4: How Rivers Work* that discharge can fluctuate daily, seasonally, and show varied responses to storms. Understanding regional weather patterns, vegetation, geology, and topography will help you determine when to visit a river, as discussed in the next section. It can help to determine both the seasonal trends and the response to precipitation. Knowing how the river responds to rain can help you choose where to camp and when to stay off the water.

MOVING CAMP ON THE FIRTH RIVER

After decades of experience as a river guide based out of Fairbanks, Alaska, John Schauer was still caught off-guard by how quickly the Firth River rose:

An already high Firth came up probably 15 feet (5 m) in the canyon at Sheep Creek in a matter of hours in 2016. Unfortunately, the gauge was off-line when I checked it after returning, but [the nearby] Kongakut and Hulahula [rivers] showed huge spikes from about 2000 cfs [57 cumecs] to 14000 cfs [400 cumecs] around the same time.

We pulled off the river at the Sheep Creek confluence for lunch and discovered a hole in the raft from hitting a wall in Ram rapid. We decided to set up camp right there on the gravel bar to repair the boat but then had to move three times until we were way up in the boreal forest. We camped in the trees for three days until the water came down to about the level it was at when we arrived.

-John Schauer

Gradient: As with discharge, a sense of gradient based on your local rivers will help you assess remote rivers. If the measured gradient on a remote river is less than what you've been paddling, the remote river might be an appropriate destination. This general sense for river character is often more useful than trying to correlate gradient to river difficulty: the same gradient can have a wide range in difficulty depending on discharge and geologic setting, as shown in the figure below.

Guidebooks and online resources provide some gradients, or you can measure it yourself. You can determine a river's gradient by measuring the distance between contours on a topo map, but I prefer using Google Earth. In addition to the gradient, try to determine if the river is continuous or pool-drop in nature.

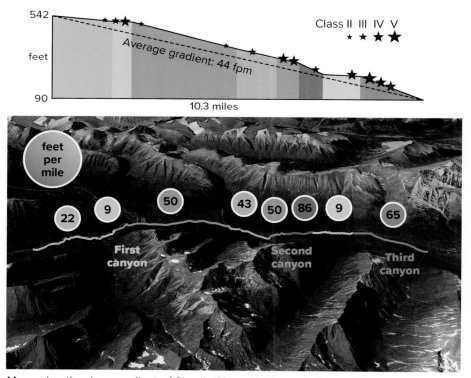

Measuring the river gradient of Sixmile River, Alaska, with Google Earth. Top: Average gradient (change in elevation divided by river length) compared with gradient along segments. Note that there isn't a consistent relationship between gradient and rapid difficulty. Bottom: Google Earth screen capture featuring river segments color coded from low (yellow) to high (red) gradients. Map data: Google, ©2021 CNES / Airbus, Maxar Technologies. See Appendix for full citation.

386 THE PACKRAFT HANDBOOK

Measuring river gradient with Google Earth:

1. Create a table with columns for river segment identifier, segment length, start elevation, end elevation, drop in elevation, and gradient.
2. Determine your segment interval. You might choose to calculate the gradient for each mile, every 10 miles, or most likely, as governed by natural transitions, such as the start and end of canyons, campsites, or other landmarks.
3. Select the *Path* tool and trace the river from start to end, creating a separate path for each segment. Use the *Measurements* tab in the *New Path* window to view and record the length of each river segment.
4. Zoom in and use the mouse to hover over the start and end point of each segment. Read the elevation value ("elev") from the bottom of the screen. Record the start and end point elevation values in your table.
5. Calculate the change in elevation for each segment and divide the change by the segment's length. Record this value in the gradient column.

Segment ID	Length (mile)	Start elev. (ft)	End elev. (ft)	Drop (ft)	Gradient (fpm)
put-in to first canyon	1.7	542	504	38	22
first canyon	0.55	504	499	5	9
first to elbows	2.93	499	352	147	50
elbows to second	1.18	352	301	51	43
second canyon	0.48	301	277	24	50
second to surf wave	0.71	277	216	61	86
surf wave to third	0.99	216	207	9	9
third canyon	1.79	207	90	117	65
entire run	**10.33**	**542**	**90**	**452**	**44**

Calculating the gradient for multiple segments might be overkill for your application. For a quick and easy exploration of the gradient, zoom to the area of interest and use the steps above to calculate a single segment's gradient.

Regional Water Level Trends

Understanding regional water level trends can help you choose when to start your trip. For example, if you want to paddle Class III water in freshwater basins (no glaciers), aim for high water levels in late spring. If you want to paddle clear Class II water in glacial basins, go in the autumn.

Temperate climates (freshwater basins): Water levels in freshwater basins mostly respond to rain, unless snow is also a significant source, in which case seasonal and daily fluxes of snowmelt are likely.

Water level trends when rain is the dominant water source:

- Water levels at high elevations typically show more rapid rising and lowering in response to rain, as water is quickly funneled into drainages.
- If the soil is wet, precipitation will more quickly end up in the river. If the soil is dry, heavy rain might run off quickly, but slow precipitation will saturate the soil first. If one storm saturates the soil, a close second storm of the same magnitude will raise the water more than the first.
- Large and dry drainages might be boatable for several days after a rain event and then return to pre-storm levels.

Josh Mumm and John Sykes getting soaked. Russell Fjord, Alaska.

Water level trends when snowmelt is significant:

- The water level response to rain behavior (above) still applies.
- High snow years result in high water and a longer boating season.
- Low snow years result in an early and short season.
- Rain on snow leads to rapid melting and high water.
- High temperatures can increase the water level while you are on the river.
- The timing of daily snowmelt pulses depends on your distance from the snow source. At high elevations, levels will rise in the afternoon and peak in the evening. At low elevations, the snowmelt pulse might not arrive until early morning.

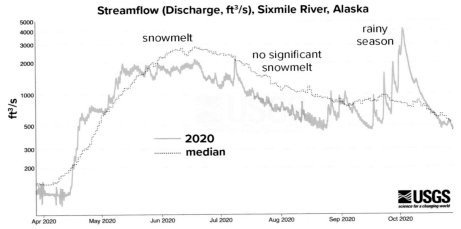

Annual discharge curves for Sixmile River, Alaska, a dominantly freshwater basin with significant snowmelt. An early-summer peak flow due to snow melt is followed by dropping water levels. 2020 featured a series of October rain events that progressively saturated the soil. Data available at https://waterdata.usgs.gov. See Appendix.

Arctic climates (glacial basins): Arctic and sub-arctic climates also feature high spring water levels due to snowmelt. If the catchment area is glacial, there can be a second peak in late July or early August (northern hemisphere) due to glacial melt during the summer's hottest days.

Water levels in glacial systems also fluctuate daily. Melt pulses originate at the glacier during the hottest hours of the day and take time to reach lower elevations. Particularly hot periods can add significant water volume to the rivers. The time for the high water pulse to reach your location downriver depends on distance and gradient but should be reasonably consistent from day to day (see the timing of daily snowmelt pulses in the previous list).

PRO TIP!

Basins with significant glacial melt or snowmelt can exhibit significant daily fluctuation. If you are confronted with a challenging water crossing or intimidating water level, set up camp and wait for the water to drop. Use a stick or rock to monitor the river stage.

Tropic and subtropic zones: The vegetation in tropical rainforests can consume a significant amount of water, resulting in lower water levels during the peak growing months. However, the soils in tropical rainforests generally have low storage capacity, so a large rain event can lead to flash flooding.

Do your homework before traveling to a destination with a monsoon season. Monsoons are seasonal events with high precipitation rates and frequent flooding.

Todd Tumolo in the tropical Barranca Grande section of Rio Antigua, Mexico.

Arid zones: Rain is uncommon in arid regions, and when it does fall, it can cause flash flooding. The soil in arid regions is generally poorly absorbent, which leads to surface flow. Hiking and boating in areas with channelized surface flow can be very dangerous.

Sarah Histand and Will Koeppen in a cold semi-arid climate zone. Coastal Plain, Alaska.

Dam-release drainages: Healthy ecological systems need continuous water flow at a range of levels. Most dams feature a baseline discharge and then additional discharge in dam-release events. Some rivers don't have enough water to float until additional water is released. In the United States, refer to American Whitewater for a list of dammed rivers and release information.

Dam-release is generally for power generation, water management, or recreational use. Many dam releases are scheduled, and their volume and timing are likely to change throughout the season. Power-generating dams may show daily water level fluctuation, similar to glacial basins or snowmelt, due to the released volume matching power demand throughout the day.

USING PACKRAFTS TO DAMN DAMS

Packrafts have a long history with dams. Dick Griffith's 1952 packrafting mission to Mexico was primarily motivated to experience Barranca Del Cobre before it was dammed. Early packrafting in Tasmania helped draw awareness to controversial damming projects, and the American Packrafting Association and American Whitewater currently use packrafts to explore threatened streams.

Weather

Most people prefer to paddle on sunny days, but in terms of river research, the weather we are most interested in is precipitation history and forecast. Precipitation forecasts and online rain gauges can help you determine if water levels are likely to rise. Refer to the storm response discussion in *Chapter 4: How Rivers Work.*

At the time of writing, www.windy.com is my go-to source for weather forecasts. Windy.com allows you to drop a virtual sensor at any location and view a 10-day forecast, including precipitation and cloud cover. Windy also includes an intuitive comparison of multiple models, which allows you to evaluate model agreement.

Your best bet for precipitation forecasts during the trip is to message your in-town contact or use a built-in weather service on a two-way satellite communication device.

DIGITAL MAPPING AND IMAGERY

Digital mapping and imagery provide the ability to plan creative journeys and be better prepared when you arrive. Digital mapping can incorporate a wealth of online geographic resources. At the time of writing, the big players in digital mapping are Google Earth, Esri, CalTopo, and Gaia GPS (or similar). All of these applications are either free or inexpensive. Visit www.thingstolucat.com for tutorials about these resources. Paper and compass skills are still important, and it would be a mistake to depend on digital equipment, especially in a wet environment.

The key benefits of digital tools include:

- Learning about current or recent conditions at the destination using historical and near-real-time imagery.
- Constructing a detailed trip plan that includes contingencies, side hikes, points of interest, expected pace, etc. Leaving this plan with your in-town contact reduces your vulnerability.
- Easy active navigation with GPS and smartphone applications.

Imagery

Satellite imagery includes historical high-resolution images on cloud-free days and recent, but lower resolution, imagery that can help determine current conditions.

Historical satellite imagery: The resolution of historic cloud-free imagery continues to improve. High-resolution imagery (0.5 m) allows you to identify constrictions, individual rapids, and other areas of interest. Google Earth is the 3D powerhouse for this kind of exploration. Esri imagery is often higher resolution than Google Earth's and can be explored in Esri applications, www.bing.com's map search, and even imported into Google Earth.

In addition to making imagery explorable, applications like Google Earth allow you to create files with waypoints and paths. These files can be emailed to partners, your in-town contact, search and rescue professionals, and uploaded to your phone or GPS unit.

I use Google Earth to sketch my intended route, as well as bail-out options and waypoints for trailheads, rapids, portages, cabins, side hikes, and other points of interest. Topographic maps at local and regional scales can be downloaded (via USGS or international equivalents), viewed in Google Earth, and printed. You can also visualize other geographic resource layers, such as land ownership and active wildfires.

Rapids in the second canyon of Sixmile River, Alaska, as featured in the ESRI World Imagery baselayer. Copyright © Esri. See Appendix for full citation.

Near-real-time imagery: Near-real-time satellite imagery doesn't have the resolution required for route planning but is useful to determine current conditions. These resources are particularly valuable for determining how much snow is in a basin, especially in spring or autumn. I use near-real-time imagery to estimate the elevation of the snowline, whether a river will have snow on the banks, if the vegetation has already leafed out in the spring, etc.

The best public (free) sources for near-real-time imagery are:

- MODIS (captured twice per day, 250 m resolution)
- Landsat (captured approximately twice per week, 30 m resolution)
- Sentinel 2-L2A (captured about four times per week, 10 m resolution)

I access this imagery with the NASA EOSDIS Worldview and Sentinel Hub websites (see Appendix). There are several private (subscription) vendors that offer higher resolution imagery. These applications are likely to become more accessible and affordable with time.

Route Planning

There are several online route planning applications and likely to be more soon. These are the applications I find most useful.

Gaia GPS: At the time of writing, and in my opinion, Gaia GPS is the most mature iPhone navigation app. Smartphones have GPS chips that do not use cellular or wireless data. In other words, your phone works as a GPS regardless of cell or WiFi connections.

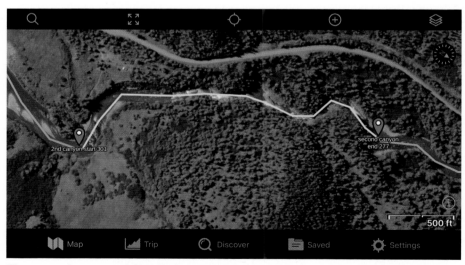

The second canyon of Sixmile River, Alaska, as viewed in the Gaia GPS smartphone application. Imagery © Esri. See Appendix.

With Gaia GPS, you can view your position or track your progress as viewed on downloaded topographic maps or satellite imagery. Routes created in Google Earth, CalTopo, or www.gaiagps.com can be imported to Gaia GPS and viewed on smartphones.

CalTopo: CalTopo is designed for the search and rescue community and offers excellent 2D mapping and route-drawing tools. CalTopo's strength is the ability to overlay topographic maps on satellite imagery and other layers of interest. Draw routes, mark waypoints, export a trip plan, and print maps.

PRO TIP!

The sharing of geotagged locations and GPS tracks is contentious within the outdoor recreation community. Sharing promotes access to the outdoors, but can also place pressure on fragile ecosystems. The guidance from the Leave No Trace Center for Outdoor Ethics is to put thought into what you choose to share, and use sharing to promote stewardship, education, safety, and legal access.

Navigation

Electronic navigation aids such as GPS units and smartphone apps enable on-the-fly navigation. Paper map and compass skills will become important if your electronic devices fail during the trip.

Handheld GPS units: Routes generated in Google Earth or other applications and saved as .kmz or .gpx files can be uploaded to GPS units. GPS brands have struggled to maintain their market in the age of smartphones, but they still offer some significant advantages: durability, battery life, and weather-resistance. Some GPS units also include built-in SOS and two-way satellite text messaging capabilities.

Smartphones: Navigating rivers is refreshingly simple: water flows downhill. But, if you've tagged rapids, points of interest, or are making an open-water crossing, you will want your phone or GPS handy. I've experienced countless instances when using my phone as a GPS helped us navigate low visibility or otherwise complicated conditions. The disadvantage of using smartphones for navigation is that they don't play well with water. If using a smartphone, keep it warm and carry it in a waterproof case inside your drysuit.

Diana Johnson in low-visibility conditions. Brooks Range, Alaska.

Rob Kehrer. Marshall Pass, Alaska.

TAKE-OUT

The years surrounding Rob Kehrer's drowning featured my own close call in an avalanche, the suicide of a paddling mentor, and the death of a former girlfriend, Amy, in an avalanche. The message couldn't be clearer: I needed to dial back my risk tolerance.

After Amy's death, I made stickers that read: "Start and end at home." I have the sticker on my paddle and skis, where I frequently see it. I appreciate this reminder that the ultimate goal is to return home safely. Training and preparation combined with capable partners and humility help us to start and end at home.

Join us in promoting the packrafting Culture of Safety. Together we can build a community that is fun, safe, and caring.

APPENDIX: SUPPLEMENTARY RESOURCES

In-person Training

In times of stress, our bodies don't want to do new things. Practicing paddle and rescue techniques in an appropriate setting will help you remember what to do in a stressful situation. If you are paddling Class III water and haven't already taken a Swiftwater Rescue Technician course, do it! You want your friends to take classes too. New packrafters will also benefit from a "Packrafting 101" course that focuses on equipment and boat control.

Packrafting Textbooks

Only a few packrafting books are currently available, but general river safety, canoe, and kayak texts are also helpful. Whitewater kayaking texts are useful for reviewing boat control, river-running, and rescue techniques.

Dial, R. (2013). *Packrafting!: An Introduction & How-To Guide.* (n.p.): Lulu.com.

> Roman Dial has done more to shape the packrafting community in North America than anyone, except the packrafting brands. His guide, while out of print, includes an excellent how-to progression section. The book takes a stronger wilderness-over-whitewater view and offers entertaining stories from the sport's early days.

Absolon, M. (2017). *Packrafting: Exploring the Wilderness by Portable Boat.* United States: Falcon Guides.

> Molly Absolon has written several guidebooks, and her professionalism comes through. Her book touches on everything lightly and will be a welcome resource to novice packrafters.

Introduction

Snyder, J. E. (1987). *The Squirt Book: The Illustrated Manual of Squirt-kayaking Technique.* United States: Menasha Ridge Press.

Chapter 1: Packrafting Equipment

Johnson, K. (2012). *Canyons and Ice: The Wilderness Travels of Dick Griffith*. United States: Ember Press.

Wikipedia contributors. "Halkett boat," January 8 2021, *Wikipedia, The Free Encyclopedia*, https://en.wikipedia.org/w/index.php?title=Halkett_boat. Accessed February 10, 2021.

Chapter 3: Risk

Canadian Avalanche Association (C. Campbell, S. Conger, B. Gould, P. Haegeli, B. Jamieson, & G. Statham Eds.). (2016). *Technical Aspects of Snow Avalanche Risk Management—Resources and Guidelines for Avalanche Practitioners in Canada*. Revelstoke, BC, Canada: Canadian Avalanche Association.

Csikszentmihalyi, M. (2009). *Flow: The Psychology of Optimal Experience*. United Kingdom: HarperCollins e-books.

McCammon, I. (2002, September). *Evidence of heuristic traps in recreational avalanche accidents.* In Proceedings of the International Snow Science Workshop (Vol. 30).

Statham, Grant. (2008). "Avalanche hazard, danger and risk–a practical explanation." Proceedings International Snow Science Workshop.

The Global Facility for Disaster Reduction and Recovery. "What is disaster risk?" *Understanding Risk*, www.understandrisk.org/vizrisk/what-is-risk. Accessed February 10, 2021.

Chapter 4: How Rivers Work

Bennett, J. (1999). *The Essential Whitewater Kayaker: A Complete Course*. United Kingdom: McGraw-Hill.

Davis, A., Davis, L. (2010). *The River Gypsies' Guide to North America*. United States: Brushy Mountain Publishing, Incorporated.

Sixmile river gauge figure: RAWS USA Climate Archive. "Station Monthly Summary: Granite Alaska," *RAWS USA Climate Archive*, https://raws.dri.edu/cgi-bin/rawMAIN.pl?akAGRN. Accessed February 10, 2021.

Sixmile river gauge figure: U.S. Geological Survey. "USGS 15271000 SIXMILE C NR HOPE AK," *National Water Information System: Web Interface,* https://nwis.waterdata.usgs.gov/ak/nwis/uv/?site_no=15271000. Accessed February 10, 2021.

Chapter 5: The Principles of River-running

Nealy, W. (1986). *Kayak: The Animated Manual of Intermediate and Advanced Whitewater Technique.* United States: Menasha Ridge Press.

> Fans of Sarah K. Glaser's illustrations in *The Packraft Handbook* will appreciate William Nealy's texts.

Oates, Mark. "Whitewater Packrafting Skills," *Mark Oates Exposure,* www.markoates.exposure.co/whitewater-packrafting-skills. Accessed February 10, 2021.

> All of Mark Oates' online resources are excellent. This is a must-visit site for anyone seeking the thrills of whitewater.

Chapter 6: Navigating River Features

Bennett, J. (1999). *The Essential Whitewater Kayaker: A Complete Course.* United Kingdom: McGraw-Hill.

Nealy, W. (1986). *Kayak: The Animated Manual of Intermediate and Advanced Whitewater Technique.* United States: Menasha Ridge Press.

Chapter 7: Open-water Crossings

Higman, B. "Packrafting Oceans," August 19 2019, *Ground Truth Alaska,* www.groundtruthalaska.org/articles/packrafting-oceans-marine-packraft-safety-skills-gear. Accessed February 10, 2021.

Chapter 8: River Rescue from the Water

Ostis, N. (2015). *NOLS River Rescue Guide.* United States: Stackpole Books.

> I reviewed several river safety resources to prepare this text, and the NOLS guide was my favorite. I was particularly impressed

with the quality of instruction and emphasis on risk and group management.

Riley, E. (2011). *Swift Water Rescue Training: Field Training Manual.* Swiftwater Safety Institute.

Chapter 9: River Rescue from Shore

Kauffman, R. "Swiftwater Rescue Course Manual," Fall 2018, *Frostburg State University*, www.frostburg.edu/faculty/rkauffman/writings-and-essays/writing-and-essays---swiftwater-rescue.php. Accessed February 10, 2021.

> Dr. Robert Kauffman's online swiftwater rescue manuals are very well presented.

Ostis, N. (2015). *NOLS River Rescue Guide.* United States: Stackpole Books.

Ray, S. (2013). *Swiftwater Rescue.* United States: CFS Press(NC).

Riley, E. (2011). *Swift Water Rescue Training: Field Training Manual.* Swiftwater Safety Institute.

Chapter 11: Medical Emergencies

American Whitewater. "Accident Database," *American Whitewater*, www.americanwhitewater.org/content/Accident/view. Accessed February 10, 2021.

Davis, Chris. "Drowning | River Guide Education Seminars - YouTube." *YouTube*, 2021, www.youtube.com/watch?v=yp9ITaROWDU. Accessed February 10, 2021.

DeWitt, G. "Whitewater Accident and Fatality Sankey Visualization." *Tableau Public*, www./public.tableau.com/profile/gabe.dewitt#!/vizhome/Whitewater-AccidentandFatalitySankeyVisualization/WhitewaterAccidentFatalitySankey. Accessed February 10, 2021.

Isaac, J., Johnson, D. E. (2011). *Wilderness and Rescue Medicine.* United States: Jones & Bartlett Learning.

Chapter 12: Backpacking, Camping, and Cargo

Leave No Trace Center for Outdoor Ethics. *Leave No Trace*, www.lnt.org. Accessed February 10, 2021.

Mehl, L. "Bear Awareness and Safety." *Things to Luc at*, www.thingstolucat. com/2019/11/01/bear-awareness-and-safety. Accessed February 10, 2021.

Chapter 13: Research and Trip Planning

American Packrafting Association. (2021). "Packrafting in the Brooks Range." Informational flier, www.packraft.org.

American Packrafting Association. (2021). "Packrafting in Remote Places." Informational flier, www.packraft.org.

American Whitewater. "Leave No Trace: The Paddlers' Footprint," *American Whitewater*, www.americanwhitewater.org/content/Wiki/stewardship:lnt. Accessed February 10, 2021.

Esri imagery featured in this chapter was created using ArcGIS® software by Esri. ArcGIS® and ArcMap™ are the intellectual property of Esri and are used herein under license. Copyright © Esri. All rights reserved. For more information about Esri® software, please visit www.esri.com.

Google Earth Pro V 7.3.3.7786. (May 5, 2020). Sixmile River, Alaska. 60.824787 N, -149.373302 E, Eye alt 31172 feet. ©2020 Google, ©2021 Maxar Technologies, NCES / Airbus. www.google.com/earth. Accessed February 10, 2021.

Leave No Trace Center for Outdoor Ethics. "Social Media Guidance," *Leave No Trace*, www.lnt.org/social-media-guidance. Accessed February 10, 2021.

Mehl, L. "Trip Planning." *Things to Luc at*, www.thingstolucat.com/category/ trip-planning. Accessed February 10, 2021.

National Aeronautics and Space Administration. "Worldview," *NASA's EOSDIS Worldview*, https://worldview.earthdata.nasa.gov. Accessed February 10, 2021.

Sentinel Hub. "EO Browser," *Sentinel Hub*, https://apps.sentinel-hub.com/ eo-browser/. Accessed February 10, 2021.

GLOSSARY

Active blade: Constant movement of the paddle blade in the water.

Active navigation: Monitoring your position and progress while traveling.

Aeration: Saturation of water with trapped air bubbles.

Anchor: An object, typically on shore, used to stop the motion of a person or equipment in the water. *Also*: Using a paddle stroke to grab and connect to the river.

Attachment point: A plate attached to the packraft's hull that allows attachment of accessories.

Back stroke: A paddle stroke that results in backward propulsion.

Back surf: Surfing while facing downriver.

Back ferry: Paddling across the river while facing downriver.

Backband: Accessory behind the seat that supports the paddler's lower back.

Backwash: The zone where the current recirculates into a hole.

Bander-snatched: Pulled backwards into a hole by the backwash, most common in boats with stubby sterns. Coined by Cody Roman Dial.

Bank (Riverbank): The solid ground at the river's edge.

Bar (River bar, Gravel bar): A shallow part of a river that often exposes sand or gravel.

Baseball stitch: A sewing stitch that pulls the edges of the material together.

Bear spray: Pressurized propellant with capsaicin (pepper) used as a bear deterrent.

Bedrock: Exposed solid rock.

Bedrock rapid: Rapids that flow over a solid rock riverbed.

Belay: Controlling the position or motion of a person or equipment by creating friction within a rope system.

Belayed rescuer: A rescuer lowered to a rescuee on a rope system.

Bend (Riverbend): A curve in a river channel.

Big water: Large and deep rivers with high volume.

Bight: A bend in rope, cord, or webbing where the lines don't cross. If the lines do cross, it is a loop.

Bikerafting: Combining bikes and packrafts for multi-sport travel.

Blade: The wide and flat part of the paddle.

Boat scouting: Inspecting the river for hazards while in the boat.

Boil line: The line separating the backwash (upstream flow) from the main current (downstream flow).

Boils: Upwelling currents that elevate the surface of the water.

Bony rapids: Shallow and rocky rapids.

Boof: A forward stroke that launches your packraft, typically from a rock or ledge.

Boogie water: Splashy water without distinct rapids.

Bootie beer: The (kayak) tradition of drinking a beer from a neoprene shoe if you capsized earlier in the day.

Boulder garden: *See*: Rock garden.

Bow: The front of the packraft.

Bow draw: A draw paddle stroke placed toward the bow.

Brace: A paddle stroke and hip movement that restores an unstable boat to an upright position.

Braided river: A river featuring multiple channels that weave together.

Breaking wave: A river or ocean wave that collapses upon itself.

Broach: Drifting sideways into an obstacle.

C-to-C roll: A capsize recovery technique to turn your boat upright without having to exit the boat.

Canister stove: A stove that runs on an isobutane-propane mix of fuel.

Capsize: To overturn a boat in water.

Carabiner: A metal loop with a spring-loaded gate used to connect rope and other loops.

Cargo: The load carried in or on a packraft.

Cargo zipper: A zipper on the packraft's hull that allows storage of equipment in or on the hull.

Catchment: The area of drainage for a body of water.

Cfs: Cubic feet per second, a measure of discharge.

Chamber: An isolated and enclosed volume of air in a packraft.

Chute: *See*: Tongue.

Cinch: A strong girth (loop) used to secure an object.

Class (I-VI): A rating of river difficulty.

Clean line: A line through rapids without rocks. *Also*: A knotless end of a throw rope.

Coaming: A raised border around the edge of a deck that prevents water from flowing into the cockpit.

Cockpit: The open well in the deck of the boat where a passenger sits.

Cold water immersion syndrome: Stages of reflexive behavior in cold water that can lead to drowning.

Combat roll: A packraft roll performed in the middle of a rapid.

Confluence: The point where two channels merge.

Constriction: A narrowing of the river between banks.

Conveyor belt: A width of water with predictable (laminar) flow that allows transport similar to an industrial conveyor belt.

Cork-screw current: *See*: Helical current.

CPR: Cardiopulmonary resuscitation; an emergency lifesaving procedure.

Creek: A low-volume constricted river, often with steep drops.

Creeking: Navigating steep and low-volume whitewater.

Crux: The hardest maneuver in a section of rapids.

Culture of Safety: An intentional effort to normalize safety and preparedness.

Current (River current): Moving water.

Cushion: A stack of water that piles up on top of an obstacle.

Cutbank: A riverbank with a steep face due to erosion.

D-ring: *See*: Tie-down.

Dam-release: Drainages where scheduled releases from dams govern water flow.

Dead reckoning: Monitoring your position relative to a fixed marker. See: Active navigation.

Deck: The top surface of the packraft.

Deck bag: A cargo back that can be attached to the bow or stern deck.

Defensive swimming: Swimming on your back, feet first and at the surface of the water.

Diagonal hole: A hole oriented at an angle to the flow of the river.

Digital mapping: The use of online mapping and navigation resources such as Google Earth, Esri, CalTopo, and Gaia GPS.

Discharge: The volume of water that moves through the river in a unit of time.

Dislocated shoulder: When the humeral head pops out of the shoulder socket.

Diurnal wind: Daily wind patterns commonly due to variable surface heating near open water.

Downstream: The part of the river at lower elevations.

Downstream V: *See*: Tongue.

Draft: The distance between the waterline and the bottom of the boat.

Draw stroke: A paddle stroke used to move the boat sideways or anchor into the river's current.

Drop: A section of river or single feature with steep elevation loss.

Drowning: The process of experiencing respiratory impairment from submersion/immersion in liquid.

Drybag: A waterproof cargo bag designed to keep contents from getting wet.

Drysuit: Fully waterproof, one-piece layer that has latex gaskets at every opening.

Ebb current: Fast tidal current during the falling tide.

Eddy: A pocket of water downstream of an obstacle that flows in an elliptical path opposite to the main current.

Eddy line: The boundary between the main current and the eddy current.

Eddy out: Paddling into an eddy.

Eddy turn: The maneuver of crossing out of the main current to catch an eddy.

Eddy-hopping: Paddling from eddy to eddy to control your downstream progression.

Edging: Pushing one side of the boat deeper into the water to give the river more to grab.

Entanglement: The hazard of getting twisted by cord, rope, or other loop-forming materials.

Entrapment: The hazard of getting pinned or trapped by equipment or against a river obstacle.

Equation of continuity: Water flowing in a channel must maintain a constant mass. If the channel area decreases, the water's velocity must increase.

Exposure: The people and possessions that hazards can influence.

Extension rescue: Extending an arm or paddle to a swimmer to pull them to safety.

Fall (Waterfall): The zone where water falls into a hole.

Feather angle: The angle of rotation between the two paddle blades.

Ferrying: Paddling across the current.

Fetch (Wind fetch): The distance that wind travels over open water.

Flashy (Flashy river): Rivers that show a rapid water level rise in response to precipitation.

Flatwater: A section of water without rapids.

Flood current: Fast tidal current during the rising tide.

Flow: Passage of water, specifically laminar or turbulent. *Also:* An "in-the-zone" mental state.

Foam: Frothy aerated water. *Also:* An extruded substance generated in the lungs of some drowning patients.

Foot brace: An accessory that provides a connection point between your feet and the packraft.

Foot entrapment: Lodging a foot in rocks or other debris on the riverbed.

Forward stroke: A paddle stroke that propels the boat forward.

Forward sweep: An arcing paddle stroke that turns the boat, starting at the bow.

Friendliness (Friendly hole): A description of a hole's direction of kick toward or away from the sides of the hole. *See also:* Smiling hole and Frowning hole.

Front surfing: Surfing while facing upriver.

Front ferry: Paddling across the current while facing upstream.

Frowning hole: Holes with kick toward the center of the hole, which can be hard to escape.

Gasket: A latex cuff that keeps water out of a drysuit. *Also:* A washer that keeps air from leaking through valves.

Gauge (River gauge): A device used to measure the water level or discharge of a river.

Glacial basin or river: Regions with slow-moving multi-year ice that contribute melt to the waterways.

Grabbing the river: Connecting with the river's current with a paddle stroke or edge control.

Gradient: A quantitative measure of river steepness.

Green water: Dense water with little aeration that provides resistance to the paddle blade.

Groundwater runoff: Draining of groundwater reservoirs during periods without precipitation.

Hand signal: Communication through body language when the volume of the river prohibits speaking and hearing. Often utilizes the paddle.

Harbor: A place on the coast that offers shelter.

Hard water: *See*: Green water.

Hazard: Environmental dangers and river features, the things we can't control.

Head-down rescuee: An unresponsive person in the water.

Helical current: Spiral-shaped water flow, typically along the banks of high-volume channels.

Heuristic trap: A mental short-cut such as a rule-of-thumb that can influence a decision despite actual observations and conditions.

High brace: A recovery and stability stroke that places the paddle's power face against the water.

High water: A water level or volume above normal values.

Hip snap: The motion used to overturn a capsized boat or stabilize a boat on edge.

Hole: Any feature where water recirculates on itself.

Horizon line: A horizontal line beyond which (downstream) the river can't be visualized, usually indicating a steep drop or waterfall.

Hull: The part of the packraft that displaces water.

Hydraulic: *See*: Hole.

Hypothermia: A dangerous drop in body temperature due to prolonged exposure to cold.

Inflatable kayak: A kayak-shaped inflatable boat, typically too heavy to carry significant distances.

In-town contact: A person (non-participant) that can coordinate communication and a rescue effort during your trip.

Keeper hole: A hole with strong recirculation that might be impossible to escape.

Kick: The component of the recirculating water in the hole that flows laterally, toward the center or sides of the hole.

Laminar flow: The linear movement of particles along straight or curved pathlines.

Landing: Paddling to shore.

Lapel: The fabric along the shoulders of a life vest.

Lateral wave: A wave that breaks at an angle to the main current.

Launching: Pushing off from shore.

Lead paddler: The paddler that descends the river first.

Leading with your head: An athletic paddling position with gaze focused on your objective.

Leash: A lanyard to connect a paddle, paddler, or cargo to the boat. Leashes are not appropriate in moving water.

Leave No Trace Principles: Guidelines to responsibly enjoy the outdoors through low-impact and respectful visitation.

Ledge: A wide rock platform that forms a drop.

Life vest: A type of personal flotation device designed to keep a swimmer afloat.

Lily-dipping: Powerless paddling strokes that barely scratch the surface of the water.

Line: A path through a rapid.

Line-of-sight: Maintaining visual contact with the paddler in front and behind you.

Log jam: A pile of driftwood.

Low brace: A recovery and stability stroke that places the back of the paddle's blade against the water.

Low-head dam: Human-made features with a uniform horizontal ledge and very dangerous recirculation (no kick).

Maneuvering: Moving skillfully and intentionally through river or open water hazards.

Meandering river: A river featuring a series of sinuous curves and bends.

Mechanical advantage: Rope systems that use pulleys to magnify the pulling force.

Merging channels: The confluence of separate river channels, often marked by a seam.

Momentum: Mass in motion; force or speed of movement.

Mother Duck: A capable partner who is excited to teach you and who can provide a safety net.

Offensive swimming: Swimming on your stomach, head first, often with an overhead crawl stroke.

Open water: Ponds, lakes, oceans and large rivers where you can potentially be far from shore.

Outcrop: Exposed bedrock that may indicate a canyon or bedrock rapids.

Outfitting: Equipment and adjustments that provide a proper fit and cargo-carrying capacity.

Packraft: An inflatable boat small and lightweight enough to be carried in a backpack.

Paddle dexterity: Manipulating the angle of the paddle blade by bending your wrists.

Pathline: The path an object travels in the water, such as a thrown branch.

Peeling out: Exiting an eddy to join the main current in the river.

Perimeter lines: Cord, rope, or webbing secured along the boat's perimeter.

PFD: *See*: Life vest.

Picking a line: Identifying a route to maneuver down the river.

Pillow: A vertical pile-up of water over an obstacle in the river.

Pinned: A packraft or person stuck against an obstacle and held in place by the river's force.

Play hole: A hole with an ideal geometry for surfing.

Pogies: Insulated hand-warming sleeves that attach to the paddle.

Point bar: River features that form at the inside bank of riverbends due to sediment deposition.

Point positive: The convention of always pointing the direction of safety, away from the hazard.

Pool: A flat section of water with no rapids.

Pool-drop gradient: A type of river gradient consisting of alternating steep drops and calm pools.

Portage: To carry a packraft around a rapid.

Power face: The concave side of the paddle that is used to pull against the current.

Powering on and off: Timing pulses of effort to build momentum or allow the boat to get entrained in the current.

Primary stability: The boat's stability when sitting flat in the water.

Progress capture: Maintaining tension on a load as a rope is pulled taut. Progress capture requires a mechanism to secure the load while resting or resetting the system.

Proper paddling position: The seated position that enables effective boat control.

Pushiness: The force of the river felt by a paddler at different water levels.

Put-in: The location where the boating part of your trip begins.

Range marker: A stationary landmark used in active navigation during open-water crossings.

Rapid: A section of water or individual river feature with three-dimensional flow (often turbulent) and aerated (white) water.

Rapid coil: Fast coiling of a rope to be thrown to a swimmer. Typically performed if a throw bag missed the mark and there isn't time to re-stuff the bag.

Read-and-run: Reading the water as you paddle downriver.

Reading the river: Scanning the water to identify hazards and features and get a sense of where the water flows.

Recirculation: A cyclical flow pattern of downwelling current that continuously feeds a hole.

Recovery zone: A stretch of calm water that allows a paddler to regain boat control or re-enter a boat.

Rescue breathing: Providing a drowned patient with exhaled air. Also known as positive pressure ventilation and mouth-to-mouth resuscitation.

Rescuee: A swimmer or patient that needs rescue.

Rescue swimmer: A rescuer who intentionally swims to assist a rescuee.

Rescue vest: Coast Guard-approved Type V life vest with rescue features such as a releasable belt.

Responding to the river's force: Maneuvering by working with the river's power rather than opposing it.

Reverse sweep: An arcing paddle stroke that turns the boat, starting at the stern.

Riffle: A gentle rapid formed over shallow water.

Rigging: *See*: Outfitting.

Rip current: A strong and localized ocean current that moves directly away from the shore.

Risk: The likelihood of harm due to exposure to a hazard. The degree of risk depends on hazard, exposure, and vulnerability.

Risk assessment: The process of identifying hazards and their associated consequences.

Risk tolerance: The level of consent to accept that something might go wrong.

River character: The nature of the river, typically described in terms of the riverbed's surface and shape.

River diary: A record of river conditions collected after paddling sessions.

River left: The left side of the river looking downriver.

River right: The right side of the river while looking downriver.

Substrate (River substrate): The material on the riverbed: sand, gravel, bedrock, etc.

River-running: Paddling down a river. Typically referring to sections with rapids that require maneuvering.

River-wide: A feature that extends across the river.

Rock garden: A section of river densely packed with rocks or boulders.

Roll: Folding the packraft for carrying in a pack or storage. *Also*: A capsize recovery technique to turn your boat upright without having to exit the boat ("C-to-C roll").

Route planning: Identifying an intended route of travel based on maps, satellite imagery, and guidebooks.

Rudder: A vertical blade at the stern of a boat that reduces rotation while paddling.

Rudder stroke: A paddle stroke that uses the blade like a rudder near the stern.

Runoff: Water flow that can feed into a river: rain, snowmelt, glacier melt, etc.

Safety boat: A paddler and boat with the expertise and positioning to assist others. Safety boat roles include coaching, assisting, providing a resting platform, towing, and managing gear.

Safety drift: The cumulative effect of decisions that gradually increases your exposure or vulnerability.

Safety net: A metaphorical description of the measures taken to reduce the consequences of being exposed to river and open-water hazards.

Scouting: Inspecting the river for hazards while walking the shore.

Sculling draw: A side draw with active paddle dexterity in a figure-eight pattern that moves a boat sideways in the water.

Seal launch: Entering the water by sliding down a smooth riverbank, rock, or snow.

Seam: The boundary between converging currents.

Secondary stability: The boat's ability to stay stable when on edge.

Sediment: Silt and rock deposited by rivers.

Self-bailing floor: Packrafts with perforated floors that allow water to drain.

Self-rescue: Unassisted recovery from capsizing by swimming, wet re-entry, or rolling.

Setting safety: Making a plan and positioning people and boats for rescue.

Shaft (Paddle shaft): The section of the paddle between the blades.

Shallow water crossings: Techniques for wading into swift water.

Shoal: A place where a sea, river, or other body of water is shallow.

Shoulder reduction: The process of easing a dislocated humeral head back into the shoulder socket.

Shuttle: The method of returning to the put-in after running a river.

Side surfing: Surfing with the boat's side parallel to the hole or wave.

Side draw: A draw paddle stroke placed in line with the hips.

Sieve: A pile of rocks that allows water to pass through but not a person or equipment.

Slack tide: A time without tidal current.

Slide: A river feature with a non-vertical elevation drop, typically over a boulder or bedrock.

Smiling hole: A hole with kick toward the sides of the hole, which helps push a boat or person out.

Spray skirt: A waterproof cover worn by a paddler to keep water from flowing into the cockpit.

Squirrelly water: Turbulent and unpredictable water.

Stability (Boat stability): A boat's ability to resist capsizing.

Stage (River stage): The height of water relative to an arbitrary reference.

Starfishing: Shifting your weight off the seat and onto the tubes in a sprawled starfish shape to decrease the boat's draft in shallow water.

Stern: The back of the packraft.

Stern draw: A draw stroke placed toward the stern.

Stewardship: The responsible protection and visitation of wild places.

Stickiness: The ability of a hole to trap a swimmer or equipment, generally indicated by the width of the backwash.

Storm response: How a river's water level and nature change in response to precipitation.

Strainer: Objects in the river, such as wood debris, that let water pass through but not people or equipment.

Sudden deflation: Rapid deflation of a packraft due to a large leak in the hull.

Surface runoff: The transportation of water along the surface rather than through the soil.

Surfing: Riding in place on a hole or wave.

Sweep paddler: The paddler that descends last and can help others in need.

Sweeper: An overhanging tree with branches that sweep the surface of the water.

Swiftwater: Water in which you can't fully control your movement.

Swiftwater entry: An aggressive technique for a rescue swimmer to quickly enter the water and make contact with a swimmer.

T-boning: Orienting a boat perpendicular to a hole or other linear feature to pass over the feature as quickly as possible.

Tail line: A strap or cord attached to the stern of the packraft to aid in equipment recovery.

Take-out: The location where the boating part of your trip ends.

Tension diagonal: A zip-line that uses the river's force to transport equipment or people across the channel.

Thigh straps: Accessories that connect your legs to the packraft allowing you to use your lower body to assist with boat control.

Throw bag: A bag stuffed with a rope that can be thrown to a swimmer.

Throw rope: A floating hydrophobic rope used in river rescues.

Tidal current: Periodic movement of water due to the gravitational interaction of the Earth, sun, and moon.

Tie-down: An accessory plate that provides an attachment point to the packraft.

Tongue: The water diverted between rocks or other river features, typically forming a pathway of deep and laminar flow ("downstream V").

Topping off: Adding additional air to a packraft through a mouth valve, commonly done several times during a long descent.

Torque: Producing rotation with a twisting force.

Trailing wake: Waves left behind an object that diverts the river's flow ("upstream V").

Trip plan: Documentation of the route plan, logistics, schedule, contacts, and other information to be left with an in-town contact to coordinate help.

Turbulent flow: Unsteady flow with water particles following random or chaotic pathlines.

Undercurrent: Three-dimensional currents of water that flow under the surface.

Undercut: A rock or bank that allows water to flow underneath and out the other side.

Universal River Signals: *See*: Hand signals.

Upstream: The part of the river at higher elevations.

Upstream V: *See*: Trailing wake.

Upwelling: Three dimensional currents of water that flow up from depth.

Valve: A nozzle that allows passage of air.

Vector pull: A technique to increase the leverage (mechanical advantage) on an object by pushing or pulling a taut line between two objects.

Volume: The amount of water in the river in cubic feet or cubic meters.

Vulnerability: The likelihood that exposure to a hazard will have harmful consequences.

Wading: Walking into swift water. *Also*: Shallow water crossings.

Walking the dog: Dragging the boat through shallow water like walking a dog on a leash.

Water level: The amount of water flowing in a river, typically described by stage or discharge.

Waterfall: A river feature with vertically falling water.

Wave: A pile-up of water that forms where the river current slows down; a disturbance on the surface of open water.

Wave train: A series of river waves that dissipate the water's energy.

Wet exit: The act of swimming out of the packraft.

Wet re-entry: The technique of climbing back into a packraft after capsizing.

Whitecaps: Waves with a broken and foaming white crest, a good indication of wind.

Whitewater: A creek or river with several rapids.

Z-pull: A 3:1 mechanical advantage pulley system used to dislodge a load or pull a rope tight.

INDEX

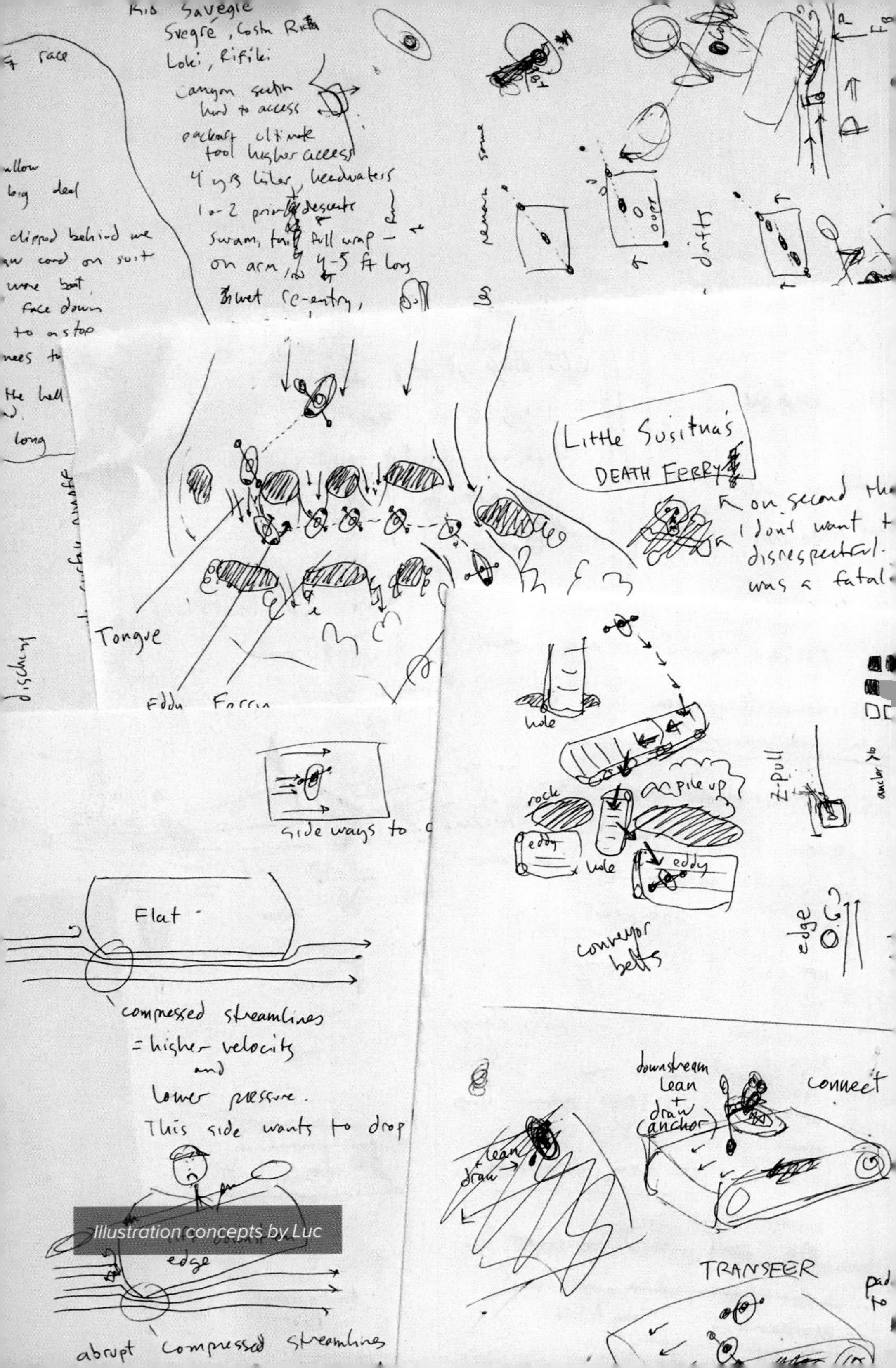

Kid Savegre
Svegre, Costa Rica
Loki, Rifiki

Canyon section
hard to access
packraft ultimate
tool higher access
4 wß liter headwaters
1 or 2 priority descents
swam, tried full wrap —
on arm 4-5 ft long
wet re-entry,

race

mellow
big deal

clipped behind me
raw cord on suit
wore boat,
face down
to on top
knees to
the hell
long

discharge

Little Susitna's
DEATH FERRY

on second th
I don't want t
disrespectful
was a fatal

Tongue

Eddy Ferrin

sideways to

hole

rock

pile up

eddy

hole

eddy

conveyor belts

Z-Pull

anchor

edge

Flat

compressed streamlines
= higher velocity
and
lower pressure.
This side wants to drop

edge

abrupt compressed streamlines

downstream
lean +
draw
(anchor)

connect

lean +
draw

TRANSFER

"I love me!"

"I love my crew"

my crew

the victim

1
2
3

(sitting on rock)

RESCUE
PRIORITIES

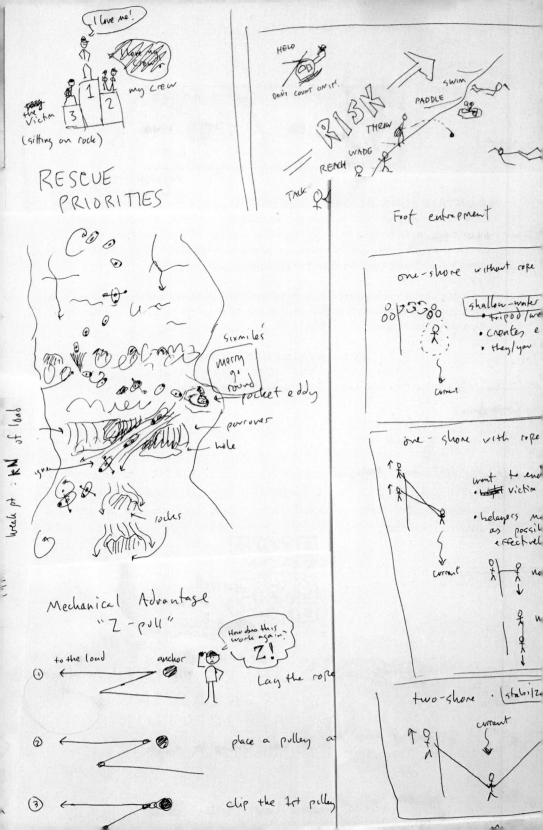

HELO

DON'T COUNT ON IT.

RISK

SWIM
PADDLE
THROW
WADE
REACH
TALK

sixmiles

merry go round

pocket eddy

pourover

hole

rocks

Weak pt : kN of load

Mechanical Advantage
"Z-pull"

"How does this work again?"

"Z!"

① to the load   anchor   Lay the rope

② place a pulley a

③ clip the 1st pulley

Foot entrapment

one-shore without rope

shallow-water
• tripod/we
• creates e
• they/you

current

one-shore with rope

want to en
• victim

• belayers m
  as possi
  effectiv

current

two-shore · stabilize

current

Thank you for reading *The Packraft Handbook* and helping to develop the packrafting Culture of Safety. Please visit *www.thingstolucat.com/packraft -handbook-resources* for instructional videos, training opportunities, updates, and additional resources.

Sincerely,
Luc Mehl

www.thingstolucat.com

Join the American Packrafting Association at www.packraft.org